Sutton Hoo and its Landscape

The Context of Monuments

Tom Williamson

Windgather Press
is an imprint of
Oxbow Books, Oxford

ISBN 978-1-90511-925-7

A CIP record for this book is available from the British Library

This book is available direct from

Oxbow Books, Oxford, UK
(Phone: 01865-241249; Fax: 01865-794449)

and

The David Brown Book Company
PO Box 511, Oakville, CT 06779, USA
(Phone: 860-945-9329; Fax: 860-945-9468)

or from our website

www.oxbowbooks.com

Printed in Singapore by
KHL Printing Co Pte Ltd

Contents

List of Figures

Abbreviations

IRO	Ipswich Record Office
TNA: PRO	The National Archives: Public Record Office, London
BL	British Library
CUL	Cambridge University Library

Acknowledgements

My greatest debt is to the Sutton Hoo Society, who in 2003 asked me to examine the landscape context of the Sutton Hoo burial mounds, and paid Sarah Harrison to act as my research assistant. My second great debt is to Sarah herself, who fulfilled her allotted role with customary ability and enthusiasm, transcribing a wide range of documents and maps, placing much of this information on a GIS database, and analysing it. None of this work would, however, have been possible without the active support and encouragement of John Newman of the Suffolk Archaeological Unit, who made freely available all the results of his painstaking fieldwalking survey of the area around Sutton Hoo. John also read, and made many useful comments on, the text. I also owe a great deal to Peter Warner, who provided much useful documentary information based on his work for the Sutton Hoo Research Project, including a transcription of the Melton 'dragge'. Thanks to Ipswich Record Office, for permission to reproduce Figures 17, 18, 26, 29 and 46; and to Cliff Hoppitt, for Figure 2.

Many other people have provided help, advice and inspiration, particularly Edward Martin and the staff of the Suffolk Archaeological Unit; Rosemary Hoppitt; Sam Newton; and Lindsay Lee. The viewshed analyses were done by James Butler, and much GIS assistance was also supplied by Rik Hoggett, then at the University of East Anglia. Tracey Partida provided much invaluable advice on the use of GIS, and saved me from panic at numerous points of crisis, and Phillip Judge drew most of the diagrams. Thanks also to Robert Liddiard, who made many useful comments on this text, and who provided sound advice and encouragement when my nerve failed me.

CHAPTER ONE

The Sutton Hoo Cemetery

Introduction

The cemetery at Sutton Hoo in south-east Suffolk is one of the best-known Anglo-Saxon sites in England. It is perhaps most famous for the magnificent grave goods recovered in the late 1930s from what is known as 'Mound 1', which are now displayed in the British Museum; but a series of investigations and excavations here, culminating in Martin Carver's campaign between 1983 and 2001, have perhaps more importantly produced a wide range of information about the character of English society at the point when this began to emerge, fitfully, into the light of history. The site of the cemetery is itself striking and evocative, and is now preserved for the nation under the care of the National Trust.

This short book is about the location of this important site. It tries to answer a superficially simple question: why are the famous Anglo-Saxon burial mounds at Sutton Hoo located where they are, in what is today a rather remote corner of Suffolk? It does so by examining the geographical context, or rather contexts, of the cemetery: by looking at where the monuments are positioned in the landscape, and at how that landscape has changed over time.

The Sutton Hoo barrows

The Sutton Hoo barrows – now known to number around nineteen in all – occupy an area of poor, heathy soil on a spur of land overlooking the estuary of the river Deben (Figs 1 and 2). The site lies towards the southern end of a much larger area of acid, sandy soils – traditionally known as the 'Sandlings' or 'Sandlands' – which runs all the way down the coast of Suffolk. The cemetery is thus located, rather curiously, only a short distance from the present county boundary between Suffolk and Essex, and therefore close to the edge of the Anglo-Saxon kingdom of East Anglia – curiously, because most people have interpreted the cemetery as the burial ground of the early, pre-Christian rulers of the latter polity.

The mounds have been noted as a feature of the landscape from at least the seventeenth century. They appear to be prominently labelled as 'Mathers Hoe' on a map of the Stanhope estates, surveyed by John Norden in 1601, even though they actually lay outside the bounds of the estate (IRO EE5/11/1). They are also marked clearly on a slightly later map, a survey of the parish of Sutton

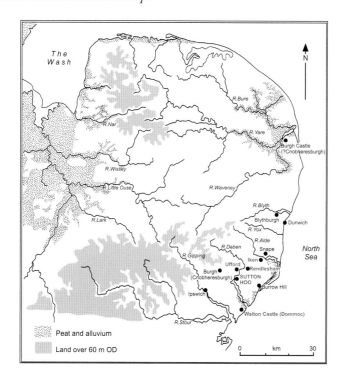

FIGURE 1. The Land of the Wuffingas: the location of the Sutton Hoo cemetery and related sites within East Anglia.

FIGURE 2. Aerial view of the Sutton Hoo cemetery (courtesy Cliff Hoppitt), looking west. Mound 1 is the large barrow towards the wood; Mound 2 is on the extreme right. Top Hat Wood occupies the sloping ground to the west, with the river Deben beyond, in the far distance.

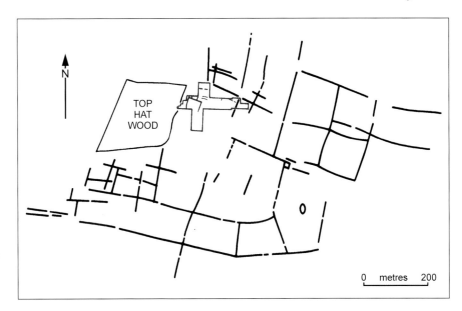

FIGURE 3. The late prehistoric co-axial field system at Sutton Hoo. The area outlined in red represents the excavated section of the cemetery, while the red lines within represent excavated portions of the field system.

surveyed by William Haiward in 1629: four mounds are shown, and labelled as 'Howhills' (IRO JA1/54/182). The barrows were also, unfortunately, noticed by early treasure hunters and antiquarians, and dug into on a number of occasions in the sixteenth century and later. One was opened in 1860, as described in an account in the *Ipswich Journal*:

> It is not known by many that not less than five Roman Barrows, lying close to each other, may be seen on a farm occupied by Mr Barritt, at Sutton, about 500 yards from the banks of the Deben, immediately opposite Woodbridge. One of these mounds was recently opened, when a considerable number (nearly two bushels) of iron screw bolts were found, all of which were sent to the blacksmith to be converted into horse shoes. It is hoped that, when leave is granted, to open the others, some more important antiquities may be discovered. The barrows were laid down in the Admiralty surveys by Captain Stanley during the stay of the Blazer, when taking soundings of the above named river some few years since.

The 'iron screw bolts' were presumably clench nails from a ship (Hoppitt 1985, 41). But the barrows first came to the attention of a wider community of archaeologists on the eve of the Second World War, when local archaeologist Basil Brown was invited by the owner of the land, Mrs Edith Pretty, to excavate them (Bruce-Mitford 1974, 141–69). It soon became apparent that rather than being prehistoric or Roman features, the burial mounds were of early Anglo-Saxon date. Three of the barrows opened in 1938 by Brown (now known as Mounds 2, 3 and 4) had already been robbed (Fig. 4). Mound 3 contained traces of the cremated bones of an adult and a horse, placed on a wooden 'tray' or platform measuring 5′ 6″ by 1′ 10″: the few remaining grave goods included some small decorated sheets of bone, perhaps from a casket; a piece of Roman or Byzantine carved ivory; the bronze lid of a jug and the remains of a *francisca* or throwing axe. Mound 2 overlay a pit which contained a scatter of rivets, the remains of the ship burial excavated in 1860, and a few grave goods which the earlier excavators had missed, and which had accompanied an inhumation: a silver gilt mount from a drinking horn; gilt-bronze mounts, probably from a sword; a silver buckle; fragments of a sword; the remains of an iron-bound wooden tub; and knife blades. Mound 4 contained rather less: within the pit were fragments of cremated bone (from the bodies of a youth and a horse), scraps of textile and fragments of sheet bronze. These results, while by no means uninteresting, were relatively disappointing. The following year, however, the largest mound – Mound 1 – was excavated, and was found to contain an intact ship burial (Bruce-Mitford 1975). The boat itself had not survived – all that remained were the rivets, and an impression where a thin layer of sand had been hardened through contact with the wood – but it was evidently in broad terms similar to the vessel discovered beneath a mound at Snape, some sixteen kilometres to the north-east, in 1862, although rather larger.

The excavations were soon taken over by C.P. Phillips, a professional archaeologist, and a magnificent range of finds was recovered from a central burial chamber within the mound. Grave robbers had tried this barrow, too, but the depth of the burial chamber had ensured that they had given up digging a few inches above it, probably because their shaft had begun to collapse. No evidence of a burial was discovered, but the rich grave goods included features which have since become famous. The excavations were abandoned with the outbreak of the Second World War. There was a certain ironic symbolism in this: the threat of invasion from Europe prevented the investigation of the most striking archaeological remains so far discovered of the last wave of Germanic invaders to arrive in this country. A few years later anti-glider defences were cut across the site, and still form a prominent feature. In spite of this interruption, Phillips did manage to produce an account of the excavations in 1940, which presented his initial findings, and those of a variety of experts in the field (Phillips 1940).

The finds from the excavations were presented by Mrs Pretty to the British Museum and were, over the following years, the subject of intense study (Bruce-Mitford 1978 and 1983; Evans 1986). Their wealth and sophistication were unparalleled in an Anglo-Saxon context. In the centre of the chamber, around the probable site of the body, were found the now famous helmet; a set of ten silver bowls, nested one inside the other, probably manufactured in the eastern Empire in the sixth century; and, beneath these, a pair of matching silver spoons, probably made in Byzantium, one with the word 'Paul' [PAVLOC] in Greek, the other modified – probably in Francia – to read 'Saul' [CAVLOC]. The body was accompanied by a range of jewellery and ornaments, including shoulder clasps and the famous gold buckle; drinking vessels; a sword with a pommel of gold and garnets; spears; a wand with a mount carrying the design of a wolf; and a purse. This had an elaborate lid of gold and garnet cloisonné work and contained 37 gold shillings or *tremisses*, each of which came from a different Frankish mint, together with two small ingots and three blank coins.

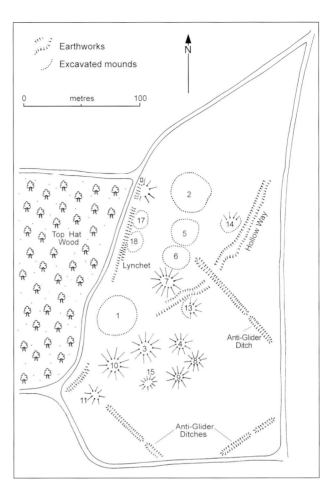

FIGURE 4. Plan of the
Sutton Hoo cemetery
(after Carver 2005).

On the eastern side of the burial chamber there was a Coptic bronze bowl, the remains of a lyre in a beaver-skin bag, and an elaborate bronze hanging bowl, probably manufactured somewhere in western Britain. There were also several bronze cauldrons. On the western side there was an iron stand with a grid near the top, beside which was a large circular shield, elaborately decorated. There was also a curious whetstone, ornamented on each side with a human face; and a ring mount, with the figure of a bronze stag fixed to its upper end, resembling the kind of sceptre carried by late Roman consuls. Elsewhere in the chamber there were the traces left by piles of textiles, a suit of chain mail, and much else. Nothing like it had been found in Britain before: nothing like it has been found since.

What was particularly striking was the way in which the grave goods had been drawn from all over Europe. The helmet, for example, has its closest parallels in Sweden, but the coins were from Francia, the hanging bowls from the Celtic west, and the silver bowls and spoons from the eastern Roman empire. The burial was interpreted as that of a king, or of someone aspiring to kingly status.

The sceptre, whetstone and other features certainly seemed symbolic of royal authority. But in addition the spoons, and perhaps the cruciform decoration on the nested silver bowls, hinted at conversion to Christianity. In spite of some initial problems with the dating of the coins, it was soon concluded that the burial was that of King Rædwald, who ruled East Anglia between c.599 and 624/5, and was the first of his line to accept the Christian faith although – as we shall see – a half-hearted convert according to our only historical source (Chadwick 1940, 87) (the coins in the purse accompanying the burial were initially dated to the mid-seventh century (Grierson 1952), but subsequent studies confirmed that they had been deposited between 620 and 625 (Kent 1975) or between 622 and 629 (Brown 1981)). The absence of a body meant that the burial deposit was initially interpreted as a 'cenotaph', presumably raised by pagan members of his family or entourage when the body itself was laid to rest in hallowed Christian ground. In reality, as later became clear, the extreme acid conditions in the subsoil had simply removed all obvious traces of the body, even the skeleton.

The boat was also the subject of careful analysis, by a team from the Science Museum directed by Lieutenant-Commander J.K.D. Hutchison (Carver 2005, 177–9). The vessel was a large one, rowed by forty oarsmen and with a large steering paddle at the rear. The hull was built around twenty-six frames. Its overall length was over 27 metres and its width 4.5 metres. It was evident that the vessel had not been specially built as a burial repository for there were signs of repair in several places. Indeed, she may have been used for burial in part because of her age.

Between 1965 and 1971 there were further investigations of the site, directed by Rupert Bruce-Mitford on behalf of the British Museum (Bruce-Mitford 1975). The area was fully surveyed for the first time and a total of fifteen certain and two possible burial mounds identified. The remains of the ship and chamber were re-examined and, under the direction of Paul Ashbee, the rest of Mound 1 was excavated, the underlying ground surfaces examined, and evidence for prehistoric occupation recovered. Excavations were also carried out in the area around Mound 1; Mound 5 was excavated, but found to have been robbed; and a number of cremations and inhumations were discovered beneath the flat ground lying between the mounds. By the time that Bruce-Mitford, Longworth and Innes published their accounts of these various interventions, between 1975 and 1983, the broad outlines of the site's development were tolerably clear (Bruce Mitford 1975, 1978 and 1983; Longworth and Innes 1980). The area occupied by the mounds had been cleared of woodland long before their construction: there was evidence of settlement from the Neolithic and the Bronze Age. The mounds, of late sixth- and early seventh-century date, were accepted as a royal cemetery, the burial place of the Wuffingas, rulers of the Anglo-Saxon kingdom of East Anglia; and the burial in Mound 1 was again identified as that of Rædwald. Nevertheless, many issues remained unresolved. Had the cemetery been associated with a settlement site? And was it solely reserved for the royal family and its entourage? Or did it form part of a larger burial ground, serving a wider community? To answer these and other questions, but also to recover evidence of burials in the other mounds before these were robbed by treasure hunters or otherwise damaged, a further series of investigations was carried out at Sutton Hoo between 1983 and 2001 under the direction of Martin Carver (Carver 1992a, 1998 and 2005). These included excavation, extensive survey work both on and off site, and a programme of palaeoenvironmental research. This campaign cast a mass of new light on the cemetery.

Firstly, much additional information was obtained about the development of the site before the erection of the mounds. It was shown that the immediate area had been cleared of woodland in the early Bronze Age, at which time it had been subdivided by substantial linear land boundaries. Both arable and pastoral farming had been practised, leading to a steady deterioration in the quality of the soils, which began to podzolise and erode. A number of separate settlement foci were identified, in the form of clusters of pits and post-holes, one group of which was interpreted as the base of a round house (Carver 2005, 391–447). Such remains were best preserved beneath the much later burial mounds, where they had been protected from plough-damage and erosion.

In the late Bronze Age or the early Iron Age the linear boundaries were abandoned and their ditches filled in, and a fenced enclosure constructed across the northern and western section of the excavated area, probably associated with stock management, as arable husbandry appears to have come to an end at this time (Carver 2005, 447–51). Nevertheless, in the later Iron Age cultivation returned. A pattern of small fields was laid out in a fairly regular, 'co-axial' pattern across the site, within which mixed farming continued into the Roman period (Carver 2005, 451–57)(Fig. 3). By the time the mounds were erected, however, further deterioration in the soil had occurred, arable farming had long been abandoned and the area was under turf.

More important than all this, however, was the new information which Carver's campaign produced concerning the cemetery itself. Meticulous survey work located further, much denuded mounds, bringing the total to nineteen (Fig. 4). Seven of the barrows were excavated or re-excavated. Four were found to cover cremations in bronze bowls (Mounds 5, 6, 7, and 18); three contained, or had once contained, inhumations. Mound 17 covered the burial of a young man, accompanied by a horse bridle and weapons, and the burial of a horse in an adjacent pit (Carver 2005, 115–136) (the skeletons here were better preserved than elsewhere on the site, where the acidic conditions had usually left only traces of the body as a stain in the sand). Mound 14 had been robbed but contained the remains of a woman's burial in a chamber, made in the mid-seventh century and thus after the main period of use of the burial ground (Carver 2005, 107–15). Mound 2, as already noted, had also been robbed, although traces remained of the elaborate ship burial, which had contained the inhumation of a male accompanied by feasting equipment and weapons (Carver 2005, 153–76). Carver's re-excavation suggested that it had been 'comparable to the Mound 1 burial in style and wealth' (Carver 2005, 10). Three contemporary burials were also discovered, without mounds, beneath the level ground to the east of Mound 5. These were simple and sparsely furnished inhumations. Including the cremations and inhumations discovered during the earlier excavations, this brought the total of furnished late sixth- and seventh-century burials known from the site to sixteen. In addition, however, a further thirty-nine rather later, unfurnished inhumations (again surviving essentially as stains in the sand) were found. These were concentrated in two groups. One lay towards the eastern edge of the cemetery; the other was clustered around Mound 5. Many of the burials had been beheaded or hanged, or showed other signs of deliberate killing, but they do not seem (as was briefly mooted by the excavation team) to have been sacrificial victims contemporary with the barrows themselves. All were probably of eighth- to eleventh-century date. Execution thus 'most probably began at Sutton Hoo after the mound cemetery had ceased to be used for mound burial, but while it remained in popular memory'. The place had become a *cwealmstow*, a place for judicial execution and presumably the site of a gallows. A map by John Norden, surveyed in 1601, shows a gallows on the rising ground of Gallows Hill, over a kilometre to the north, overlooking Wilford Bridge. The execution site was presumably moved to this place, from Sutton Hoo, some time in the twelfth century (Carver 2005, 315–49).

For much of the Middle Ages, as Carver was able to show, the site remained as pasture, grazed by sheep and by rabbits. Carver suggested that the burial mounds had actually been used to farm the latter animals. Some time in the post-medieval period, however, the area – including the mounds themselves – was ploughed, after which time many of the mounds were plundered by treasure hunters. Further phases of ploughing occurred in the eighteenth and nineteenth centuries, and an excavation, as already noted, in 1860 (Fig. 5).

Carver's excavation, and wider research project, were not the end of the story. In 2000 the questions surrounding the context of Sutton Hoo were made more complicated – or at least, more interesting – by the excavation of another Anglo-Saxon cemetery, some 600 metres to the north, during the construction of the car park associated with the new visitors' centre, erected after ownership of the site had been transferred to the National Trust. This new burial ground occupies a similar position to that of the barrows, on the level shelf above the 30-metre contour and facing towards the river Deben. It had already been known as a site of potential archaeological significance due to the accidental discovery in 1986 of a decorated Coptic bucket – the 'Bromeswell Bucket' – at a point some sixty metres to the west, and the recovery by the archaeologist John Newman in 1986 of early and middle Saxon sherds here. In 2000 the area was systematically metal-detected and various finds of late sixth-century date were recovered, while before the start of construction work the area to be occupied by the car park was geophysically surveyed, and a number of evaluation trenches dug. Following this, the entire area was stripped by the Suffolk County Council

FIGURE 5. General view of Sutton Hoo, looking towards Mounds 6 and 7. The barrows were substantially taller before being truncated by ploughing in the Middle Ages and after.

Archaeological Services field team. A diminutive Bronze Age ring-ditch and the ditches of an Iron Age field system were discovered, the latter sharing the same general orientation as, and probably forming a continuation of, that discovered beneath the Sutton Hoo mounds. In addition, seventeen cremations and nineteen inhumations, nine of which lay within small ring-ditches, were found thinly scattered across the northern and eastern sections of the excavated area. The burials, evidently the edge of a larger cemetery, were of sixth- and early seventh-century date, beginning before but perhaps overlapping in time with the main cemetery to the south. The cemetery contained some wealthy burials – one cremation was contained within a bronze hanging bowl – but for the most part it was a normal 'folk cemetery', the burial ground for some section of the 'general Anglo-Saxon population in the area' (Newman 2005, 486). The Sutton Hoo cemetery did not stand alone.

The Wuffingas

The burial mounds at Sutton Hoo have, right from the time of the 1930s excavations, been firmly linked by almost all historians and archaeologists with the *Wuffingas*, the ruling dynasty of the kingdom of the East Angles from at least the late sixth century; and the burial in Mound 1, in particular, has been identified as that of the great early seventh-century king Rædwald – an attribution first suggested in print by the great Anglo-Saxon historian, H.M. Chadwick, in 1940. True, other members of the Wuffingas dynasty have been proposed for the burial in Mound 1 (Wallace-Hadrill 1975; Wood 1983; Page 1976); and some archaeologists have even queried whether the interment here was that of an East Angle at all, but rather a Swedish king (Nerman 1948) or a member of the East Saxon dynasty (Parker Pearson *et al.* 1993). But for the most part, and for reasons that will become apparent, there is broad agreement that the cemetery does indeed represent the burial ground of the East Anglian royal house.

Comparatively little is known about the Wuffingas, about their rise to power and the formation of the East Anglian kingdom – a polity which, like the other kingdoms in seventh-century England, probably developed in the course of the sixth century out of a constellation of much smaller tribal territories into which the Province of Britannia had disintegrated at the end of the Roman occupation (Bassett 1989; Williamson 1993, 62–5; Scull 1992). The bulk of what is known about these matters comes from the historian Bede, whose *Ecclesiastical History of the English People* was written in Northumbria in the early eighth century. The *Anglo-Saxon Chronicle* also contains a number of references to events in East Anglia but most, although not all, of these seem to be derived from Bede. The *Chronicle*, although it is a record of contemporary events from the mid-ninth century, is for earlier periods a retrospective account, derived from a range of sources, many of dubious veracity. Beyond this, our knowledge of early East Anglian history rests on a small number of references in much later, medieval texts – saint's lives and histories (especially those by Roger of Wendover and Matthew Paris) – which may or may not incorporate early material; and on the genealogy of the Wuffingas, as preserved in the pedigree of King Ælfwald (c.713–49), which survives in a copy of the early ninth century (BL, Cotton Vespasian B.vi) and – a more abbreviated version – in the work of the ninth-century historian Nennius (*Historia Brittonum*, chapter 9: see Chadwick 1940; Yorke 1990, 67–71; Newton 1993, 77–81).

Bede's main interest was in the conversion to Christianity of the various English kingdoms, and the subsequent history of the English church, and much of what he tells us about other aspects of history is incidental to this greater theme. Moreover, living in Northumbria (created, during the seventh century, from the union of the two smaller polities of Bernicia and Deira) Bede was especially interested in the history of that kingdom and its church. But he does discuss the gradual triumph of Christianity in the other Anglo-Saxon kingdoms, and of necessity describes aspects of their political history, not least because conversion was often the sign of the dominance of one ruler over another, as the various small kingdoms into which England was divided in the period between the later sixth and ninth centuries jostled for power and supremacy. He describes how Kent was the first kingdom to be converted, King Æthelberht receiving, as early as 597, a mission from Rome led by St Augustine. The royal house of the East Saxons was briefly converted in 604, under King Sæberht, but reverted to paganism under his sons and only accepted the faith as late as c.653 under Sigeberht 'Sanctus', acting under the influence of his Northumbrian overlord King Oswiu.

Rædwald is discussed in connection with the conversion both of Northumbria and of East Anglia itself. He first appears in Chapter 5 of the second book of the *History*, in a short digression which follows Bede's account of the death of King Æthelberht of Kent in 616:

He was the third English king to rule over all the southern kingdoms, which are divided from the north by the river Humber and the surrounding territory; but he was the first to enter the kingdom of heaven. The first king to hold the like sovereignty was Ælle, king of the South Saxons; the second was Cælin, king of the West-Saxons, known in their own language as Ceawlin; the third, as we have said, was Æthelbert, king of Kent; the fourth was Rædwald, king of the East Angles, who even during the lifetime of Æthelbert was gaining the leadership. The fifth was Edwin, king of the Northumbrians, the nation inhabiting the district north of the Humber. (Mclure and Collins 1994, 78)

The *Anglo-Saxon Chronicle*, in an entry for 827 – perhaps derived in part from Bede – describes these men as *Bretwaldas*, a much debated term which probably means something like 'wide ruler' or 'overlord' (Swanton 1996, 61). It was a title which was not in continuous use, an honorary epithet applied to men whose political dominance extended, as Bede notes, over the whole of southern Britain.

More detailed information about Rædwald comes in Chapter 12 of Book 2 of the *History*, where Bede describes how King Edwin of Deira, driven into exile by the invasion of King Æthelfrith of Bernicia, eventually sought refuge at the East Anglian court. According to Bede, Æthelfrith tried to persuade Rædwald to kill his rival, offering him:

Large sums of money to put Edwin to death. But it had no effect. He sent a second and third time, offering even larger gifts of silver and further threatening to make war on him if Rædwald refused his offer. (Mclure and Collins 1994, 92)

Rædwald was eventually persuaded to accede to Æthelfrith's requests, agreeing to kill Edwin, or to deliver him up to his representatives: but his wife persuaded him not to follow such a dishonourable course (Edwin meanwhile, alerted to the possibility of Rædwald's treachery and musing on his fate, had been visited by an angel – the beginning of his conversion, and Bede's main interest in the story). Indeed, according to Bede not only did Rædwald reject Æthelfrith's demands, but he amassed an army and marched on Northumbria (in 616, according to other sources), defeating and killing Æthelfrith in a great battle on the river Idle. Edwin was able to take control of both Deira and Bernicia but Rædwald's own son, Rægenhere, was also slain in the battle. Several years later Edwin and his kingdom formally converted to Christianity.

A little later in his *History* Bede returns again to Rædwald, informing us that at an early stage of his reign he had 'been initiated into the mysteries of the Christian faith in Kent', presumably under the influence of King Æthelberht, his overlord and at the time the dominant power in southern Britain. But his conversion was equivocal, and his subsequent actions evidently filled Bede with some horror:

For on his return home, he was seduced by his wife and by certain evil teachers and perverted, turned back from the sincerity of the faith, so that his last state was worse than his first. After the manner of the ancient Samaritans, he seemed to be serving both Christ and the gods whom he had previously served; and in the same temple he had one altar for the Christian sacrifice and another small altar on which to offer victims to devils. (Mclure and Collins 1994, 98)

Bede then adds some important information about Rædwald's descent: 'The aforesaid King Rædwald was noble by birth, though ignoble in his actions, being the son of Tytilus, whose father was Uuffa, from whom the kings of the East Angles are called Uuffings' (Mclure and Collins 1994, 98).

The ninth-century pedigree of the early eighth-century King Ælfwald provides more information about the Uuffingas, or Wuffingas. This does not mention Rædwald himself, because Ælfwald traced his descent, and claim to the throne, through Rædwald's brother Eni. In a similar way, Rædwald's son Eorpwald (who reigned c.625–7) and Sigeberht (who acceded to the throne in c.630), together with Anna (who died in c.653/4), Æthelhere (who ruled from c.653/4 to 655) and Æthelwald (c.655–663) are missing, for all were direct descendants of Rædwald, rather than of Eni. But the genealogy is nevertheless of some interest. It lists Ælfwald's pedigree as follows:

> Ælfwald alduulfing (i.e., 'Ælfwald son of Aluulf')
> Alduulf eðilricing
> Eðilric ening
> Eni tyttling
> Tyttla wuffing
> Wuffa wehing
> Wehha wilhelming
> Wilhelm hryping
> Hryp hroðmunding
> Hroðmund trygling
> Trygil tyttmaning
> Tyttman casering
> Caser wodning
> Woden
>
> (Newton 1993, 77–8; Yorke 1990, 67–9)

As Sam Newton has pointed out, this genealogy – like most examples of Old English king lists – covers fourteen generations, a practice probably derived from biblical precedents (Newton 1993, 59). Moreover, like similar lists it was probably based on earlier, pre-literate verse traditions cataloguing the rulers of the East Angles, or of some section of them. The suggestion that one man was the 'son' of another need not be taken literally, of course, as the statement that Caesar was Woden's son indicates. Nor, again as the names 'Woden' and 'Caesar' indicate, should we assume that all the people listed in the genealogy were real.

> Indeed, as recent work suggests, the pedigree's pre- and proto-historic 'generations' may be more accurately understood to represent symbolically filiated conventions and figures from origin-legends deemed to be relevant to dynastic authority at the time of compilation. (Newton 1993, 105)

At one end of this list we have historical figures, who certainly existed, such as Ælfwald (713–49) or Alduulf (663–713). At the other end, however, are figures which are clearly mythical (or at least, have no part in the ancestry of the East Anglian kings): Woden, Caesar. At what point we move from figures of myth and legend to 'real' people is uncertain, but Newton and others have suggested that historical accuracy need be expected for no more than four generations before the first written version of a pedigree (Newton 1993, 105). In which case, with Wuffa himself, we enter the world of legend and origin-myth. Bede, as we have seen, suggests that Wuffa was the founder of the dynasty: Nennius suggests that Wilhelm, Wehha's predecessor in the list (*Guechan* in his version) was the first to rule over the *gens Eastanglorum* (Chadwick 1940, 59): but either way the name 'Wuffingas' indicates that Uffa was regarded as the dynasty's founder.

The fact that Wuffa was almost certainly a mythical figure has encouraged some historians to suggest other derivations for the family name. In particular, Sam Newton has argued persuasively that the name *Wuffingas* is, in fact, identical with that of the *Wulfingas*, 'the people of the wolf', a group who appear in the Old English poems *Widsith* and *Beowulf* as a tribe living in southern Sweden. Newton suggests, as part of a wider argument that the latter poem was composed at the East Anglian court, that these people migrated to England some time in the sixth century and settled in the area around Sutton Hoo (Newton 1993, 105–10). This suggestion receives some support from the archaeological evidence. Not only does the style of the earliest of the burials within the Sutton Hoo mounds signal, in Martin Carver's words, 'affiliation to the cultural practices of Scandinavia and north Germany' (Carver 2005, 490), but more specifically the rite of ship burial evident in Mounds 1 and 2 has its closest parallels in southern Scandinavia, in the rather similar burials thinly scattered along the coast of the Baltic and the North Sea.

I have described Rædwald and Tyttla as 'Kings of East Anglia', or 'Kings of the East Angles', but it is not in fact entirely clear what such titles would have meant in the late sixth or early seventh centuries, if they had indeed been used then. The character of kingship was closely bound up with the character of kingdoms at different points in the past. A minority of historians and archaeologist believe that some at least of the Old English kingdoms were directly descended from Iron Age tribal territories, and the Romano-British administrative divisions into which these developed: the East Saxon kingdom was thus the land of the Trinovantes by another name, East Anglia the old territory of the Iceni (Bassett 1989, 24; Blair 1947; Brooks 1989, 57–8). Most, however, would probably follow the ideas developed by scholars like Stephen Bassett, who have argued that the end of Roman rule was followed by a period of extreme political fragmentation (Bassett 1989). Lowland England in the fifth and early sixth centuries was thus divided into a myriad of diminutive tribal territories, each extending over tens rather than hundreds of square kilometres. Particular tribal leaders may have exercised some temporary supremacy over wider areas but political power was essentially personal, temporary and transient, and the geographies of power mutable. By the time that Bede was writing in the eighth century larger political units had emerged, and more permanent systems of dominance were imposed across extensive areas – the kingdoms of Kent, Essex, Mercia, Northumbria, East Anglia and the rest. Yet how far this process had really progressed by the early seventh century, at the time of Sutton Hoo, remains very unclear. It is possible that Rædwald, for all his prestige as *Bretwalda*, exercised even in East Anglia what was an essentially personal dominance over a constellation of semi-autonomous territories which recognised him as overlord, and rendered him tribute, but which still retained their own ruling families and a measure of political independence. As we shall see, the geographically restricted distribution of places certainly or probably associated with Rædwald and his immediate successors certainly supports such an idea.

Bede's account of Rædwald's apostasy comes as an aside in a story about his son Eorpwald, who succeeded to the throne following his father's death in c.625. Unlike his father, Eorpwald was a wholehearted convert to Christianity, strongly encouraged in his faith by King Edwin of Northumbria. But, as Bede explains:

> Eorpwald was killed not long after he had accepted the faith, by a heathen called Ricberht. Thereupon the Kingdom remained in error for three years, until Eopwald's brother Sigeberht came to the throne. The latter was a devout Christian and a very learned man in all respects; while his brother was alive he had been in exile in Gaul, where he had been initiated into the mysteries of the Christian faith. (Mclure and Collins 1994, 99)

Bede does not tell us that Ricberht was a member of the same family or dynasty, but the implication is that he probably was. Either way, Sigeberht – a saintly individual whom Bede describes in glowing terms – immediately set about the systematic evangelisation of the East Angles. Bishop Felix, a Burgundian by birth, came from Kent and established the first bishopric in the kingdom, at a place called *Dommoc*; a little later, in c.633, the Irish missionary Fursa arrived and established a monastery at a place called *Cnobheresburgh*. But, like a number of other newly converted Anglo-Saxon kings, Sigeberht's enthusiasm for the new faith eventually impacted on his role as ruler:

> So greatly did he love the kingdom of heaven that at last he resigned his kingly office and entrusted it to his kinsman Ecgric, who had previously ruled over part of the kingdom. He thereupon entered a monastery which he himself had founded. (Mclure and Collins 1994, 138)

The reference to Ecgric is notable, for it indicates that structures of authority in the early seventh century were somewhat different from those familiar from later Saxon times, and could evidently involve the sharing of power, and its geographical division, among members of a ruling family.

Some time after this East Anglia was attacked by an army from the Midland kingdom of Mercia, a growing power in the mid-seventh century, led by the still-pagan King Penda. Sigeberht was dragged from the monastery to fulfil his inherited role as war-leader but, although the East Angles were victorious, both he and Ecgrig were killed in the battle. He was succeeded by another saintly king, his son Anna, who continued his father's work of conversion, further endowing the monastery at *Cnobheresburgh* and establishing others. In 654 the *Anglo-Saxon Chronicle* (but not Bede) records that 'Botolph began to build a monastery at *Icanho*' (Swanton 1996, 29). This was almost certainly Iken, a short distance to the north-east of Sutton Hoo (Cramp 1984; West 1984; Scarfe 1986, 39–51).

Anna was killed in the same year, together with his son, fighting against Penda. The later political history of East Anglia need not concern us here: suffice it to say that the kingdom never again achieved the prominence it had enjoyed under Rædwald. For much of its subsequent history it was dominated by, although never quite fully absorbed into, its more powerful neighbours, Mercia and then Wessex. It remained then, more or less independent until 869 when, with the death of King Edward at the hands of the Danes, it fell first under Danish control, and, following the reconquest of eastern England, was absorbed into Wessex, and thus within the new unified English state.

The cemetery at Sutton Hoo cannot be understood in isolation from the early political history of East Anglia, however imperfectly recorded and understood. The question of whether or not the burial in Mound 1 can be identified with Rædwald is, in the last analysis, impossible to answer, although we will have cause to return to it at a later stage. But more important is the way in which the cemetery fits in well, in broader terms, not only with the history of the Wuffingas but also with models for social and political development which most historians and archaeologists accept for the later sixth and seventh century. This, as I have noted, was a time in which a more complex and hierarchical society was developing in England, and when certain rulers were beginning to establish permanent dominance over extensive tracts of land. Kings, and kingdoms, were emerging from a more decentralised, and probably more egalitarian, society. The grave goods found at the site, in Mound 1 especially, are not only evidence of the vast wealth of the individual interred here, and that of his family. They also demonstrate contacts with a world extending far beyond the shores of East Anglia – Scandinavia, Francia, Byzantium. The rite of ship-burial is itself of some importance here, for it is only known from a few other sites in England, all in East Anglia. It is otherwise characteristic of northern Europe in this period, of the Baltic and eastern Scandinavia. Burial under barrows was also relatively rare in England at this time, and geographically limited in Continental Europe to southern Scandinavia, the Rhineland, and northern Switzerland – areas fringing the core of the Christian, Frankish world. The construction of a barrow took time and labour, and seems only to have developed as a burial practice as new elites emerged in these areas, keen and able to demand 'monumental expressions of status' (Blair 2005, 78). And it was a short-lived phenomenon: for almost as soon as kingdoms developed in these peripheral zones, their rulers sought membership of the wider club of European rulers, and additional support for their claims to supremacy, by converting to Christianity. Soon, they were being buried in the various monasteries which they had themselves founded.

Other aspects of the burial rites employed at the site, and how they fit in with the wider development of funerary practices in Anglo-Saxon England, must also be briefly considered. Sutton Hoo, like a number of other cemeteries in eastern England, contains both inhumations and cremations. The former rite involved placing the dead in the ground accompanied by a range of offerings and grave goods which exhibited, in their styles, clear regional differences. The latter – which usually involved the placing of the ashes of the deceased, together with the remains of food-offerings and grave goods, in some kind of receptacle (generally a ceramic urn) – was always more popular in East Anglia, the Midlands and the north-east of England than it was in the south. It was also a practice that declined in importance over time, and especially after the start of the seventh century, so that the cremations at Sutton Hoo are amongst the latest known. Its rapid fall from popularity has been associated with the growing influence of Christianity, for the strong belief of the early church in bodily resurrection made it particular hostile to the practice (Hoggett 2007). In the same period, there were also important changes in the character of inhumation burials. Indeed, so different in character are the inhumation grounds of the seventh and early eighth centuries that they have, since the time of Leeds (1936), been described as 'final phase' cemeteries. More graves were now completely unfurnished than before: yet, at the same time, those which *were* furnished often contained some very wealthy grave goods. There were fewer burials with foodstuffs and other apparently 'practical' equipment, while traditional (and to some extent regional) styles of brooch and dress accessories vanished 'almost overnight' (Geake 1999, 204). They were replaced by a range of new types of ornament, including pairs of pins linked by chains, necklaces with pendants, and single disk brooches, all with close parallels in Francia, Byzantium and the late Roman world. Some archaeologists have seen these changes as an indication of the growing political and cultural influence of the Franks but Geake, the leading authority on this material, has interpreted them as a manifestation of a more general increase in late classical cultural influence, closely linked to the rise of regional kingship in England (Geake 1997, 133). Hoggett, more recently, has seen both the disappearance of cremation and the 'final phase' inhumations as being closely connected with the arrival of Christianity (Hoggett 2007). Grave goods were now mainly restricted to clothes and ornaments, and were more about displaying status than equipping the deceased for the journey to the afterlife. Geake, in contrast, has argued that 'final phase' burials represented an *alternative* to Christian burial (Geake 1992), while Carver, taking this argument further, has seen the more elaborate burials found at the start of this phase – like the later mounds at Sutton Hoo – as representing 'defiant paganism' (Carver 1992b, 181).

Yet it is perhaps worth noting here that interment with elaborate grave goods was, in certain parts of Europe, considered perfectly compatible with

FIGURE 6. Iken church, the site of the monastery at Icanho founded by Botolph in 653. The church, dedicated appropriately to St Botolph, stands on a virtual island beside the river Alde: a classic site for an early monastery. The great estuaries of the Sandlings still make a strong visual and emotional impact on the viewer.

Christianity (Blair 2005, 59–61), and it is arguable that we should see (as Geake has elsewhere implied: 1997, 133–4) the advent of new fashions from the world of late antiquity, and the arrival of the church, as to some extent connected, and both associated with increasing social stratification and the emergence of kings and kingdoms. Looked at in another way, however, we might also say that after two centuries in which much of lowland England had been drawn into the cultural orbit of the pagan north – of north Germany and Scandinavia – older patterns of influence were now reasserting themselves. In the words of John Blair, 'Suddenly, the English turned their backs on a range of cultural markers from their Germanic inheritance, and replaced them with new ones redolent of Frankish and eventually Mediterranean culture' (Blair 2005, 40). The later burials at Sutton Hoo mark the point at which these new influences, already established in southern England, were beginning to affect the east.

The land of the Wuffingas

I noted earlier that 'kingdoms' in the early seventh century probably represented little more than tracts of territory across which a particular family managed to maintain a sustained supremacy. Their direct political control was at first more limited, perhaps to the lands of the tribal group from which they had emerged, and over which they had first come to rule. What is particularly striking in this context is that, even under Rædwald's immediate successors, the Wuffingas remained closely associated with one small and rather marginal portion of the East Anglian kingdom – south-eastern Suffolk. Indeed, it is remarkable just how many sites with royal associations, mentioned in the *Anglo-Saxon Chronicle* or by Bede, or otherwise known to have been important in the early or middle Saxon period, are located within a short distance of Sutton Hoo (see Fig. 1). Some five kilometres north-east of the burial ground lies the village of Rendlesham, where there was a major residence – if not *the* major residence – of the Wuffingas. It was here, according to Bede, that Swidhelm, a King of the East Saxons, was baptised by Bishop Cedd in 655, with Æthelwald, the brother of King Anna, acting as his sponsor. Bede describes the place as a *vicus regius*, a 'royal estate' or 'royal residence', perhaps 'palace' (Bruce-Mitford 1974, 75). Whether, as is often assumed, Rendlesham had already been a place of importance more than three decades earlier, at the time of Rædwald, is uncertain: but the place's proximity to Sutton Hoo is striking. So too is the location of the parish and Domesday vill of Ufford, immediately across the Deben from Rendlesham. The name means 'Uffa's ford' or, just possibly, 'Uffa's enclosure'. In spite of what has been suggested by some scholars (Parker Pearson *et al.* 1993, 29) it is unlikely to be a coincidence that a place with such a name should be found so close to both Rendlesham and Sutton Hoo. A number of early ecclesiastical sites, founded after the final triumph of Christianity in the kingdom under Sigeberht, were likewise located in the immediate area. Much academic ink has been spilled over the precise location of *Dommoc*, where Felix established his episcopal see. Some historians still argue that it was at Dunwich, later a major city (but now largely eroded by the sea) on the coast some thirty kilometres north-east of Sutton Hoo (Whitelock 1972; Haslam 1972). But most now agree that it was within the old Roman Saxon Shore fort at Walton, at the mouth of the river Deben, only thirteen kilometres south of Sutton Hoo – a site now unfortunately completely destroyed by the waves (Rigold 1961 and 1974). The parish church of Walton is dedicated to St Felix. Early monasteries and bishoprics were often placed within abandoned walled Roman forts or towns, possibly because these provided ready-made enclosures of the kind deemed necessary for ecclesiastical sites, but mainly perhaps to symbolically affirm continuity with the Imperial, Christian past. The monastery established some twenty-five years later by Botolph at *Icanho* has been variously identified, but was almost certainly at Iken, a mere fifteen kilometres north-east of Sutton Hoo. The isolated church here, dedicated appropriately to St Botolph, stands on a virtual island, prominently positioned overlooking the estuary of the river Alde, a classic site for an early monastery (Pestell 2004, 24–5) (Fig. 6). In 1972 the base of a late ninth-century cross was discovered here, built into the medieval church tower, and subsequent excavations revealed evidence of middle Saxon activity on the site (Cramp 1984; West 1984; Scarfe 1986, 39–51). Other early monastic sites in the area were probably established by Sigeberht and his successors, to judge from the results of excavations undertaken at Burrow Hill, a former island in the marshes at Butley, twelve kilometres east of Sutton Hoo: for the middle Saxon settlement here, again located in a classic position for an early monastery, included a cemetery containing a high proportion of male burials (Fenwick 1984). It is possible that the site of *Cnobheresburgh* – where, according to Bede, the Irish missionary Fursa was invited to establish a monastery by Sigeberht – was also in south-east Suffolk. Bede describes how:

> The monastery was pleasantly situated close to woods and the sea, in a Roman camp which is called in English Cnobheresburg, that is, the city of Cnobher. The king of that realm, Anna, and his nobles afterwards endowed it with still finer buildings and gifts. (McClure and Collins 1994, 139)

The word here translated 'Roman camp' is the Latin *castrum*, 'fortified place', and the site is normally identified with Burgh Castle in the far north of the county (it is now in Norfolk). But the use of the term *urbs*, here translated simply as 'city', as well as the fact that the name incorporates the English term *burh,* has suggested to some that the place was not an obvious Roman site, for which Bede would have been more likely to use the term 'civitas' (Campbell 1979, 36). Hoggett has suggested that the place called Burgh, some seven kilometres to the west of Sutton Hoo, where a church dedicated to St Botolph lies within an Iron Age enclosure containing evidence for Roman occupation, is perhaps a stronger candidate (Hoggett 2007, 114–15). Lastly, attention should be drawn to the town of Ipswich, a mere fifteen kilometres to the south-west of Sutton Hoo, a place which evidently had a significant role in the consolidation of the Wuffingas' power over East Anglia. It was a *wic*, the term used by archaeologists to describe the coastal entrepots through which early Anglo-Saxon kings controlled long-distance exchange, some of which subsequently developed as centres of production. In its earliest phases, dating to the later sixth century, the place was no more than an open settlement, perhaps only occupied intermittently, where boats could unload on a sheltered beach beside the river Orwell (Scull 2002; Wade 1988a, 1993). At this time it may not have been the only such place in East Anglia. Minor rulers of subordinate territories may also have had their own controlled landing places, on rivers or the coast. A territory centred on Blything, for example, may have had one at Dunwich (Haslam 1993) and others, to judge from the archaeological evidence, perhaps existed at places like Burnham and Bawsey in Norfolk. As the Wuffingas consolidated their hold over East Anglia, however, Ipswich became the principal *wic* for the whole kingdom and during the seventh and eighth centuries it became larger and more urban in character. Occupation spread across most of the area of the present town centre and over the river, into the parish of Stoke. By the 720s a special form of pottery was being produced here, Ipswich Ware, which was used throughout the kingdom, and a variety of other goods was manufactured and distributed under royal control. Much of the street system of the town may date back to middle Saxon times and some of the churches – including St Mildred's and St Augustine's – almost certainly originated then (Wade 1993). Yet at this time, it must be emphasised, Ipswich was not a town in the modern or, indeed, in the medieval sense, and did not exist within a true market economy. It was

a centre for royal import and production, from which prestige goods could be distributed to a favoured elite.

Not all of the major early and middle Saxon sites in eastern Suffolk can be associated with the Wuffingas. The great sixth- and early seventh-century cemetery at Snape, for example, which lies some sixteen kilometres to the north-west of Sutton Hoo, and which includes a number of elaborate ship and boat burials (Filmer Sankey and Pestell 2001), is unlikely to represent another of the dynasty's burial grounds, and was presumably associated with some subordinate social group in the locality, although evidently one of some wealth. Moreover, not all of the places associated with the Wuffingas lay in this far south-eastern corner of Suffolk. Blythburgh, some thirty kilometres to the north of Sutton Hoo, had evidently become a significant centre of royal power by the mid-seventh century, for it was probably while defending this place against a Mercian army led by King Penda that King Anna and his son were killed at nearby Bulcamp in 654 (Warner 1996, 120–1). Anna himself is said to have been buried at Blythburgh, probably another early monastery, and, according to the medieval *Liber Eliensis*, was still being venerated there in the twelfth century (Blake 1962, 18) (Fig. 7). The place originally, however, almost certainly lay within the territory of a quite different tribal group, the *Blythingas*, whose name – preserved in that of the later administrative territory Blything Hundred – means 'the people of the river Blyth' (Warner 1996, 120–1). Like the people who buried at Snape, they were presumably absorbed into the territory of the Wuffingas in the course of the sixth and seventh centuries. The *Liber Eliensis* also credits Sigeberht with founding the monastery at Bury St Edmunds, on the far side of the county, but the story is almost certainly a medieval invention.

The Wuffingas, in origin at least, were thus associated with only the southern section of the Suffolk coastal heathlands. They do not, at least under Rædwald and his immediate successors, appear to have had direct control over the whole

FIGURE 7. The church at Blythburgh, overlooking drained grazing marshes – the former estuary of the river Blyth. The church is traditionally said to have been the burial place of King Anna, who was killed fighting the Mercian army at nearby Bulcamp in 654.

of the Sandlings. Nor do they seem to have been associated with any other district in East Anglia. This is spite of the fact that, although in the immediate post-Roman period much of Norfolk and Suffolk (especially the heavier clays) seem to have been only thinly settled, several extensive areas of lighter soils, such as Breckland or north Norfolk, have produced abundant evidence for early Anglo-Saxon settlement, especially in the form of cemeteries. The places which our admittedly meagre documentary sources directly associate with the Wuffingas – Rendlesham, Iken, *Dommoc*, perhaps *Cnobheresburgh* and Ufford – were all concentrated, quite close together, in the south, together with Ipswich which a little later became the great entrepot of the kingdom. It is for this reason that the identification of Sutton Hoo as the burial ground of the Wuffingas is so plausible. It is theoretically possible that some other immensely wealthy and well-connected group lived in this district in the late sixth and seventh centuries, unnoticed by Bede and our other sources: but on balance unlikely. The southern portion of the Sandlings was the original land of the Wuffingas.

And this in turn means that the question posed at the start of this chapter, and the subject of this short volume – 'why is the Sutton Hoo cemetery found in this particular place?' – is really two rather different questions. At one level we need to view the cemetery as part of this wider concentration of early and middle Saxon sites in south-east Suffolk, and this involves explaining why the dynasty which came to dominate the whole of East Anglia originated *here*, on the very edge of the kingdom. Of course the explanation may turn out to be simply chance: the dominance of an extensive area by one family was the result of the luck or prowess of a particular individual or group of individuals who fortuitously originated in this district. But the question is nevertheless one worth asking. But at a second level we need to explain why, of all the places within this district in which the barrow cemetery could have been placed, it was located on this piece of high ground overlooking the Deben. Why was it *here*, rather than five, ten or more kilometres to the north, east or west? Again, pure chance, serendipity, the quirky initial decision of one individual, may be the explanation: but, once again, the question is worth asking.

Approaches to landscape

These two questions not only involve examining the location of Sutton Hoo at two distinct spatial levels and in two rather different landscape contexts. Perhaps more importantly, as I shall argue, they invite us to look at the site's location in two rather different ways. To explain the remarkable concentration of middle Saxon sites in south-east Suffolk, and the close association of the Wuffingas with this rather marginal part of their kingdom, we need to think in terms of broad patterns of geography, movement, power politics, and communication – the kinds of matters which archaeologists and historians have long been concerned with. In the later sections of this text I will return to such issues. But, given that it is written from the perspective of landscape history, I will emphasise more than is perhaps usual in such studies the role of topography and natural landforms in generating regional and national patterns of contact, allegiance and association. In essence, I shall argue that patterns of territorial and political organisation, and of social identity, were to a significant extent structured by natural topography: by the disposition of different kinds of soil, and by the arrangement of drainage systems and river valleys, interfluves and watersheds, and coastlines. This was true at a very local level, at a regional level and even at a national level: and a consideration of broad as much as of localised geographies may help to explain the power and wealth of those who were buried at Sutton Hoo. Indeed, it is only by looking at these various geographical contexts that can we make any real sense of Sutton Hoo. Otherwise, as Catherine Hills has emphasised, the location of these rich burials in this superficially remote and unremarkable location is surprising, and hard to explain.

> The Sutton Hoo treasure springs unexpectedly out of a rural agricultural society, in part of this region [East Anglia] where there is no very obvious density of population, nor immediate source of wealth. … There is nothing comparable in East Anglia. (Hills 1983, 103)

When considering the precise location of the Sutton Hoo cemetery within the heartland of the Wuffingas, in contrast, I shall employ some perhaps less familiar approaches, ones which take us into more debatable intellectual territory. For this question demands that we consider the mind-set and motivations of the individual or individuals who chose this particular place as an appropriate site for a cemetery, forcing us to speculate on questions of status and politics, religious beliefs and even aesthetics. This study is thus, in part, an exercise in that genre or range of genres in landscape archaeology usually referred to as 'phenomenology'.

The term perhaps requires some explanation. 'Phenomenological' approaches form part of a wider 'post-processual' archaeology which emerged in the 1980s and 90s. During the previous decades the discipline had tried to make itself into a science – not simply in terms of its methods, such as radiocarbon dating, but also in terms of its aims and objectives. Its more ambitious theorists believed it should aspire to being a kind of scientific long-term history, capable of providing 'laws' of human social development; and they argued that it should follow the rules of the empiricist natural sciences, in the sense that it should advance hypotheses – ideas or suggestions – which would then be rigorously tested against new or existing data. 'Post-processualists' reacted against these developments and accused the 'new' archaeology, in effect, of de-humanising the past, or losing sight of ordinary people and of seeing society as a kind of vast and complex machine. Individuals, they claimed, had been marginalised in favour of what Thomas described as the 'titanic forces' which surrounded them – demographic and technological change, political developments and climatic change (Thomas 1993). 'Post-processual' archaeologists also accused the academic establishment of failing to acknowledge the extent to which the discipline was embedded in, and conditioned by, current norms and social values. Its scientific 'objectivity' was a sham. Archaeology, in short, had become hamstrung by its addiction to positivism, empiricism and scientific method. The approaches to landscape archaeology with which I am here concerned arose as part of this vigorous reaction.

Landscape archaeologists usually look at the physical structures, spaces and distributions left by past societies as reflections, traces and by-products of social and economic activities, activities which were themselves moulded and structured, to some extent, by aspects of the environment. The location of ceremonial monuments in the landscape might thus be interpreted in terms of social territories and patterns of social organisation: burial mounds might serve to legitimise claims to land, and therefore be positioned on the edges of a group's territory, striking symbols of appropriation. In such approaches the landscape is examined, as it were, from above, as depicted on maps and plans or in aerial photographs. The distribution of barrows would thus be considered in terms of the location of contemporary settlements and types of land use, as suggested by different kinds of soil, for example.

'Phenomenological' and 'experiential' approaches start from a different range of premises (Barrett 1994; Bender 1998; Bradley 2000a; Edmonds 1999; Tilley 1994, 2004). People inhabiting a particular landscape invested both natural and man-made features with a range of symbolic associations and meanings. Anthropological studies show that for non-western peoples the landscape is alive with stories, myths, memories, through which individuals and societies construct their identity and self-image, and through which they relate to the cosmos. The location, as much as the design, of early monuments was the outcome of a similar range of ideas and beliefs, rather than a simple consequence of the social and economic patterns supposedly reconstructed by archaeologists. Indeed, much of the two-dimensional mapping of monuments and their distributions tends to hinder rather than help our attempts to understand their meaning. As John Barrett and others have strongly argued, such representations tell us next to nothing about how monuments and places were perceived in the past, because their creators never saw them from the air, only from ground level (Barrett 1994). In short, we need to try to get inside the heads of the people of the past, and understand how they experienced the landscape. We need, in Bradley's words, to consider 'the superstructure of meanings and values through which particular landscapes were experienced' (Bradley 2000a, 2).

Some historians and historical geographers, especially those studying the early modern period, have developed similar approaches. Denis Cosgrove, for example, has emphasised the way in which the very concept of 'landscape' arose as part of a complex nexus of ideological change in the sixteenth and seventeenth centuries. It was associated with a way of viewing the physical environment that developed, alongside cartography, in association with new concepts of ownership, capitalist forms of production, and novel modes of political power (Cosgrove 1984). Some scholars believe that the very tools employed by modern students of the past – plans, maps, aerial photographs

– are themselves 'Cartesian devices' which stand in direct lineal descent to the modes of representation which accompanied the emergence of capitalism. To cultural geographers Daniels and Cosgrove, moreover, the landscape has an 'iconography' which needs to be read and interpreted like a painting or a text (Cosgrove and Daniels 1988). Features such as trees or woodlands, or certain kinds of land use, had a symbolic meaning to contemporaries (Daniels 1988). Dave Rollison, meanwhile, has argued that people in early modern England used the landscape as a 'memory palace'. Meanings attached to the physical environment, through folk stories and popular sayings, were one of the ways in which social knowledge was passed from one generation to the next (Rollison 1992: see also Whyte 2006).

The construction of monuments, their maintenance, and their subsequent use and interpretation by later societies have been matters of concern to many archaeologists interested in these approaches. Monuments were integrated into patterns of ritual, and often seasonal, movement:

> While places and movement between them are intimately related to the formation of personal biographies, places themselves may be said to acquire a history, sedimented layers of meaning by virtue of the actions and events that take place in them. Personal biographies, social identities and a biography of place are intimately connected. (Tilley 1994, 27)

Monuments and places thus need to be understood in terms of the activities which took place at and around them, activities which in turn shaped the way in which they were experienced. Once they had been constructed, moreover, many monuments had as it were an afterlife: they continued to be powerful presences in the landscape, and might often be invested with entirely new meanings (Bradley 2002a). In the early Anglo-Saxon period, for example, features like Bronze Age round barrows were frequently chosen as places for burial, because individuals or communities consciously associated themselves with the remote past in an attempt to legitimate claims to land or resources (Bradley 1987 and 1993; Harke 1994; Lucy 1992; Williams 1988). Conversely, when Anglo-Saxon England was evangelised in the course of the seventh century, Christian missionaries – as we have seen – frequently chose abandoned Roman forts, and similar sites associated with the imperial past, as places in which to establish churches and monasteries.

Not every historian or archaeologist concerned with the landscape has welcomed this 'phenomenological' agenda. Some believe that the experience of individuals represents only a part of what we should be studying. People in the past, as much as people in the present, did not know – could not know – about the complex, multifarious influences on their world. We often know far more about their world than they ever could and to concentrate *only* on their experiences, as some phenomenologists seem to want us to do, appears to many students of the past to be a rather odd way of trying to understand how and why early people lived the lives they did. Reconstructing past experiences might be important, but it should not necessarily be the *most* important concern of the archaeologist or historian. But many people, more importantly, simply doubt whether it is possible to know how people in the remote past experienced or thought about their environment. Anthropological studies, as archaeologists like Christopher Tilley are keen to point out, reveal the richly textured character of the associations placed upon the landscape by non-western cultures, in the form of legends, songs, rituals, customs, stories, social and individual memories. The very extent of this complexity makes it unlikely that we can ever really recover more than fragments of the experience of landscape in the past.

But there are some more specific conceptual problems with phenomenological approaches to landscape. As noted earlier, post-processualists share the idea that, in the 1960s and 70s, archaeology became hamstrung by its addiction to positivism, empiricism, and scientific method – including the idea that claims to truth had to be based on the rigorous testing of hypotheses against the evidence. Scientific caution, they suggest, can be both illusory and intellectually limiting. As Barbara Bender has put it, 'we *have* to go beyond the evidence … [it] does not of itself deliver an understanding … it is open to any number of interpretations' (Bender 1998, 7). Julian Thomas has similarly argued that empirical verification can never deliver a full understanding and that instead we should aim at a 'plausible account produced in and for the present' (Thomas 1996, 89). Indeed, those who espouse phenomenological approaches normally place considerable emphasis on how *we* experience archaeological monuments and their surroundings today: what we can see from them, where they can be seen from. Many, for example, are concerned with the way they seem to mimic natural landforms, or to be intentionally shaped in such a way as to contrast with them. Personal observation and experience in the present, they argue, can often help us to understand the kind of ways these places might have been thought about in the past. But there are obvious dangers here. As Andrew Fleming recently put it: 'Having largely freed themselves from traditional concerns with verification, post-processualists had given themselves permission to say more or less whatever they liked' about the past (Fleming 2006, 269). It may be completely misleading to assume that our own responses to ancient sites and their settings can tell us much about the attitudes and experiences of those who built them. Or to put it another way, they *might* do – but how would we know? If the response of two archaeologists to a particular monument or landscape were radically different, how would we be able to chose which provided the most valuable insights into the ideas and experiences of people living in the past? To quote Fleming again:

> If 'trained' phenomenologists studied the same landscapes independently … would they achieve similar outcomes? Suppose I walked the Dorset Ridgeway as a phenomenologist and developed very different insights … should anyone, could anyone, try to decide on the basis of the 'evidence' which of us has produced the better account of the prehistoric past? Post-processual logic suggests that the answer should be no. This is partly because, as we have seen, we are expected to go *beyond* the evidence. (Fleming 2006, 273)

But we should not, as Fleming elsewhere argues, throw the phenomenological baby out with the proverbial bathwater. In rejecting the normal procedures of the natural sciences – especially the rigorous testing of hypotheses – in favour of more intuitive and subjective approaches, phenomenologists can quite legitimately be criticised for producing ideas about the past which they are incapable of showing are in any way superior to those thought up by anybody else. But the unfortunate reality is that, when we are obliged to engage with the spiritual and emotional aspects of past societies, strict scientific procedures – at least in the sense of confirming a hypothesis by repeating an experiment and obtaining the same results – are not always of much help.

Early Anglo-Saxon religion, for example, seems to have lacked a set of firm doctrines which were so widely shared that the same practices, leaving the same kinds of archaeological traces, can be found in all parts of the country. Burial practices thus display considerable variation not only between but also within communities. Cremation and inhumation were often practised at the same time, within the same cemetery: but the range of variation went well beyond this initial choice. At Snape, some sixteen kilometres north-east of Sutton Hoo, for example, animals were sometimes placed on the cremation pyre and sometimes not; the ashes from the pyre were sometimes placed directly in the ground, sometimes into a variety of containers. Inhumations might be placed directly into an unlined grave; into a grave lined with fabric; into a coffin; or into a boat. The sites of graves might be marked with a mound or posts, but might not. 'In short, burying a pagan Anglo-Saxon required a huge number of choices' (Filmer-Sankey and Pestell 2001, 262). In a similar way, there were no simple rules about where to place a cemetery. Some communities evidently thought it important to bury their dead near an ancient monument – around a quarter of known cemeteries seem to display this preference, according to Williams (1998, 92). Bronze Age round barrows were the most popular option, but a wide range of prehistoric and Romano-British sites might also be chosen as suitable locations. Some communities, in contrast, were attracted to striking natural landforms, such as prominent hills; others placed their burial grounds in commanding positions with wide views across the landscape; others still preferred low terraces above rivers. In many cases there is no obvious reason why a cemetery should have been in one place rather than another, a hundred or even a thousand metres to the north, south, east or west. Perhaps those burying in such places were drawn by some feature of the landscape which has since vanished without trace, such as an ancient or prominent tree: place-name and other evidence suggests that natural features like these were often imbued with a spiritual significance by the early Anglo-Saxons. In short, any explanation for why a community chose a particular site to bury its dead cannot be verified, 'tested', simply by seeing whether their neighbours did the same. In this sense, at least, any suggestions advanced about the location of Sutton Hoo will, of necessity, be 'unscientific'.

There are obvious dangers in 'phenomenological' approaches, and there are good reasons for doubting whether these should take priority over more conventional perspectives. Yet in understanding past landscapes it is, perhaps, a matter of horses for courses. If we are interested in economic or agrarian aspects of past societies, then speculating on how their members viewed the cosmos and conceived the rhythm of the seasons might well play a part in our research. We would, however, probably learn more by considering where they settled, and how they used soils of different kinds. On the one hand, if our main concern was with the ceremonial monuments they erected, or with other aspects of their spiritual experience or behaviour, we would of necessity be forced to think in more speculative ways, producing hypotheses less susceptible to conventional 'testing'. Yet it is important to emphasise that, in reality, 'practical' and 'religious' aspects of life will never have been entirely discrete and separate. Cosmological beliefs – about the 'correct' foods to eat, the right way to plant and harvest – might well have informed and affected agricultural practices. But conversely, how people ordered their agricultural activities will have impacted on their religious and ceremonial practices – how they divided up time, how they organised the festivals that punctuated their year. And in a similar way, how the environment was shaped by strategies of subsistence and other economic activities will, to judge from the experience of more recent times (Daniels 1988) have created an iconography of landscape, which will in turn have affected how different places were experienced in emotional and perhaps cosmological terms, thus influencing decisions about the location of burial places or ceremonial monuments. Forms of land use and systems of exploitation, and the daily and seasonal patterns of movement associated with these, will likewise have helped to determine which areas of the landscape appeared central, which were peripheral and perhaps lonely; which everyday and humdrum, which separate and special. Of course, meanings attached to landscape will also have been influenced by the characteristics of topography: the height of hills, the extent and character of the views which could be enjoyed from a particular point. Yet even these were, to some extent, affected by patterns of contemporary land use and exploitation. It might be possible to enjoy an extensive panorama from a certain place *today*, but during the period in which we are interested such a prospect might (for example) have been completely obscured by tracts of woodland.

In order to understand how local people in the sixth and seventh centuries might have thought about the landscape around Sutton Hoo, and about the particular spot occupied by the cemetery itself, we cannot therefore simply walk around the area today, soaking up the atmosphere and admiring the view, and assume that we are experiencing more or less what they did. We instead need to first attempt, in so far as this is possible, to reconstruct the physical appearance of the landscape at the time, and the ways in which it was used. We are thus fortunate in that, as part of the Sutton Hoo research project headed by Martin Carver, Sutton and the surrounding parishes were systematically fieldwalked by the noted Suffolk archaeologist John Newman. By painstakingly examining the surface of ploughed fields he was able to discover large numbers of early settlement sites: and a number of others are known in the area from chance finds and aerial photography. We thus know a great deal about patterns of settlement in the area around Sutton Hoo before, during and after the Anglo-Saxon period. In addition, we are in a more fortunate position than prehistoric archaeologists attempting to understand the context of Neolithic and Bronze Age monuments in that, while we may lack any *direct* documentary evidence for the character of the early or middle Saxon landscape, some important *indirect* light can be shed on this by a range of important medieval and early post-medieval sources. Although these may date from a period long after the time of Sutton Hoo they can still be used, in association with the archaeological evidence, to tell us something about how the landscape of that period might have been exploited and experienced. Of particular importance are a number of surveys or extents made in the fifteenth or sixteenth centuries: those for Rendlesham (IRO HB416/B4/1/30); Kingston (CUL Mss C328, 311); and for Butley, Boyton and Tangham (BL Eg 2784); the maps made by William Haiward of Sutton itself (surveyed in 1629, drawn up in 1631) and Shottisham (1631) (IRO SA1/54/182 and IRO HA 24:50/19 1.11); and the survey of the Stanhope estates, covering land in Tunstall, Bromeswell, Eyke, Wantisden, and other parishes in the area around Sutton Hoo, made by John Norden in 1601 (IRO V5/22/1; EE5/11/1). The historian Peter Warner, working in association with the Sutton Hoo research project, has already made important use of much of this material, and his comments and advice have proved invaluable in this research, although my interpretations differ in some respects from his.

Phenomenological approaches, if adopted uncritically, can easily become no more than exercises in misinformed speculation. The central section of this book will, I hope, at least represent an exercise in *partially informed* speculation. For I cannot pretend that, even with all this evidence, we can arrive at ideas about the experience of the Sutton Hoo landscape in the sixth and seventh centuries which are in any way susceptible to rigorous scientific testing. But we can go some way of the way towards understanding how contemporaries *may* have thought about the local landscape, and why they thus chose to place the Sutton Hoo cemetery where they did.

CHAPTER TWO

The Changing Landscape

....

The Sandlands

Sutton Hoo stands on the edge of a wide shelf of fairly level land which lies at around thirty metres OD. Immediately to the west the ground falls away steeply towards the estuary of the river Deben: the water's edge today lies some 800 metres away. The mounds are carefully preserved in a landscape of grass which extends along and above the slope, northwards to Tranmer House, the National Trust visitors' centre and associated car parks. But immediately to the east the land lies under the plough, in wide fields fringed in part by rows of conifers, and with a distant backdrop of pine forests. Immediately to the west of the mounds is a plantation – Top Hat Wood – composed of oak and sweet chestnut. This occupies the slope below the cemetery but has grown high enough to almost completely block out any view of the river. Other woods are visible from the site on the sloping ground further to the north.

The prospects from the Sutton Hoo cemetery, with acid grassland, wide arable fields, pines and plantations, is typical of the district known as the 'Sandlings' or 'Sandlands'. But the landscape did not, of course, always look like this and to understand the context of Sutton Hoo we first need to examine how it developed in the course of the medieval and post-medieval periods. The aim of this chapter is thus simply to provide a broad overview of the history of the local landscape: but before we can do this we need first to note some significant features of the natural environment and topography of the area.

The Sandlands, or Sandlings, is the name given to the strip of light land lying between the North Sea to the east and the great dissected clay plateau, which occupies the centre of Suffolk, to the west. The solid geology of this distinctive area is mainly characterised by the formation known as the *crag*, a complex sequence of shelly sands, gravels and clays which was laid down in the late Pliocene and early Pleistocene periods, between 3.5 and 1.6 million years ago (Chatwin 1961). In a number of places in the area around Sutton Hoo, however, and further south towards the county boundary with Essex, earlier Tertiary deposits, principally the London clay, are exposed at or come near to the surface.

Important though this solid geology has been in the development of the landscape, across much of the Sandlings it is obscured by glacial sands and gravels, left by streams running out from the ice sheet which, during the Anglian glaciation, occupied the central areas of Suffolk, and which deposited the extensive areas of boulder clay there (Wymer 1999). On the higher ground these fluvioglacial deposits form a continuous blanket, as much as thirty metres thick in places, but averaging around ten metres. They give rise to the most acidic and infertile soils of the district, those of the *Newport 4 Association* (Hodge *et al.* 1984, 277–8). On the lower ground, in contrast, rather more fertile (although still very sandy) soils are found: those of the *Newport 2 Association*, formed in deposits of the underlying crag as well as in glacial sands (Hodge *et al.* 1984, 272–3); and those of the *Newport 3 Association*, which are loamy as well as sandy, being formed in both fluvio-glacial sands and in patches of boulder clay and 'head' (i.e., glacially redeposited clay material) (Hodge *et al.* 1984, 274–7) (Fig. 8).

The geology of the region is thus varied but all the formations are, in geological terms, comparatively young and soft, and thus eroded with relative ease by the action of the sea. The coastline of Suffolk has been subject to considerable change since the end of the glaciations. Popular mythology, it is true, tends to exaggerate the rate of coastal erosion but the soft mud cliffs are constantly falling into the sea. To the south of Southwold, the town of Dunwich – a substantial trading settlement in early medieval times and, as we have noted, one possible candidate for the place called *Dommoc* – has disappeared almost entirely beneath the waves; while to the north of this, the parish of Easton Bavents has been mostly lost and that of Covehithe greatly reduced in area. But of far more importance in the making of the local landscape has been the fate of the eroded material, which is moved southwards by currents and by longshore drift, forming mobile 'spits' of sand and shingle which gradually intrude on the estuaries of the streams and rivers which run eastwards off the boulder clays, cutting through the strip of coastal sands, to the sea (Steers 1925 and 1926). Towards the north of the district especially, some of the mouths of the streams and smaller rivers have been entirely blocked, their water reaching the sea by seeping through banks of sand and shingle. Their lower valleys are thus very poorly drained and largely filled with deposits of peat, which has formed in the lagoons of fresh water ponded back behind these natural dams. Such areas often remained as unreclaimed fen until well into the post-medieval period. The mouths of larger rivers like the Blyth and the Alde, in contrast, have been only partially blocked in this manner. Instead, constriction of their outflows, coupled with changes in relative land/sea levels in the course of the post-glacial period, has created wide stretches of water resembling inland estuaries. Two kilometres inland from its mouth the river Blyth thus opens into a great area of mudflats and open water which extends for some three kilometres inland as far as Bulcamp and Blythburgh. More dramatically, the growth of the great spit of Orford Ness has deflected the outfall of the river Alde for more than twelve kilometres to the south. The river would once have entered the sea just to the south of what is now the town of Aldeburgh. It now turns abruptly southwards within a few metres of the sea, and then runs parallel with the coast before finally entering it at Shingle Street. Upstream from the point of deflection the river has been ponded back, again creating a wide inland expanse of water and mudflats.

These processes have ensured that these two estuaries are particularly dramatic incidents in the landscape, although that of the Deben itself, largely unaffected by such changes, is also striking. Given that the land, throughout the coastal strip, never rises much above thirty metres OD, and that landforms are generally soft and gentle, the great valleys and estuaries provide the only really dramatic changes in relief. Indeed, even where the difference in height between valley floor and adjacent upland is negligible, the contrast between the rising slopes and the flat, level expanses of water makes it appear greater than it really is. Travelling by land along the coastline these great lateral interruptions in an otherwise topographically uneventful countryside thus make a profound, moving impact on the observer: and it is hard to believe that they would not always have done so.

The formation of spits across estuaries, and in more general terms in long bands parallel to the coast, also led to the creation of extensive areas of salt marsh in their lee, areas which were in most cases progressively embanked and reclaimed, as fresh-water grazing marsh, in the course of the medieval and post-medieval periods. In these situations, peat deposits are largely restricted to narrow bands of poorly draining land immediately adjacent to the uplands, or to the higher reaches of the valleys, and the reclaimed areas principally comprise fertile silts and clays. How far the shifting sands had progressed at the time of Sutton Hoo is uncertain. Some of the region's rivers were probably blocked in relatively recent times. In the area to the north of Southwold, Domesday records a port at Frostenden. This place now lies several kilometres inland, and presumably the stream flowing into Easton Broad was at that time a tidal estuary (Morley and Cooper 1922). Thirteenth-century documents in the cartulary of Butley Priory appear to describe the mouths of the Kessingland, Benacre, Dunwich, and Minsmere Rivers, as well as that of the Hundred River to the north of Aldeburgh, as still open to the sea and used as havens for boats. Even in the seventeenth century some may have remained open. The anonymous author of the *Chorography of Suffolk*, writing in 1605, described how 'At Yoxford springs a little river [i.e., the Minsmere River] that floweth to Fordley and to Theberton … and so directly into the sea where it maketh the haven called Minsmere haven' (MacCulloch 1976, 21). On the other hand, the formation of spits in the south of the region, in the area closer to Sutton Hoo, must have been far advanced by late Saxon times for early medieval documents make it clear that large areas of salt marsh were already being embanked and reclaimed by the twelfth century, especially around Orford (Allen, Potter and Poulter 2002, 21).

In general, the relative proportion of wetland taking the form of salt marsh, embanked and reclaimed at a relatively early date to form grazing marsh, and peat, generally only drained in the eighteenth and nineteenth centuries, changes from the north to the south of the Sandlings region, with marsh more dominant in the south and peat fen in the north. In other ways, too, the natural landscape of the Sandlings changes as we move from north to south. The agriculturalist Arthur Young described in 1797 how the term 'Sandlings' was not then generally used for the entire strip of poor soils running down the coast of Suffolk, but was 'given peculiarly to the country south of the line of Woodbridge and Orford, where a large extent of poor, and even blowing sands is found' (Young 1797). To the north of this the soils were loamier and more fertile: 'there are few districts in the county, if any, abounding with wealthier farmers'. The reason for this distinction is apparent from the modern maps produced by the Soil Survey: moving towards the south, the coastal strip of sands becomes steadily wider (Fig. 8). While parishes lying to the north of Aldeburgh generally extend up onto the heavier but more fertile claylands to the west, many of those in the south are entirely confined to the sands, although usually including within their area some low-lying coastal wetlands.

The area in the immediate vicinity of Sutton Hoo which forms the focus for most of the discussion in this and the following chapters is typical of the southern section of the Sandlings. Bounded to the west by the river Deben and its estuary, it corresponds with the medieval parishes of Sutton itself, Shottisham, Eyke, Hollesley, Ramsholt, Alderton and Bawdsey, together with parts of Butley, Capel St Andrew, Boyton, Wantisden and Rendlesham (Fig. 9). These parishes vary considerably in size but are, in general, rather larger than the average for Suffolk: in broad terms, in East Anglia as elsewhere areas of poor, acidic soils generally have larger parishes than those on more fertile land, although the reasons for this are complex and there are many exceptions. Sutton itself is one of the largest parishes in the county and, as Figure 10 suggests, a high proportion of its area is occupied by particularly poor soils. The parochial system developed in the centuries either side of the Norman Conquest, as local churches were erected within larger, older ecclesiastical territories, usually by manorial lords but sometimes by groups of free men. Where land was poor, levels of local wealth low and/or populations small, parishes tended, for obvious reasons, to be larger than in wealthier and more densely settled districts, for a number of local lords and communities might have to combine together in order to endow a church.

The majority of the area – mostly lying above twenty metres OD but occasionally, as in the vicinity of Sutton Hoo, rising above thirty metres – is occupied by soils of the Newport 4 Association, large areas of which remained as open heathland until reclaimed for agriculture in the twentieth century or, more usually, planted up as conifer plantations by the Forestry Commission. The more fertile Newport 2 soils cover a smaller area, on the lower slopes, while on the lowest ground, close to sea level, areas of silt and estuarine clay – now grazing marsh, and most probably already salt marsh in Saxon times – occur, separated by narrow strips of sand and shingle from the estuary of the Deben or the North Sea.

The relative agricultural importance of the Newport 2 soils, at least in the period since the Middle Ages, is clear from the fact that today all the parish churches in this area, and all the main settlements, are located on or beside them. The poor sandy uplands, in contrast, are largely devoid of settlement. This does not, however, mean that they were considered economically unimportant in the Middle Ages, or even in the post-medieval period. The configuration of parishes – which in part, as we shall see, fossilised that of early medieval agricultural territories – ensured that each community had access to a portion of these poorer soils. Indeed, the way that parish boundaries often converge near the central points of the main upland masses suggests a degree of competition over access to, and negotiation to ensure a fair division of, this resource (Fig. 10). Of course, it is likely that the character of the local soils, and especially those formed in the upland sands, has changed over time, and that the latter were originally less leached and acidic than today, and included layers of humus and perhaps deposits of the fertile, wind-blown, silty material called *loess*. The archaeological evidence does, however, suggest that the uplands were already less favoured for farming and settlement by the Roman period, and they were certainly, by the early Middle Ages, occupied by extensive areas of heathland.

Figure 10 shows that the district around Sutton Hoo also included, some five kilometres to the north-west of the cemetery, a small area of clay soil. Indeed, although the immediate hinterland of Sutton Hoo comprises extensive tracts of sand, the boulder clay plateau of central Suffolk lies at no great distance to the west and north, and the parish of Rendlesham – which included, as we have seen, the site of an early *vicus regius* – lies largely on clay. In this context it is important to note that the soils derived from the local boulder clays display as much variation as those formed in sands and gravels. Generally speaking, where the clay plateau is dissected by significant valleys they are generally lighter and/or more calcareous than on the level plateaux above, where the poorly draining and sometimes acidic soils of the Beccles and Ragdale Associations are dominant. The clay soils found within Rendlesham parish are, not surprisingly, of the former variety (they are classified by the Soil Survey as falling within the Burlingham 3 Association). Variations in the characteristics of the clay soils in the area thus replicate, in some respects, those of the sands. In both cases there is a marked contrast between the soils of the valley sides, which were at least moderately fertile, and those of the uplands, which – at least by Saxon times – were less tractable and/or less fertile, and better suited to pasture or woodland than to arable.

Early settlement

Although this chapter is mainly concerned with the ways in which the local landscape developed in medieval and later times a brief consideration of earlier developments is unavoidable, for the simple reason that certain important features – the location of many settlements, the sites of parish churches – were shaped and decided before the Norman Conquest.

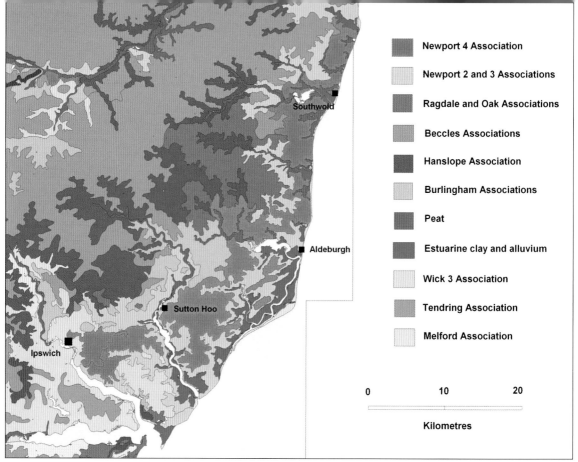

Newport 4 Association

Newport 2 and 3 Associations

Ragdale and Oak Associations

Beccles Associations

Hanslope Association

Burlingham Associations

Peat

Estuarine clay and alluvium

Wick 3 Association

Tendring Association

Melford Association

0   10   20

Kilometres

FIGURE 8 (*above*). The Sandlings, showing principal soil types and the location of Sutton Hoo.

FIGURE 9 (*left*). The boundaries of the area discussed in Chapters 2 and 3.

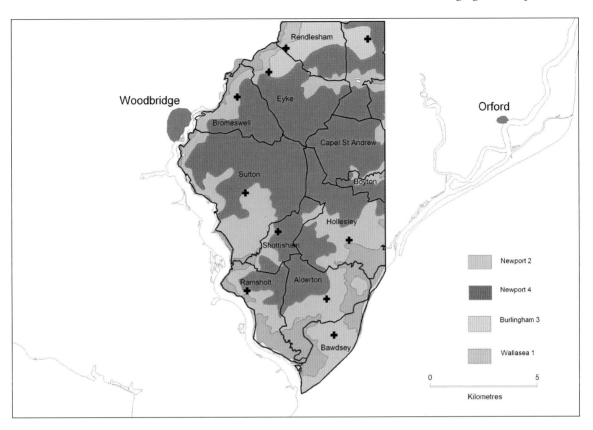

FIGURE 10. The location
of parish churches, and
the configuration of
parish boundaries in
relation to soil types, in
the area around Sutton
Hoo.

As already noted, as part of the Sutton Hoo research project the archaeologist John Newman undertook a systematic fieldwalking survey of the area around Sutton Hoo, which extended into most, but not all, of the area shown in Figure 9. By carefully examining the surface of the ploughsoil he was able to discover spreads of pottery and other debris marking the sites of settlements of prehistoric, Roman, Saxon and medieval date. In addition, various archaeological sites – for the most part, farms or small hamlets – have also been discovered over the years by chance. But even the results of Newman's meticulous survey do not provide a complete picture of settlement history. Some periods are more archaeologically 'visible' than others. Romano-British and medieval settlements are usually marked by significant concentrations of pottery sherds which are well made and generally survive well on the surface of the ploughsoil: the only problem here is that some concentrations of material may indicate, not the sites of settlements, but areas of arable land which were being intensively manured with material brought from middens on nearby farms. Late prehistoric and early Anglo-Saxon sites, in contrast, are usually less visible. The friable, poorly fired pottery used in these periods often disintegrates rapidly when exposed to frost and rain, especially in areas of acidic soils. The pottery produced in other periods, to give a third alternative – most notably, the distinctive middle Saxon Ipswich Ware – although durable and capable of surviving well on the surface, is often present in only relatively small quantities. More important than questions of artefact survival, however, is the fact that many settlements of Saxon or medieval date are still occupied today, and their origins are therefore obscured by houses, outbuildings, gardens and paddocks. Some areas, moreover, are unavailable for archaeological inspection because they lie beneath pasture or woodland. For all these reasons, even intensive field surveys of the kind carried out by Newman cannot usually recover a complete picture of early settlement history: but they do permit us to reconstruct the broad patterns of past settlement and land use.

As Figure 11 shows, prehistoric material – principally flint tools and flakes – is widely scattered, with some concentrations occurring even on the sandy uplands, although usually towards their margins. A number of round barrows, or the cropmarks marking their sites, are also known from these locations. The presence of such sites, especially the flint scatters, on the upland soils perhaps indicates that their quality has indeed deteriorated over time, and Carver's excavations showed that the area around the Sutton Hoo cemetery was farmed, to some extent as arable, in the prehistoric and Roman periods, before erosion and podzolisation (Carver 2005, 391–458). But Sutton Hoo, it should be emphasised, lies on the very edge of the sandy uplands, and most of the prehistoric sites known from fieldwork and chance finds are similarly positioned. Away from these locations, where the sands lie deeper, prehistoric settlements seem to have been rare. While to some extent this absence of upland settlements might be an illusion – a consequence of the fact that large areas are today occupied by conifer plantations, and thus unavailable for archaeological inspection – this cannot be the main reason for this striking *lacuna* because extensive arable fields also occur today in many places on these soils, as for example in the area immediately to the east of Sutton Hoo itself.

With few exceptions, Roman and post-Roman settlements are even more noticeably clustered on the more fertile soils of the Newport 2 Association, or around their upper or lower margins (Figs 12, 13 and 14). This pattern is especially marked in the southern portion of Sutton parish, in the adjacent parts of Shottisham and Ramsholt, and in the adjoining portions of Alderton, where sites of various periods form an almost (but never quite) continuous band of settlement. But there are some marked interruptions in the distribution, most notably in the area to the north of Alderton village. Here, a broad belt of Newport 2 soils, running north for two kilometres or more between the heathy uplands to the west and the drained marshes to the east, is almost devoid of settlement. This empty zone is terminated to the north by a cluster of sites around Brew House and Poplar Farm, beside the headwaters of the Black Ditch, to the north-west of Hollesley village; but to the east of this, as the band of Newport 2 soils swings eastwards, just to the north of Hollesley, sites are again few and far between. There is nothing in modern land use patterns to explain these gaps and, while it is true that this particular area was not intensively fieldwalked by Newman, the *lacuna* is noticeable and suggests that soils alone are not enough to account for the distribution of early settlements.

Figure 15, showing aspects of the area's hydrology, goes some way towards supplying an explanation. Almost all the known Roman and Saxon sites are located beside running water, or else in low-lying areas beside the coast where the London clay outcrops at the surface or is only thinly buried beneath the crag. Here, shallow wells could be constructed with relative ease to exploit the perched water table. Virtually no sites of Roman or Anglo-Saxon date known from archaeological fieldwork or documents lie more than c.200 metres from an obvious water source, and most if not all of the exceptions appear to be associated with watercourses which have failed in modern times, or which have been culverted; or with patches of clay outlying from the main masses, missed by the broad and generalising sweeps of the geological survey. Both soils *and* water supply were thus key determinants of settlement location: an obvious and unremarkable observation, perhaps, but one worth emphasising simply because some landscape archaeologists, as we have seen, castigate those who attempt to understand the lives of past peoples by examining soil maps, distribution maps, and other 'Cartesian devices'. In reality people in the past would not, and could not, live in any location. They chose the places where crops could best be grown, and where people and stock could be supplied with water with relative ease.

One last point must be briefly emphasised, although there is no space to discuss it in detail here. The way in which early medieval settlement developed in the area around Sutton Hoo, as across much of East Anglia, was clearly rather different from what is often (and wrongly) considered the 'norm', as exemplified by the Midland areas of England. There, settlement in the middle and later Saxon periods tended to develop along increasingly 'nucleated' lines, so that by the twelfth century most people lived in sizeable villages. In the area under discussion, in contrast, middle and later Saxon settlement remained fairly dispersed, in small hamlets and individual farms. As we shall see, it was to become increasingly scattered in character in the period after the Norman Conquest.

The later Saxon landscape

It is only in the later Saxon period that we begin to get a clear picture of the pattern of settlement, and to some extent the appearance of the landscape, in the area around Sutton Hoo. This is because, as well as having archaeological evidence, we have for the first time a documentary source, Domesday Book. This describes the various manors (estates) and vills (townships) in the district, and provides information about their tenant populations and resources.

Domesday shows us a landscape in which there was little woodland. Whereas vills on the claylands to the west and north-west might have woodland sufficient for a thousand swine or more (the normal way in which Domesday records woodland in this part of the country), Staverton had only enough for thirty swine and other vills in the area less, or none at all. The survey also suggests

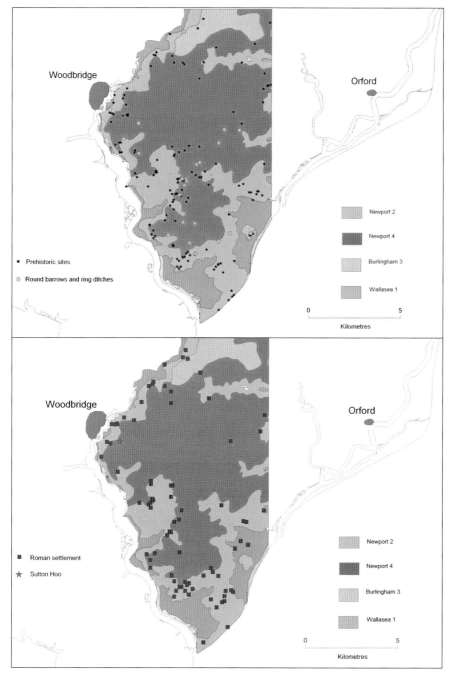

FIGURE 11. The location of known prehistoric sites in relation to soil types in the area around Sutton Hoo.

FIGURE 12. The location of known Romano-British settlements in relation to soil types in the area around Sutton Hoo.

FIGURE 13 (*facing*). The location of known Anglo-Saxon settlements in relation to soils types in the area around Sutton Hoo.

FIGURE 14 (*facing*). Medieval settlements known from archaeological evidence in the area around Sutton Hoo.

that, in spite of the fact that the local soils are often described as poor, the area around Sutton actually had a rather dense population at the time of Domesday, with just under 20 recorded individuals per square mile (implying a real population, for the survey only records landholders, of perhaps 80 per square mile – among the highest densities in England). In addition, the survey informs us that there were around four plough teams per square mile, above average for Suffolk. But it tells us little else about local agriculture because only the livestock on the home farms or demesnes of manorial lords were listed, and

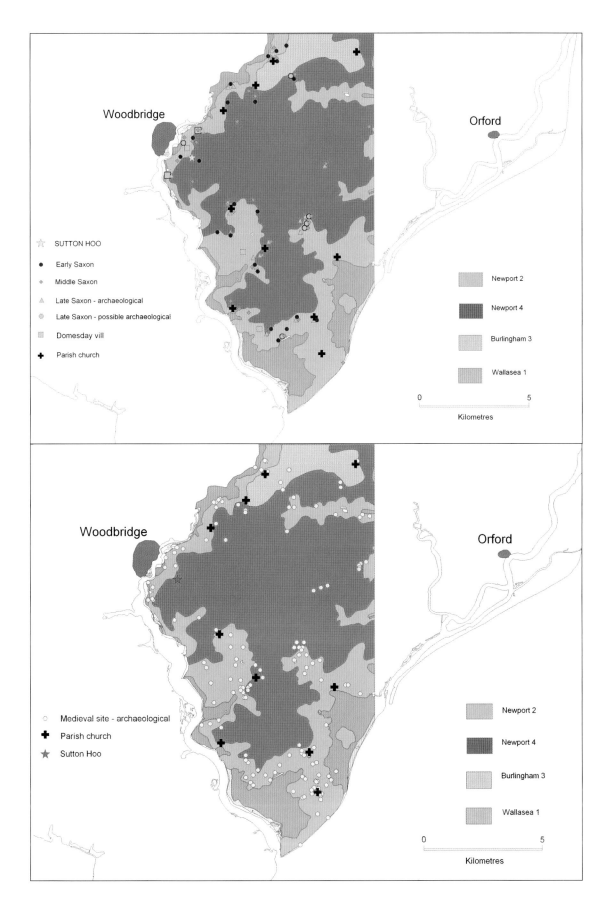

Woodbridge

Orford

☆ SUTTON HOO

● Early Saxon

◆ Middle Saxon

△ Late Saxon - archaeological

◉ Late Saxon - possible archaeological

▢ Domesday vill

✚ Parish church

Newport 2

Newport 4

Burlingham 3

Wallasea 1

0   5
Kilometres

Woodbridge

Orford

○ Medieval site - archaeological

✚ Parish church

★ Sutton Hoo

Newport 2

Newport 4

Burlingham 3

Wallasea 1

0   5
Kilometres

much of the land was held as small estates by free men, about whose farming enterprises Domesday remains silent.

Perhaps the most notable feature of the Domesday record is that is show that the district was characterised by a rather high density of named places, or vills – that is, units recognised by late Saxon administrators and tax collectors – a characteristic which it shared with the area of Colneis Hundred on the opposite side of the Deben, which has been discussed by Norman Scarfe (1988), and also with certain other areas of relatively dense population in East Anglia and elsewhere. While most of the vills which Domesday records in England continued to operate as separate administrative units into the Middle Ages and beyond, usually becoming ecclesiastical and civil parishes, some did not: and this was especially true where they were, as in the area around Sutton, particularly thick on the ground. In such districts a significant proportion were absorbed into a neighbouring place in the course of the Middle Ages and, while their names might on occasions be perpetuated by some farm, manor or 'hall', in many cases their location remains a matter for speculation and debate (Fig. 16).

In some cases, however, 'lost' vills are not in reality lost at all. They are simply places which have changed their name. Staverton is the most important local example. Its name survives on the map today only in that of Staverton Park, an area of ancient wood pasture occupying poor, heathy soils at the point where the parishes of Eyke, Butley, and Wantisden meet. No house or settlement bears this name today, but 'Staverton Hall' is depicted on John Norden's map of 1601 (IRO V5/22/1) a little to the south-east of what is now Friday Street, in the parish of Eyke but close to the boundary with Rendlesham (at c.TM 335517). Staverton was not a small place at the time of Domesday. It had a recorded population of twenty-four, equivalent to over a hundred people, and possessed a mill and a church. It even had an outlier, or dependent settlement, with the unlikely name of 'Bing'. Staverton continues to appear in documents like the *Inquisitiones Post Mortem* into the sixteenth century, although the latest references are not to a vill, or even to a manor, but rather to 'A tenement, 43a land, 10a pasture, 8a meadow, and 40a heath in Eyke, called 'Stavertons'' (HMSO 1898, 909). These later documents also show that the manor of Staverton had rights in marshes called Old Moor and 'Chisfen', the latter the area later known as Cheffyn Common beside the river Deben, on the western boundary of the parish of Eyke (HMSO 1913, 434). The advowson of Eyke church (and that of Bromeswell) also descended with the manor. The connections with Eyke are particularly interesting because that place does *not* appear by name in Domesday Book, in spite of the fact that it became a large parish and has a church which, although much altered, was evidently a substantial Norman structure with a central crossing tower. John Newman discovered small quantities of late Saxon pottery sherds in its immediate vicinity, and seventh- and eighth-century coins have been found nearby. There can be little if any doubt that Domesday's Staverton was, in reality, Eyke, and that the name of the place changed over the following centuries, perhaps as one part of the vill became more important than another.

In other cases, as already noted, vills are not entirely lost, but can be identified with later manors, modern 'halls'. The vill of Peyton (*Peituna*), for example – a relatively large place, with a recorded population in 1066 of thirty-five – can be identified with Peyton Hall, now a single farm in the south of Ramsholt parish. The place called Stockerland no longer appears on the modern map, but was presumably centred on Ferry Farm in Sutton, which the 1631 map of Sutton by William Haiward describes by this name – as Peter Warner observed in 1984 (Warner 1984, 01/2). The tiny vill of Wilford – with its four inhabitants – did not survive as a settlement into post-medieval times but can presumably be identified with a scatter of early, middle and late Saxon pottery, together with medieval material, discovered by John Newman close to Wilford Bridge (centred at TM 291498). *Udeham* – another small vill, with a recorded population of two in 1066 (seven by 1086), but relatively valuable and including a mill – can almost certainly be identified with the manor of Wood Hall, in the south of Sutton parish. The name was still used in an Inquisition Post Mortem (relating to John Wingfield) as late as 1481 (Copinger 1911, 271). The vill of Hoo also falls into this category. Domesday Book describes two separate places with this name in Suffolk. One lay in the hundred of Loess and was a substantial place, with a recorded population of twenty-three in 1066 and a church. This is the parish of Hoo near Crettingham, eight kilometres north-west of Sutton. The other, however, was in Wilford Hundred and was much smaller, with a recorded population of only two free men. There is little doubt that this was at or near the place, now a single farm, called Little Haugh, a short distance (c.600 metres) to the north-west of the Sutton Hoo cemetery, close to which John Newman recovered quantities of medieval pottery: although once again the place is never heard of again as a separate vill. The fact that one of the free men in Hoo was commended to Robert Malet in 1086 – a powerful individual who also held the principal manors in Sutton itself – suggests that the diminutive vill was simply absorbed into Sutton soon after the time of Domesday.

In several cases we can only suggest a very approximate location for a missing vill. The place called *Culeslea* continued to appear in documents into the fourteenth century and was presumably in Alderton, to judge from one reference to 'Colesle in Altherton' in an Inquisition Post Mortem of 1295 (HMSO 1912, 207), but that is all we can say. The recurrent grouping in later documents, especially Inquisitions, of *Thurstanestuna* with Alderton suggests that this, too, lay somewhere in that parish, although Darby in his *Domesday Gazetteer* suggests that it was in fact within Bromeswell (HMSO 1912, 207; Darby and Versey 1975). *Bing*, an outlier or dependent settlement of Staverton, may have been in Bawdsey (Darby and Versey 1975). The locations of other Domesday vills – mostly tiny places like *Halgestou* with a population of two, or *Hundesthoft* with only three recorded inhabitants, but including some larger ones like *Laneburc* with six recorded inhabitants or Littlecross with seven – are even less clear. All are placed in the Sutton area by modern scholars – usually in Sutton itself, although Darby places *Halgestou* in Shottisham – but on

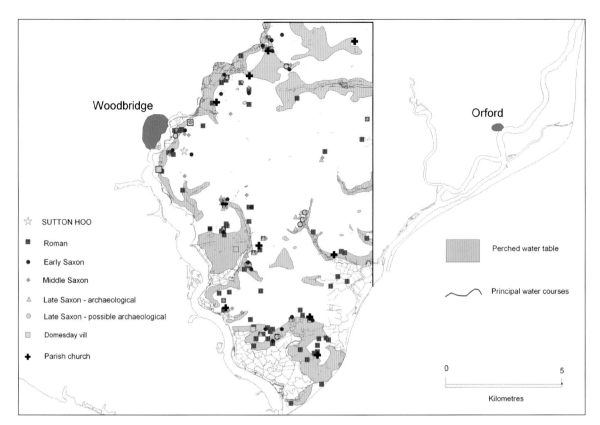

Woodbridge

Orford

☆ SUTTON HOO

■ Roman

● Early Saxon

◆ Middle Saxon

△ Late Saxon - archaeological

● Late Saxon - possible archaeological

▢ Domesday vill

✚ Parish church

▨ Perched water table

〰 Principal water courses

0   5

Kilometres

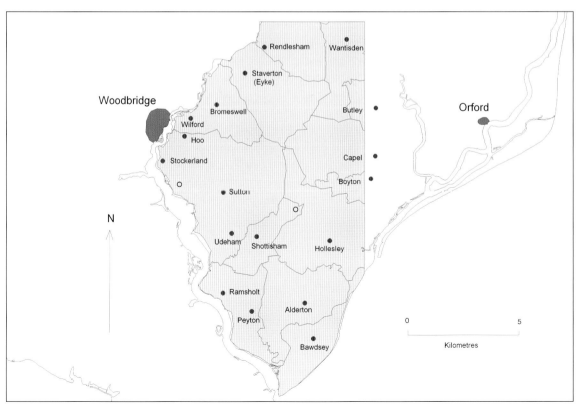

Woodbridge

Orford

● Rendlesham

● Wantisden

● Staverton (Eyke)

● Bromeswell

● Butley

● Wilford

● Hoo

● Stockerland

● Capel

○

● Sutton

● Boyton

○

● Udeham

● Shottisham

● Hollesley

● Ramsholt

● Alderton

● Peyton

● Bawdsey

N

0   5

Kilometres

very little evidence, and some of the suggested locations make little if any sense. All four of these places fail to appear in subsequent documents and they were presumably absorbed into neighbouring vills at an early date. None contained any recognised manor (merely small numbers of free men, with their undertenants) at the time of Domesday, and none possessed a church.

Precisely why this area should have been characterised by such a multiplicity of vills in later Saxon times, many of very small size, is uncertain. This was, as we have noted, a characteristic of other areas with a relatively dense population, but by no means of *all* such areas. Flegg in north-east Norfolk, for example, had a denser population than the area around Sutton Hoo but has no 'lost' vills, and few examples of these kinds of diminutive vill. To some extent the proliferation of separately named and administratively recognised places must reflect the fact that the settlement pattern of the district was already relatively dispersed. Rather than being concentrated in a few villages, that is, it was scattered in small hamlets and clusters of farms, each of which presumably had its own name. Yet even this would not necessarily have engendered a high density of individual *vills*, for we know – from archaeological and documentary research – that in other parts of the country individual vills could often embrace a plethora of spatially discrete settlements (Taylor 1983, 125–6). In all probability the answer lies in part in the character of the late Saxon settlement pattern, but in part in the character of the district's tenurial organisation. This was not only a fairly densely settled district, but one in which a high proportion of the population were described by Domesday as *liberi homines*, free men, who would have paid taxes in their own right rather than through some neighbouring manor. For this reason, perhaps, the names of the places in which many of them lived were individually recorded.

The question is, however, made slightly more complicated by the fact that some of the parishes in this area, most notably Sutton, are relatively large, and in other parts of East Anglia the area they occupied might comprise two or even more parishes. In other contexts, that is, vills like Udeham would probably have achieved parochial status. That they did not do so here was largely because, while the area was relatively populous in early medieval times, it was also by this stage relatively poor, especially when compared with the claylands lying to the west, where settlement and cultivation were now expanding fast. Where much of the land was in the hands of free but relatively poor men, under-provision of churches is perhaps unsurprising.

Most medieval parishes in the area thus probably contained – were built out of – a number of diminutive late Saxon vills: for as well as those whose sites (like Peyton, or Udeham) which we can identify, there also a number – such as Bing, or Littlecross – whose location is uncertain. Some are presumably represented by scatters of pottery and other debris found by fieldwalking, especially those which appear to have been occupied over a long period of time (notable examples include the concentration of early, middle and later Saxon pottery and metalwork in Alderton, to the east of the village, at c.TM 334416). Moreover, even where a medieval parish developed out of a single Domesday vill, this in most if not all cases will have contained two or more settlements, each perhaps with its own agricultural territory: John Newman's fieldwalking survey has recovered a number of late Saxon pottery scatters which cannot be equated with known vills; and there are more such scatters in total then there are named vills, although not all of these were necessarily occupied at the time of Domesday (the kind of pottery used to distinguish late from middle Saxon settlement first came into use in the area in the ninth century). On the other hand, some of the places which Domesday suggests were the sites of vills have produced no evidence for late Saxon occupation. Archaeological evidence alone, that is, underestimates the extent of late Saxon settlement, usually for the reason already explained – continuity of occupation at a certain place obscures the evidence of its origins and history. In the parish of Sutton itself, no late Saxon finds have been made in the area around Stockerland (although medieval and Roman material has been located nearby), nor around Wood Hall, the probable site of Udeham. This absence almost certainly reflects, not the fact that either of these places has been misidentified from the documentary evidence, but rather that the relevant archaeological material is inaccessible. What applies to Sutton is also true of the adjacent parishes. In Ramsholt, for example, Peyton Hall – as already noted – represents the vill of Peyton, but no late Saxon pottery has yet been found there. In short, at the time of Domesday the area consisted of a scatter of hamlets and farms, some of which were classified as vills, some not; and of the former, some survived into the medieval period as parishes, while others were absorbed, in administrative terms, into the territories of neighbours.

The medieval landscape: fields and settlement

Domesday Book tells us the names of places, lists their populations and provides some indication of the extent of cultivation, but tells us little more: and the same is, for the most part, true of all documentary sources before the fifteenth and sixteenth centuries. It is only then that documents were produced which provide us with relatively detailed information about the appearance and layout of the local landscape. These can also, with caution, be used to throw some light on these matters rather earlier in the Middle Ages. Firstly, as already noted, a number of important maps of the area were produced in the early seventeenth century. The famous surveyor John Norden compiled a book of surveys showing the estate of Sir John Stanhope in 1600–01, which includes parts of the study area – the family held land in Bromeswell, Eyke, Wantisden and Butley (IRO V5/22/1; EE5/11/1); while William Haiward produced detailed maps of Sutton and Shottisham in 1629 and 1631, both of which show the ownership of each minute strip of land in these parishes (IRO HA 24: 50/19/1.11; IRO JA1/54 (1)). Secondly, there are a number of important 'dragges', or extents – written surveys. One relates to Rendlesham, although it also includes some land in Tunstall and Wantisden (IRO HB 416/B4/1/30). It includes references to land transactions made as early as the twentieth year of the reign of Richard II (1396/7) but is itself of sixteenth-century date, written in English with occasional Latin, and incorporates material from the sixteenth as well as the fifteenth century. Such 'surveys' were usually compilations of material, transcribed from numerous individual copyhold entries in the manorial records, so they describe the landscape not at a particular point in time but as it was over a period of a century or more. Another 'dragge' concerns the lands of the manor of Melton, Ufford and Kingston, which included property in Bromeswell and Sutton (CUL MSS C 328, 311). The document is Elizabethan in its present form, but again incorporates earlier material. A third survey, for the manor of Butley, Boyton and Tangham, on the fringes of the area mapped in Figure 9, is again of Elizabethan date (BL Eg. 2789).

The first point to note is that Norden's survey, and the maps produced by Haiward, both show a highly scattered pattern of settlement: one which was considerably more dispersed, indeed, than that which exists in the area today (Fig. 17). Newman's fieldwalking evidence indicates that this had been even more the case in the high Middle Ages: in a manner familiar from other parts of East Anglia, population growth in the centuries after Domesday did not simply lead to the expansion of existing settlements, but rather to the spread of farms and cottages out across the landscape, and sometimes their migration away from older, late Saxon sites. The Domesday settlement pattern, in other words, already comprising a scatter of farms and hamlets, became even more scattered. Parish churches were often associated with only a handful of cottages and farms, or even lay separate from the main areas of settlement. Those at Sutton and Butley stood quite alone in the midst of the fields. Some farms and cottages were clustered – again in a pattern familiar from elsewhere in East Anglia – around the periphery of greens and commons. Most were strung out along lanes and tracks. Many of these sites had disappeared before the various maps were surveyed, leaving only scatters of debris in the midst of the fields. The large number of such sites testify to the extent to which settlement expanded, and population rose, in the two centuries between Domesday and c.1300; and also to the extent of the subsequent late medieval demographic decline. But many of these isolated farms and cottages were abandoned *after* the earliest maps were made, in the course of the seventeenth and eighteenth centuries.

By the nineteenth century the area around Sutton Hoo was, in comparison with the medieval situation, fairly thinly settled and its settlement pattern more nucleated, a salutary reminder of how we must be careful not to read the early history of the landscape too simply, or directly, from the evidence of much later maps. Indeed, several of the villages in the area only really came into existence in the course of the eighteenth, nineteenth or even twentieth centuries. In 1631 Shottisham church was thus accompanied only by a farm and three cottages, with a further three houses loosely strung out along the road approaching it from the east (IRO JA1/54 (1)). By the end of the nineteenth century this loose collection of dwellings had developed into a substantial village, with a school

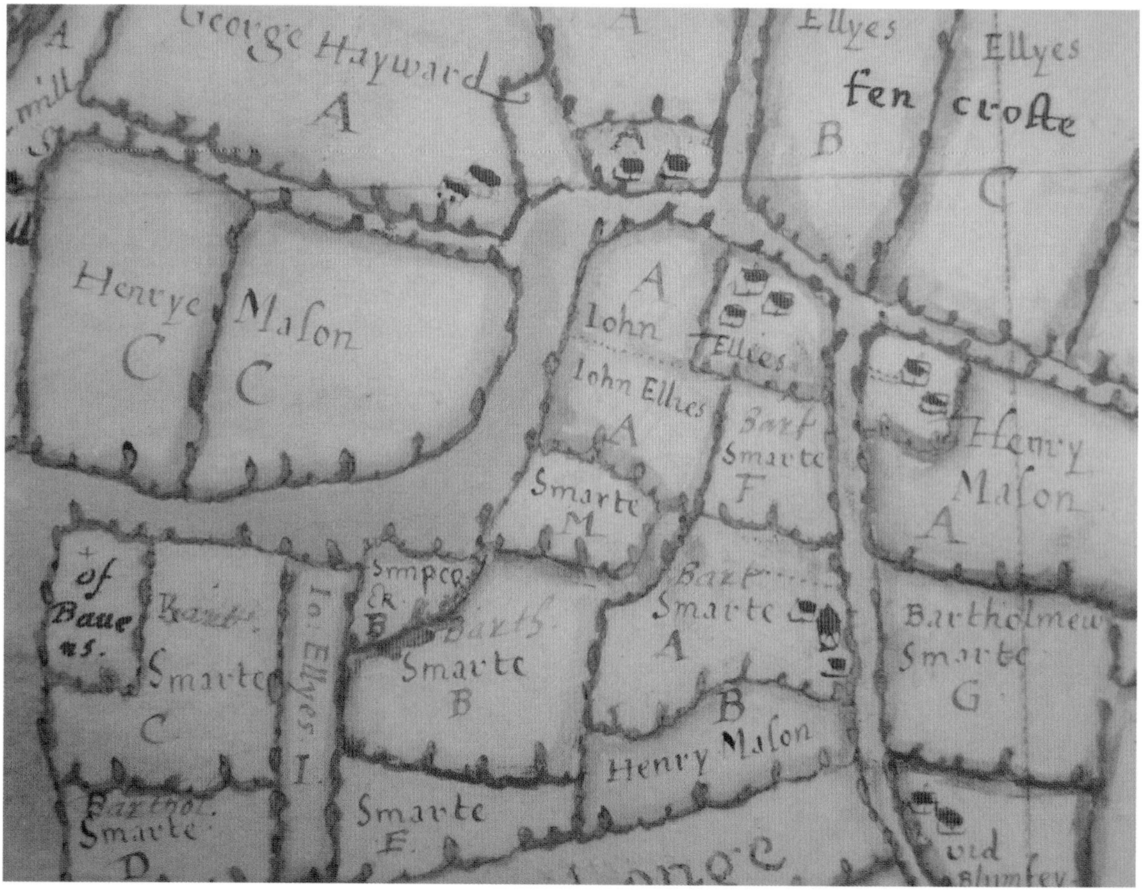
George Hayward
Ellyes
Ellyes
fen crofte
Henrye Mason
John Ellyes
John Ellyes
Bart Smarte
Henry Mason
Smarte
of Bauens
Barth Smarte
Jo: Ellyes
Barth Smarte
Bart Smarte
Bartholmew Smarte
Henry Mason
Barthol Smarte
Smarte

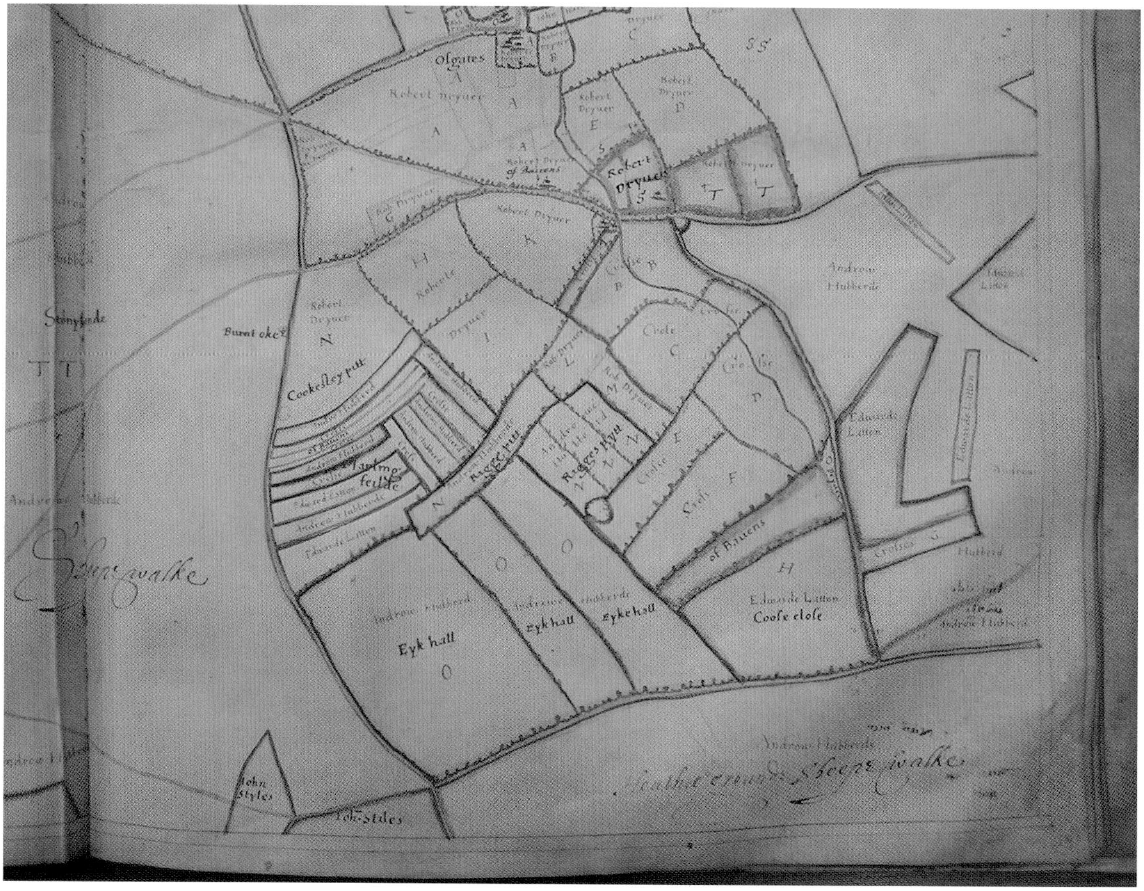
Olgates
Robert Dryuer
Robert Dryuer of Bauens
Robert Dryuer
Robert Dryuer
Andrew Hubberde
Stonyfelde
Burnt oke
Cookesley pitt
Raggespitt
Raggespytt
of Bauens
Edwarde Litton
Coose close
Eyk hall
Eyk hall
Eyke hall
Andrew Hubberd
Sheepe walke
Heathe grounde Sheepe walke
John Styles
Joh: Styles

and public house. Over the same period, several outlying farmsteads in the parish had been abandoned.

The early maps also show that by the early seventeenth century the landscape of the area around Sutton Hoo comprised a patchwork of open fields and enclosures. There were significant variations from parish to parish in the relative extents of each. In Wantisden in 1601, for example, there was no open-field land at all: in Sutton in 1629, in contrast, well over a third of the cultivable land was still open (Fig. 19). The various extents suggest that enclosure had already progressed a long way by the fifteenth and sixteenth centuries. They often refer to land in 'fields' – open fields – and make frequent use of the term 'went', the local name for a furlong or bundle of strips. But they also refer to numerous 'pightles' (small hedged pieces of land), 'crofts' and 'closes', as well as to hedged fields containing the strips of several proprietors – a kind of half-way-house between open and enclosed land. The Kingston extent thus refers to property in Bromeswell as 'six pieces of bond land … lying in the croft called Calve Croft …'. Around 38% of the land described by the extent in this parish lay in open fields, 22% in closes and perhaps 15% comprised 'subdivided closes' (in a further 25% of cases the precise status of the land in question is unclear) (CUL MSS C 328, 311). In the Rendlesham extent open fields accounted for 42% of the land

FIGURE 17. Early maps suggest that in the period before the eighteenth century the settlement pattern of the area around Sutton Hoo was more dispersed than it is today: an extract from John Norden's survey of the Stanhope estates, 1600–01, showing the area around Broom Hill in Eyke. Several of these farms and cottages have since disappeared.

FIGURE 18. Fields created by piecemeal enclosure from open arable, together with some residual open-field strips, depicted by John Norden in the south of the parish of Eyke.

FIGURE 19 (*right*). Map of the parish of Sutton, surveyed in 1629 by William Haiward, showing a mixture of open fields and hedged closes, most of the latter evidently enclosed piecemeal from the former (courtesy Peter Warner).

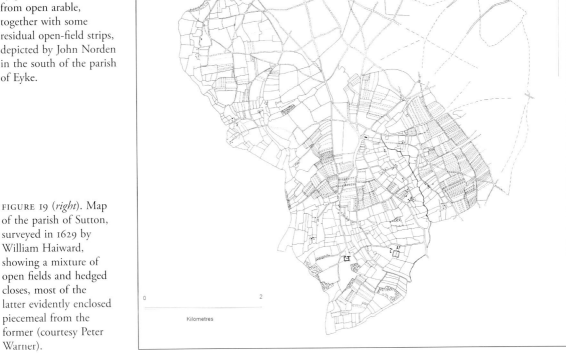

described, with enclosed land (including areas of private heath) taking up 51%, the rest being made up of turbaries, private meadows, and land of uncertain status (IRO HB 416/B4/1/30).

In all parts of the area, some enclosed fields had always existed. Some of the larger closes, like those shown around the sites of Wood Hall and Pettistree manors on the 1629/1631 map of Sutton, for example, appear always to have been farmed quite separately from the open fields, as compact blocks of demesne land; while others, fields located between the surviving open furlongs and heath, were probably enclosed directly from heathland. But the majority of hedged closes had evidently been created in the fifteenth and sixteenth centuries by enclosing former open-field land. The extents make numerous references to such recently enclosed parcels. That for Rendlesham, for example, refers to 'one piece of bond land … lying in the said field and called *le Hedwent* between the land of the lord in the tenure of Francis Gould towards the north and the land of the manor of Staverton in the tenure of Ric Balhead Galfrid Pells now newly enclosed' (IRO HB 416/B4/1/30). It is also clear that the open fields were generally removed in this district, as across much of East Anglia, by what is known as *piecemeal enclosure*. Landowners bought, sold and exchanged strips so that they acquired consolidated blocks of land, which they could then surround with a hedge and farm as they liked, free from the communal controls and uses which, to varying extents, applied to the open arable.

This method of enclosure often leaves fairly clear traces in the landscape, for the gradual establishment of hedges along the edges of contiguous groups of strips preserved the basic layout of the old landscape. Strips in the open fields were seldom straight: they were usually slightly sinuous, sometimes taking the form of a shallow 'reversed S' (caused by the need for the ploughman to move towards the left as he approached the end of the strip in order to avoid too tight a turning circle) (Eyre 1955). This shape, and the sinuosity of the strips more generally, was preserved by piecemeal enclosure. In addition, two strips running end to end were seldom enclosed in line by this method, so that the boundary of one of the new enclosures generally ran not to the corner of the next, but to a point a little way in along the boundary line: such kinks and dogs legs are another noticeable feature of these landscapes (it is noteworthy that several of the abandoned medieval sites discovered by Newman lie within fields shaped like this, indicating that consolidation and enclosure of the open arable had been continuing even before the Black Death).

We are very fortunate in having the two surveys prepared by William Haiward, and the book of maps made by John Norden, for these provide an invaluable picture of the local landscape as it was soon after the end of the Middle Ages. We are less fortunate in that for the rest of the area around Sutton Hoo the earliest available maps are of eighteenth- or nineteenth-century date. These later sources can, however, tell us something about the character of the earlier landscape for, as already intimated, certain field shapes, and certain road and boundary patterns, convey important information about previous

FIGURE 20. Field boundaries and roads shown on the earliest surviving maps in the area around Sutton Hoo. This map is based on the tithe award maps for the relevant parishes and, where available, earlier surveys in the Ipswich Record Office, viz. William Haiward's maps of Sutton, 1629 (HA 24. 50/19/1.11); and Shottisham, 1631 (JA1/54 (1)); John Norden's survey of the Stanhope estates, 1601 (V5/22/1; EE5/11/1); and estate maps for Ramsholt, 1777 (JA1/14/2); Bromeswell, 1728 (HB10.427/834), 1799–1812 (HB10.427/833), and undated nineteenth century (HD 80/1/1 (34)); Bawdsey and Alderton, late eighteenth century (HD 417/1); Bawdsey, 1727 (HA 30.50/22/26.1); Alderton, 1810 (HB 10/427/835) and 1859 (HB 26/412/1837 and HB 26/412/1840); and Butley, 1839–40 (HD 628/10).

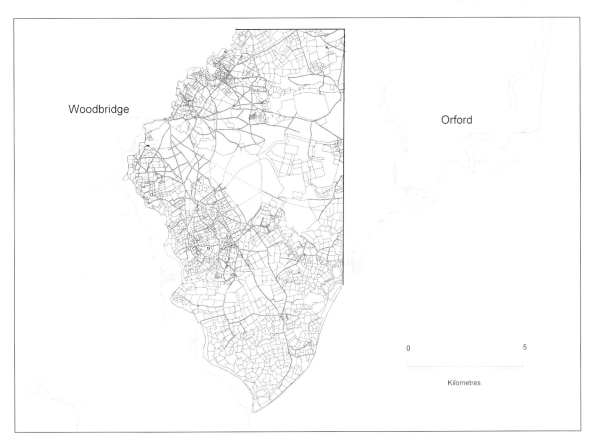

Woodbridge

Orford

0   5

Kilometres

developments. Figure 20 shows the roads and boundaries depicted on the earliest available maps for all the parishes in the area around Sutton Hoo. Figure 21 categorises or 'characterises' the different types and shapes of field, showing which areas were still occupied by open fields when the maps in question were surveyed; which by fields with boundaries created by the piecemeal enclosure of open arable; which were occupied by open heathland or by post-medieval intakes from this; and which land falls into other categories. Not surprisingly, most of the known open fields, and areas of probable former open field, lie on the Newport 2 soils, although they extend in many places up on to the fringes of the poorer soils of the sandy uplands. Indeed, in the seventeenth century a high proportion of the *surviving* open fields could be found in the latter locations, perhaps because wealthy landowners were less interested in consolidating and enclosing poorer-quality land. The map also shows, equally unsurprisingly, that the main areas of heathland in the seventeenth century, as well as the fields apparently enclosed from the heaths, were found on the Newport 4 soils, and especially towards the centres of the main blocks of higher ground.

The medieval open fields of the area were of a particular type. In the classic form of the open-field system, familiar from the textbooks and largely found in the Midland areas of England, there were usually two or three great 'fields' in

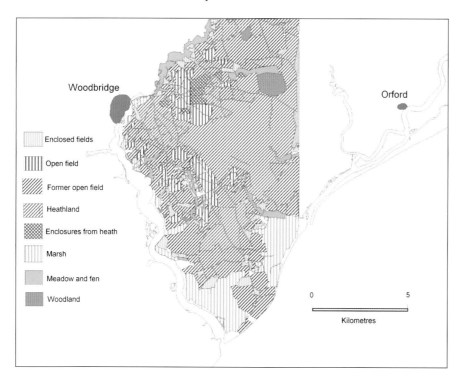

Woodbridge

Orford

Enclosed fields

Open field

Former open field

Heathland

Enclosures from heath

Marsh

Meadow and fen

Woodland

0   5

Kilometres

FIGURE 21. Principal field and landscape types shown on the earliest surviving maps in the area around Sutton Hoo. The shapes of enclosed fields suggest that extensive areas of the better soils were occupied by open arable in the Middle Ages.

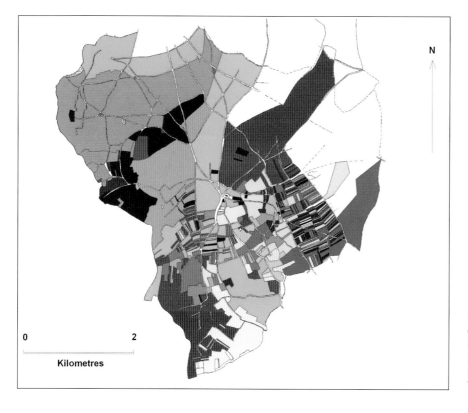

N

0   2

Kilometres

FIGURE 22. The complexity of landholding patterns in the parish of Sutton in 1629, as recorded by William Haiward.

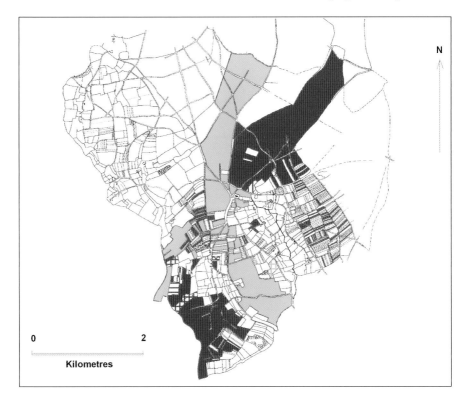

FIGURE 23. The
distribution of the
property of the largest
landowners in Sutton
in 1629. Red: Francis
Burwell; green: William
Fernley (the properties
shown hatched or
cross-hatched had been
recently acquired).

FIGURE 24. The
distribution of the
property of selected
smaller owners in Sutton
in 1629. Note how these
are concentrated in
restricted areas of the
parish.

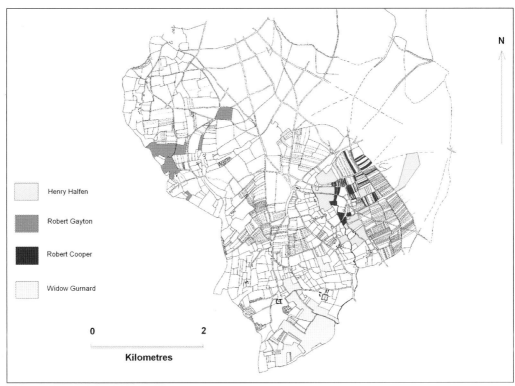

each parish, across which the holdings of particular farmers were more or less evenly scattered. Each year one would lie fallow, one would contain winter-sown and one spring-sown crops. The available evidence makes it clear that none of this can ever have been true of the area around Sutton Hoo. In Sutton itself Haiward's map (IRO HA 24: 50/19/1.11) shows that instead of being evenly scattered, the holdings of individual owners were markedly concentrated in particular areas of the parish (Fig. 22).

True, this pattern had to some extent been obscured by the fact that, in the course of the late medieval and early modern periods, some very large holdings had been created through the progressive 'engrossment' of smaller properties, something often associated with the piecemeal enclosure of the land in question. Nevertheless, even these extensive properties – the lands belonging to men like Mr Fernley or Mr Burwell – were normally concentrated in one part of the parish (Fig. 23). Where smaller holdings still survived, the concentration of strips within limited areas is usually rather clearer (Fig. 24). This pattern indicates that the open fields cannot have had an extensive and continuous area under fallow each year in the Midland manner, for if so every year some of the farmers would have been unable to grow any crops. Instead, as with most open fields in East Anglia, fallowing was organised on the basis of furlongs, or groups of furlongs, rather than by 'fields'. Within the fields themselves the boundaries of the furlongs, and in some cases those of the strips, were bounded by narrow, unploughed baulks. The legend on Haiward's map of Shottisham (Fig. 25) notes that he had marked 'the meares in the fields w[i]th a light grene the waies w[i]th a streake of yellow' (IRO JA1/54 (1)) (at Ufford in the eighteenth century fifty-three acres of open arable, divided into seventy-four strips, were said to be 'so intermixed with other lands that they could not be set out, the balks having been ploughed up' (Burrell 1960, 44)).

The lower, better soils in the district were not entirely occupied by open fields and closes in the Middle Ages. Maps and extents show that there were also a number of small greens and commons, some quite extensive but many little more than wide drove roads. These, too, were rapidly privatised from the late Middle Ages. In addition, in the minor valleys of the various streams flowing across the uplands there were ribbons of meadow and fen. The latter were found in the more waterlogged areas, where soils were peaty, and were cut for a variety of products – saw-sedge (*Cladium mariscus*) and reed for thatching, rough fen grasses and rushes for marsh hay and litter, and in some cases peat itself for fuel. They also provided grazing in the summer months, although this was often of poor quality. They could, by improving the drainage, usually be converted into better-quality grassland. John Norden noted, between Rendlesham and Butley, an area of fen beside a brook which had been recently enclosed and turned into good pasture ground (IRO 50/1/74(12)).

Heaths and marshes

In the Middle Ages much, probably most of the heathland which occupied the poorest soils in the district had been common land. But through the late Middle Ages, and into the sixteenth and seventeenth centuries, manorial lords and the larger farmers had been busy enclosing it, turning it into private sheep grounds, and the maps and extents show that much was held in severalty. The Sutton map of 1629/1631 thus shows that most of the heathland in the parish took the form of 'walks' attached to the largest farms, and only a relatively small proportion was common (IRO HA 24: 50/19/1.11), while the sixteenth-century 'dragge' of Butley, Boyton and Tangham describes numerous portions of 'bruery' or heathland held in severalty. John Norden's map of 1601 shows that one area of sheepwalk in the south-east of Bromeswell was separated from the adjoining common heath by a feature described as 'the ditch of the new Inclosure'; while in Eyke a large tract of heathland is simply described as 'Late Common' (Fig. 26). Norden's survey of the Stanhope estates was part of that revolution in attitudes to landed property which I noted briefly in the opening chapter. Mapping was about the control, expropriation and the exploitation of private property. A map was a management tool which allowed the outsider – in this case, Sir John Stanhope – to relish, as if from on high, a prospect over a landscape over which he had complete control, and helped to maximise the profits which could be derived from it.

Whether held in severalty or exploited in common, heaths were not, for the most part, natural environments. With some exceptions, they occupied areas which were originally tree-covered but, lying on easily worked sandy soils, they were attractive to early farmers. Once cleared of trees – deliberately for cultivation, by felling for wood and timber, or through the depredations of sheep and other stock – their soils deteriorated. This, coupled with sustained grazing, favoured the development of a characteristic vegetation, dominated by various combinations of heather or ling (*Calluna vulgaris*), bell heather (*Erica cinerea*), gorse or furze (*Ulex europaeus*) and broom (*Sarothamnus scoparius*). Certain grasses also thrive on such poor soils, including sheep's fescue (*Festuca ovina*), wavy hair grass (*Deschampsia flexuosa*), and common bent (*Agrostis tenuis*), while some areas become dominated by bracken. Not all English heaths are the same, however. On the surviving Sandlings heaths the dominant shrub is ling, accompanied by rather smaller amounts of bell heather and gorse. In addition, in some parts of the Sandlings grass heath – acid grassland dominated by common bent, sheep's fescue, and sheep's sorrel (*Rumex acetosella*) – also occurs (Beardall and Casey 1995, 32–3) (Fig. 27).

It is important to emphasise that the heaths were not only created, but also sustained, by human activities. If they had not been intensively exploited, the trees would have returned. In medieval and early post-medieval times furze was cut for fuel (it was the most common form of charcoal excavated at the Anglo-Saxon burial ground at Snape) (Filmer-Sankey and Pestell 2001, 259), and it could also be used for fencing. John Norden, in his *Surveyor's Dialogue*

N

0   1

Kilometres'

FIGURE 25. The open
fields of Shottisham,
as mapped by William
Haiward in 1631.

of 1618, described how it was employed 'to brew withall and bake, and to stoppe a little gap in a hedge' (Norden 1618, 234). Ling was likewise a source of fuel, and may also have been used as thatch. Some areas may have been set apart for its cultivation and protected from grazing in the Middle Ages, for it was sold in large quantities. In Staverton in 1305–6 sales of the plant bought in £2 12s (Rackham 1986, 295). It was also used in farmyards, in place of straw, to judge from the diary of Samuel Gross, who farmed in the area in the 1840s (IRO SI/8/3.2). Bracken was likewise used for fuel and for thatch, but mainly as animal litter. It was surprisingly valuable, sales at Staverton bringing in fourteen shillings in 1274–5 (Rackham 1986, 295).

Yet while the heaths thus supplied a variety of produce for the local inhabitants their main use in medieval as in post-medieval times was always for grazing sheep. These had an economic importance in their own right, but they were mainly valued as a source of fertility. The flocks were grazed on the heaths by day, and by night folded on the arable fields, when they lay fallow or after harvest, their dung keeping the poor, leached soils in heart (Kerridge 1967, 42–5). In the words of John Norden, who knew the Sandlings well, in light soil districts

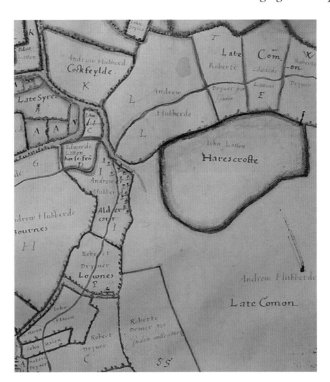

FIGURE 26. Extract from John Norden's survey of the Stanhope estates, 1600–01, showing recently enclosed heath and meadow land in the area to the west of Staverton Park, in Eyke.

FIGURE 27. Surviving open heathland on Sutton Common, two kilometres to the south-east of Sutton Hoo.

> The farmers doe much enrich their Land indeede with the sheep-fold. A most easie, and a most profitable course; and who so neglecteth it, having means, may be condemned for an ill husband (Norden 1618, 229).

In some parts of East Anglia this practice formed part of the *foldcourse system*, in which the intensive night-folding was a monopoly of the manorial lord which tenants could enjoy only in return for a cash payment, and in which the sheep were organised into communal flocks, dominated by the stock of the lord and under the care of his shepherd. Stray references show that such arrangements did exist in the Sandlings, even in the post-medieval period. In 1637 there was said to be two foldcourses in Blythburgh and Walberswick 'upon the sheepwalk or heath there, containing 500 acres' (IRO 50/22/3.1); while a sixteenth-century lease for Alderton refers to 'meadows, feedings, pastures, foldcourses …' (Burrell 1960, 34). But they never seem to have been as deeply entrenched here as in many parts of Norfolk and Suffolk.

The other main animal grazed on the heaths was the rabbit, introduced into England soon after the Norman Conquest. Rabbits were valued for their fur and meat, and kept in small enclosures, often within deer parks, or in large open warrens in areas where there were extensive areas of sand, such as coastal sand dunes. The light soils of the Sandlings, especially the poor upland sands, made ideal places in which to establish warrens. By the fourteenth century there were a number of examples in the area around Sutton Hoo, at Dunningworth (established by 1274), Iken (recorded from 1392), and within the deer park at Staverton (from c.1322). Over the following centuries examples were established at Sutton, Shottisham, Staverton, Boyton, Hollesley, and Tunstall (Hoppitt 1999; Bailey 1988). In many parts of England rabbits were provided with special accommodation in the form of earthworks which archaeologists call 'pillow mounds', partly to encourage them to burrow but also to make it easier to trap them. These features were less necessary in an area like the Sandlings, where the soils were deep, sandy and freely draining, but they were sometimes provided, either as 'clappers' for breeding does, or when new warrens were first established. A large version of such a mound, nearly two metres high, survives on Sutton Common (TM31394765) (Fig. 28). It is set within a circular earthwork enclosure covering some 1.25 hectares, probably a breeding enclosure. Two smaller mounds, also probably warren mounds, survive to the north, at TM31404806. At some point in the late medieval or, more probably, the post-medieval period a warren was evidently established on Sutton Heath, and the rabbits also seem to have burrowed freely in the barrows at Sutton Hoo. Martin Carver suggested that four medieval or post-medieval pits placed symmetrically around the margins of Mound 2 might have been dug in connection with warrening, and that rabbits might actually have been 'farmed' in the mounds (Carver 2005, 171–4). While this is possible, it is perhaps unlikely that the mounds would have been intentionally or intensively stocked with rabbits in the way that the pillow mounds further to the east presumably were, for they

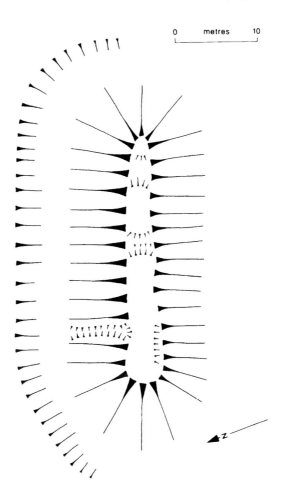

FIGURE 28. An unusually large example of a 'pillow mound', relic of the post-medieval rabbit farming industry, on Sutton Common. It stands within a circular enclosure and probably functioned as a 'clapper' for breeding does on a warren established in the seventeenth century.

lay on the margins of the heath, close to arable land, a location in which high densities of rabbits were not normally encouraged because of the damage which they caused to crops, and the legal disputes which could arise from this.

The Sandlings heaths seem to have been very intensively grazed by sheep and other stock and this probably ensured that they had a more managed appearance than the surviving fragments today, with the heather and gorse more closely cropped. John Norden, writing in 1618, noted that while in general he recommended the destruction of gorse, 'there is a kind of furze worth the preservation, if it grow in a Countrey barren of wood'. This, he noted, supplied much of the fuel used in Devon and Cornwall: it grew 'very high, and the stalke great, whereof the people make faggots'. But he went on:

> And this kind of Furse groweth also upon the Sea coast of *Suffolke*: But that the people make not the use of them, as in *Devonshire* and *Cornwalle*, for they suffer their sheep and cattell to browse and crop them when they be young, and so they grow too scrubbed and lowe tufts, seldome to that perfection that they might be. (Norden 1618, 235)

It is hardly surprising, then, that in the sixteenth and seventeenth centuries the heaths carried very few trees or shrubs. Those few areas which were scattered with thorns are clearly singled out on Norden's maps.

So far I have discussed arable land and heath as if they represented separate and distinct forms of land use. But throughout the Sandlings there is evidence that much of the heathland was subject to sporadic cultivation, at least by the sixteenth century. On several of Norden's maps of the Stanhope estates annotations indicate this clearly. One area in Chillesford was described as being 'heathye and barren yet in some places beareth indifferent good rye' (IRO EE5/11/1): while of another, to the south-east of Staverton Park, Norden noted: 'some of this is reasonable good rye ground; so more of the heath if it were used accordingly' (IRO V5/22/1) (Fig. 29). The late sixteenth-century extent of Butley, Boyton and Tangham similarly refers to areas, like 'le Sheepe Walke', which were 'part arable and part bruery'. Such sporadic and shifting cultivation continued into the nineteenth century. As late as 1885 White's Directory, discussing the local heaths, noted how 'such lands, the better spots at least, are occasionally broken up and cultivated for a few years, and then laid down again on a self-sown herbage for a ten, twenty or perhaps a thirty year rest' (White 1885, 4). Martin Carver noted phases of late medieval and post-medieval cultivation at Sutton Hoo, during which the mounds had themselves been ploughed, considerably reducing their height and thus their prominence in the landscape. Rather than representing the opportunistic expansion of the frontiers of cultivation along the margins of the heath, in response to rises in cereal prices, these episodes are probably best understood as part of the normal cycle of management to which most of the heaths in the area were subject during the historic period.

The maps produced by Norden and Haiward, as well as the extents produced in the fifteenth and sixteenth centuries, thus show that in almost all the parishes in the district the main cultivated areas, concentrated on the Newport 2 soils, were bounded on their upper margins by tracts of heathland, intensively exploited by local communities. In many parishes these arable areas were similarly bounded on their lower margins by coastal wetlands, some still in their virgin state – unreclaimed salt marsh – but mostly by this time embanked and improved. The reclamation of the Suffolk coastal marshes began at a very early date, perhaps even in the pre-Conquest period. Extensive areas were certainly being 'inned' from the tides around Orford by the 1160s, following the construction of the great castle there by Henry II. In the estuary of the Deben and around its mouth, so far as the evidence goes, much reclamation took place rather later, in the sixteenth or seventeenth centuries. The salt marshes in Alderton, Bawdsey and Butley seem to have been embanked by Butley Priory in the 1520s and 30s: prior to this they had been 'often drowned with salt water and of lyttle valuew' (TNA: PRO E134 Eliz.27/28 M15). The priory's marshes at Hollesley were probably improved around the same time, for Henry VIII's sister Mary, her husband the Duke of Suffolk, and others went to view them when they visited the area in 1528 (Dickens 1951, 50). In the 1540s four hundred acres

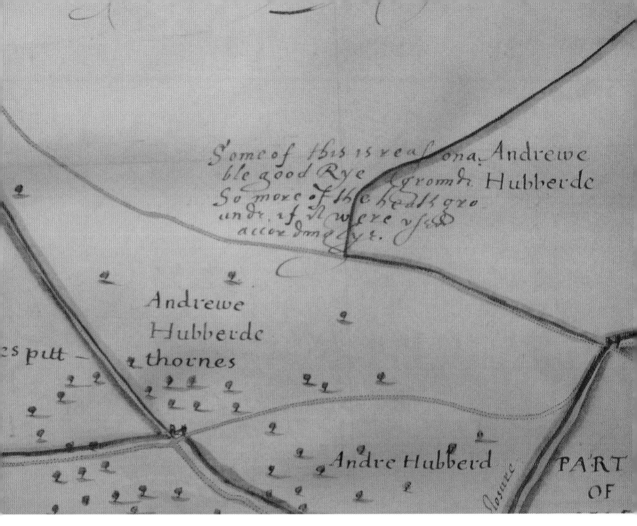

Some of this is reasona‑
ble good Rye gromd.
So more of the heath gro‑
und, if it were vsed
accordingely t.

Andrewe Hubberde

Andrewe
Hubberde
thornes

es putt

Andre Hubberd

PART
OF

FIGURE 29. Extract
from John Norden's
survey of the Stanhope
estates, 1600–01, showing
heathland in the south-
east of Bromeswell. Note
the scatter of thorns, a
relatively unusual feature;
and Norden's comments
about cultivating rye on
the heath.

(162 hectares) of the Duke of Norfolk's marshes in the same parish were reclaimed. Reclamation continued into the following century. John Norden's survey shows 'The New Inned Marsh' on the north side of the Butley River, beside the Sudbourne Fleet, as well as the dam erected across the mouth of this watercourse to prevent the ingress of the tides (IRO EE5/11/1). The main use of this reclaimed land was for grazing, initially for sheep but increasingly, by late medieval times, for cattle. The silts and clays, once effectively drained, afforded excellent grazing but some parts were sporadically ploughed and cropped: one farm in Butley had 38 acres out of 104 of its marshes in tilth in 1794 (Burrell 1960, 147).

Before reclamation these low-lying areas would have had a very different appearance – with rougher and more diverse vegetation, and dissected by creeks that filled and emptied with the tides. Their meagre, salt-tolerant vegetation would have provided some seasonal grazing, however, as well as a range of natural foodstuffs in the form of fish and shellfish. By later Saxon times – and also earlier, in the Roman period – they would also have been important for salt production. Domesday records a number of salt pans along the coast (and also in a number of inland vills, presumably detached assets of the manors in question), although none in the immediate area of Sutton Hoo.

Recent changes

The medieval and early post-medieval landscape of the district has been described in some detail because, as we shall see, its character and layout may contain clues about the local environment in early and middle Saxon times. The dissolution of this landscape in the course of the later seventeenth, eighteenth and nineteenth centuries will be described more briefly, and for a different reason. Our understanding of the context of the burial mounds at Sutton Hoo is inevitably shaped by the present appearance of their surroundings: but this, in many respects, is a creation of only the past few centuries.

The key changes in the eighteenth, nineteenth and twentieth centuries were, firstly, the enclosure of the remaining areas of open fields and an associated increase in the number of hedges and hedgerow trees. Piecemeal attrition of the open arable continued through the seventeenth and into the eighteenth century and by the nineteenth century, to judge from the available maps of the area, virtually no common arable remained in the immediate vicinity of Sutton Hoo, although in some adjacent areas small fragments remained into the nineteenth century, as at Ufford, across the Deben, where forty-four acres divided into fifteen strips still existed when the tithe award map was surveyed in 1844. What is striking is that the distinctive field patterns created by piecemeal enclosure, so evident on early maps of the area, are far less obvious in the modern landscape, which is instead dominated by ruler-straight boundaries. It appears that in the post-medieval period, as more and more land fell into the hands of large estates, the existing somewhat irregular field pattern was redrawn, presumably to fit in with contemporary notions of what a modern, 'improved' landscape should look like.

Secondly, these centuries saw a significant reduction in the area of heathland. The chronology of this is hard to estimate because of the difficulties of distinguishing shifting cultivation, which had probably always been a feature of the locality, from permanent reclamation. On the available evidence, however, it would seem that the latter increased significantly in extent during the 'agricultural revolution' period of the later eighteenth and early nineteenth centuries. In 1784 the Frenchman Francois de la Rochefoucauld, travelling through Sutton, thus described how:

> It is in the past twenty years or so that all this countryside – perhaps twenty square miles – has been inhabited. The extreme depth of the shifting sand had until then defeated the reclaimers ... I saw some very fine crops in land that – simply judged by someone who will not make a perfect connoisseur of soil – one would suppose could produce nothing. An acre is rented at five or six shillings a year ... (Scarfe 1988b, 135)

Arthur Young, writing in 1795, likewise described the recent changes made on the 'extensive wastes of Sutton': 'great tracts have been broken up within these twenty years, and are found to answer well ...' (Young 1795, 38).

Reclamation was accompanied by attempts to neutralise soil acidity, for this lowered the yields of some crops and precluded the cultivation of others (Hanley 1949, vol. 1, 138; Robinson 1949, 232). Moreover, acid land could soon become overrun again with heathland vegetation, as Norden explained:

> It is the nature of Furze, Broome, and Brakes, to keepe their standing, and hardly will yeelde the possession once gotten in a field: for commonly they like the soyle well, and the soyle them; and where there is a mutuall congruity, there is seldome a voluntary separation. And therefore, as long as there is not a disturbance of their possession with a contrary earth, they will keepe where they are … And therefore as the soyle is commonly barren, hot and dry where they live, make this ground fat and fruitful, and they will die. And therefore the greatest enemy that may be set to encounter them is good and rich Marle, and thereupon, the plough some few yeares together, and you shall see, they will shrinke away, and hide their heads. (Norden 1618, 239)

The principal method of remedying acidity was, as Norden describes, to mix the sandy soil with some kind of calcareous material. As early as 1601 there are local references to treating land with lime made from shells collected from the sea shore, and in the nineteenth century clay was brought many miles from the west to spread on the fields. Chalk was even brought from Essex and Kent in empty grain ships returning from London (Young 1797, 137). But the most important remedy for acidity was a particular form of shelly, calcareous crag which lies close to the surface in many parts of the district. This was excavated from pits and spread on the fields. The practice was an old one – Norden shows a number of examples on his map of the Stanhope lands, one lying in a close called 'Marlingfield' (IRO V5/22/1) – but it increased in scale markedly during the eighteenth and nineteenth centuries, as extensive tracts of the acid uplands were reclaimed. In the 1790s Young described how, in the area around Ramsholt, 'pits are to be seen on every farm, some very large and deep' (Young 1797, 130). In October 1808 one James Harding was killed in Sutton due to the collapse of a pit 'situate in a field called Crag Pit Hill' (IRO HB10: 50/20/9.14).

Yet in spite of the impression given by Young and other eighteenth- and nineteenth-century writers (e.g. Kirby 1829, 3) large areas of heathland survived the agricultural revolution period, unaffected by the fashionable mania for 'improvement'. Even heavy applications of 'calcareous earths' could do little to remedy the extreme droughtiness of the local soils, or their deficiency in key chemicals like boron and manganese. When the extent of heath and sheepwalk shown on Norden's 1601 survey of the Stanhope estates, and on Haiward's surveys of Sutton and Shottisham, is compared with that depicted on the tithe award maps of c.1840 or the First Edition Ordnance Survey 6″ maps of the 1880s (Fig. 30), a significant reduction is indicated in some places but overall there was only a relatively limited decrease and in some parishes none at all. Indeed, to judge from the map evidence, some areas which had been under arable cultivation in the seventeenth century had actually become heathland by the nineteenth. Certainly, extensive heaths survived in the area into the nineteenth century, and the agricultural depression which began in the late

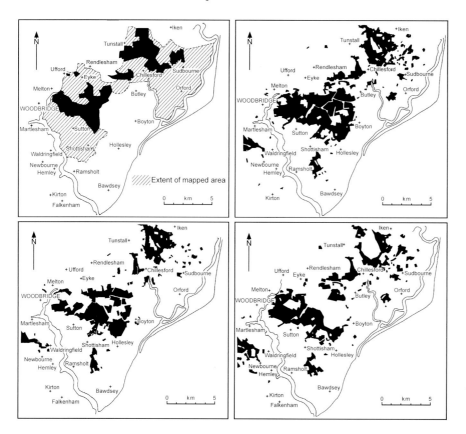

FIGURE 30. The distribution of heathland in the southern Sandlings. Top left: areas of heathland and 'walks' shown on John Norden's survey of the Stanhope estates (1600–01), and on William Haiward's maps of Sutton (1629) and Shottisham (1631). Below left: distribution of heathland on the tithe award maps, c.1840. Top right: areas of heathland and rough grazing shown on the Second Edition Ordnance Survey maps, 1905. Below right: distribution of heathland recorded by the Land Utilisation Survey in 1935.

1870s saw some reversion of arable to rough grazing. As grain prices fell, it became uneconomic to cultivate the worst soils. But the depression years also saw major changes in the character of the local heaths. Sheep numbers declined in the district, so the heaths were grazed less intensively, while at the same time the regular cutting of gorse, heather and bracken came to an end. The last of these increased in importance, and hawthorn and other scrub began to colonise in many places. Shrubs and trees find it difficult to establish themselves in dense stands of heather. But as older, larger stands develop with a decline in grazing intensity, patches of open ground are formed between them, where hawthorn, blackthorn and birch can successfully seed and, untroubled by regular grazing, grow to maturity (Fig. 31).

The disappearance of most of the heaths in the area came in the course of the twentieth century. Some simply regenerated to woodland, as birch became fully established and was joined by oak and, in places, pines. Others were obliterated through deliberate planting. Landowners had established small areas of woodland in the district throughout the post-medieval period but the rate of planting seems to have increased in the course of the nineteenth century, and especially with the onset of the agricultural depression in the decades after 1870. In the inter-war period the rate of afforestation increased markedly, however, as

FIGURE 31. Woodland regenerating over ungrazed heathland on Sutton Common.

FIGURE 32. Twentieth-century pine plantations in Capel St Andrew, part of the Forestry Commission's Rendlesham Forest.

the Forestry Commission started to acquire and plant land in the district. The extensive plantations now known as Rendlesham Forest began life in 1920 with the purchase of 1,878 acres (760 hectares) from Lord Rendlesham, followed by a spate of further purchases through the 1920s: the land was rapidly planted up. Tunstall Forest, further to the north, was built up more gradually. The Commission's first purchase was of 437 acres (177 hectares), part of the Sudbourne estate, in 1920: but no further land was bought until 1929, when 906 acres (367 hectares) of the Campsea Ashe estate was acquired, followed in 1930 by 1,600 acres (648 hectares) of the Chillesford estate. In the 1920s and 30s the two areas – Rendlesham and Tunstall – were managed as a single unit, called Rendlesham Forest (Forestry Commission archives, Santon Downham: Acquisition Files, uncatalogued). By 1926 2,302 acres (932 hectares) had been planted, rising to 3,501 acres (1,417 hectares) by 1930 (Acquisition files: Forestry Commission Archives, Santon Downham).

In addition, the post-War period saw a sustained attempt to convert much of the remaining heathland to arable. Small-scale attempts at reclamation had been made in the 1920s, and again in the 1940s (Trist 1971, 120). But from 1949 large areas were brought into cultivation. Government subsidies for liming, the widespread use of artificial fertilisers, and the availability of cheap chemical treatments to rectify the potash, boron, manganese and copper deficiencies to which these acid, leached soils were prone all made large-scale reclamation possible. So too did a range of modern machinery, including tractors and rotary cultivators, which ground up the tough stems of the outgrown heather (Trist 1971, 120–23). Irrigation began to be used in the 1950s, and on a large scale by the 1960s: once irrigated, the light soils were excellent for cultivating potatoes and other vegetables. Between 1949 and 1952 1,533 acres (620 hectares) were ploughed at Wantisden Hall, at Iken Hall, at Lodge Farm in Sudbourne, and on the Shottisham, Martlesham, and Waldringfield Heaths. By 1955 a further 1,120 acres (453 hectares) had been reclaimed around Sutton Hoo and on Sutton Hoo Common; at Methersgate Hall; and on the Kesgrave, Bromeswell, Hollesley, Nacton and Brightwell Heaths. The years between 1955 and 1964 saw a further 207 acres ploughed in Shottisham, Sutton and Hollesley (Trist 1971, 121).

Conclusion

I noted in the last chapter the dangers involved in trying to understand how ancient monuments might have been experienced by the people responsible for their construction by simply relying on how we experience them and their surroundings today. This chapter, by providing a brief overview of the development of the local landscape over the last millennium, should have served to reinforce such reservations. The landscape context of Sutton Hoo has changed considerably since medieval times. Coastal wetlands have been reclaimed; heaths have been massively reduced in area. Above all, the landscape has become much more subdivided, by hedges and pine lines, and much more wooded in appearance, especially as a consequence of the great planting campaigns of the 1920s and 30s.

Woodland now makes a major impact almost everywhere in the locality, even if only as a distant backdrop, and it comes as something of a surprise to learn that the overwhelming majority is so recent in date. As late as 1856 Glyde bemoaned the rather dull character of the scenery on the coast between Landguard Point and Dunwich, 'bleak and dreary, destitute of wood' (Glyde 1856, 28).

These changes, and especially those occurring in very recent times, had a particularly pronounced effect on the immediate environs of Sutton Hoo: so much so that it is now difficult to appreciate the significance of the cemetery's location in terms of the configuration of different types of land use, and in relation to the river Deben. In the early seventeenth century, and almost certainly for centuries before that, the mounds stood in a very open landscape, on the western edge of a large tract of heathland which extended, uninterrupted, for more than seven kilometres to the east. It thus lay in a kind of junction zone, for on the slopes to the west, and below them, lay arable land, some farmed as open fields. Moreover, the cemetery occupied a point where the band of arable on the better soils of the lower ground was considerably narrower than it was to the south, and almost certainly (for we have no early maps) than it was to the north: the point, in other words, where the high, heathy ground came closest to the water. Perhaps more importantly, in the seventeenth century – and again, probably for a long time before this – an uninterrupted view could have been enjoyed westwards from the cemetery, towards the river Deben: a view which, as I shall argue, was of some significance to those who erected the mounds.

All this changed radically in the course of the last two centuries. Firstly, the amount of woodland in the immediate area increased, closing off views in many directions. Belts were planted in the early nineteenth century on the level ground to the north-east of Sutton Hoo, presumably when the heathland here was reclaimed (Fig. 33). Plantations were also established in the course of the nineteenth century on two stretches of north-facing slope overlooking the river: one just under a kilometre to the north of the cemetery, looking towards Melton; the other ('Apricot Hill Plantation') to the west, near Ferry Hill. By 1905 more of the sloping ground had been planted up, ploughing here now making less economic sense as the agricultural depression deepened. The former plantation was expanded to form the block of woodland now known as Brown's Planting (subsequently expanded further (before 1928) to the south, with the addition of Home Wood). More importantly, the steep slope immediately to the west of the cemetery was planted up with oak, sweet chestnut and other species to create the trapezoid area of woodland known today as Top Hat Wood. It is hard to exaggerate the impact of these changes. The views from the Sutton Hoo cemetery towards the river were now almost completely blocked, while those from the Tranmer House cemetery, some 600 metres to the north, were largely obscured. Indeed, the best thing the current owners – the National Trust – could do to enhance the experience of the site would be to chop down every tree in Top Hat Wood, to restore the original character of the relationship between Sutton Hoo and the Deben.

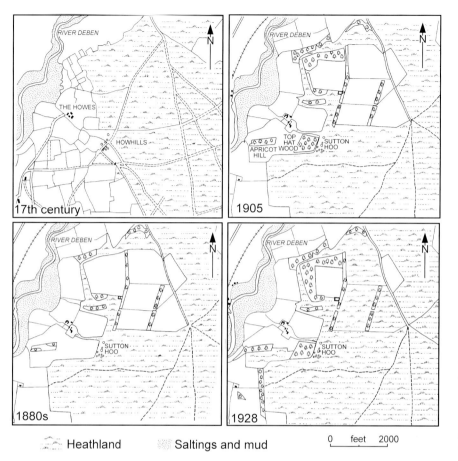

FIGURE 33. The changing setting of Sutton Hoo. In the seventeenth century the mounds stood on the western edge of an extensive area of heathland, with open views to the west over arable land and the river Deben. Over the following centuries the area of heathland has fluctuated; and the immediate environs of the mounds has become progressively more wooded, obstructing views towards the river (sources: William Haiward's 1629 map of Sutton; successive editions of the 6″ Ordnance Survey maps).

But the landscape to the east of the cemetery has also been radically changed by relatively recent developments. Although some areas of Sutton Heath – including that, surrounded by tree belts, lying to the east and north-east of Tranmer House – were reclaimed during the eighteenth and early nineteenth centuries, the Ordnance Survey 6″ map of 1889 shows that most of the area cemetery still comprised a vast tract of open heathland. Indeed, by the late 1920s much of the reclaimed land to the east of Tranmer House had reverted to rough grazing once more. In the post-War period, however, much of this heathland – and all that portion lying to the east of the mounds – was ploughed up. The cemetery's age-old location, close to the junction of arable and heath, was thus completely altered.

To understand the landscape context of monuments like the barrows at Sutton Hoo, therefore, it is not enough to walk around them today, looking at them from different angles within their modern landscape context, hoping that this will help to elucidate their meaning: for that context has changed dramatically with the passage of time. To reconstruct the broad outline of these changes, in the course of the medieval and post-medieval periods, is relatively easy. To gain an impression of the appearance and structure of earlier landscapes, and in particular of that which existed when the burial mounds themselves were erected, is a much more difficult task. But it is one which we must attempt, if we wish to understand the significance of the cemetery.

CHAPTER THREE

The Experience of Landscape

In the previous chapter I presented a brief, general account of the landscape history of the area around Sutton Hoo. I now want to examine in more detail the contemporary landscape context of the barrow cemetery in the early and middle Saxon periods. This is not an easy task. There are no documentary records which might throw direct light on this subject, and for the reasons already noted – continuity of occupation, and the low visibility of early Saxon sites in fieldwalking surveys – the interpretation of the archaeological evidence is by no means straightforward. It is, moreover, dangerous to simply back-project into the sixth and seventh centuries the kind of landscape which we can reconstruct on the basis of medieval and post-medieval sources. Because of all this, much of what follows is of necessity speculative – but not, I hope, wildly so. It rests on the belief that while we cannot recover the precise *details* of the landscape – the layout of roads and fields, and the disposition of settlements – at the time that the Sutton Hoo cemetery was in use, we can say something in more general terms about the development of land use and territorial organisation in the surrounding area over the longer Saxon period: and from this we may begin to understand certain aspects of the cemetery's location. Patterns of settlement, resource exploitation and movement which we can reconstruct for the later Saxon period may, that is, tell us something about the way the local environment was used and experienced in the late sixth and early seventh centuries.

Settlement clusters

I noted in the previous chapter that the majority of Roman and Anglo-Saxon settlement sites, and a high proportion of medieval ones, were concentrated within particular topographic zones. They avoided the dry, acid soils of the uplands, above twenty metres OD. And they were positioned in places where water was freely available, either beside watercourses and springs, or where the London clay lies close to the surface, providing a perched water table. Yet within this preferred zone there are signs of a more restricted clustering of settlement. Particular places were repeatedly occupied over several centuries (Fig. 34).

The most striking aspect of this phenomenon is the way in which Roman and late Saxon settlements are often found in close proximity; early and/or middle Saxon material is also frequently present on such sites, to fill the gap

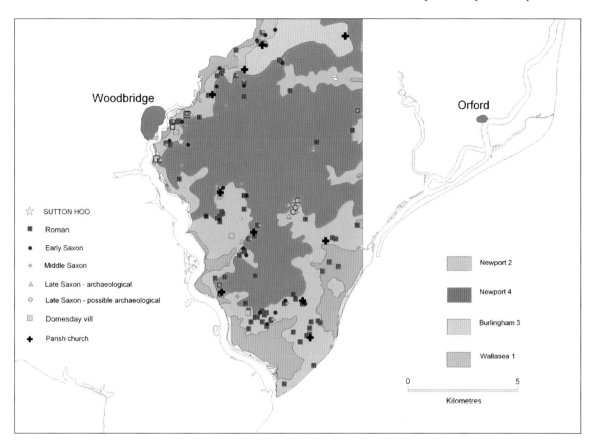

Woodbridge

Orford

☆ SUTTON HOO

■ Roman

● Early Saxon

◆ Middle Saxon

△ Late Saxon - archaeological

◎ Late Saxon - possible archaeological

▢ Domesday vill

✚ Parish church

Newport 2

Newport 4

Burlingham 3

Wallasea 1

0   5

Kilometres

FIGURE 34. Roman and Anglo-Saxon settlements in the area around Sutton Hoo, showing the apparent 'clustering' of sites.

between the two periods, although where it has not been recorded we should not necessarily take this as evidence of absence. Of particular note is the close proximity of Roman sites and parish churches, most of which were probably established by the later eleventh century, within or beside existing settlements, even if the direct archaeological evidence for these now lies obscured beneath adjacent settlements, or under the churchyard itself. At Alderton, a Roman site – with evidence of early and middle Saxon occupation   lies only fifty metres to the south of the churchyard; at Sutton another lies a mere forty metres from the church. Ramsholt has a Roman settlement 100 metres from the churchyard, Rendlesham has one 120 metres to the north-east (again with evidence of early and middle Saxon occupation); while the churches at both Shottisham and Bawdsey lie within 150 metres of Roman sites. At Bromeswell and Hollesley the distance is rather greater, at 200 metres and 300 respectively, but the association is still suggestive, given the overall density of Roman sites in the area. What is also striking is that Roman settlements likewise occur in close proximity to a range of other late Saxon settlements, but especially those which represent the sites of 'lost' Domesday vills, places which never acquired a church and became parishes in their own right. Peyton Hall, for example, the settlement focus for the vill of Peyton, is surrounded by grass paddocks but has Roman material in the field some sixty metres to the north-east: Stockerland in the north of Sutton has a Roman site c.250 metres away. Late Roman occupation is also perhaps indicated close to Sutton Hall, if Warner is correct in his identification of this as the place where a late Roman coin hoard was uncovered by workmen in 1871 (1984, 04/1 and 2). Certain of the other, apparently large later Saxon settlements which might be identified with some of the major manors listed in Domesday also seem to be associated with Roman sites or multi-period 'clusters', such as Alderton Hall, which lies some 800 metres to the south-east of Peyton.

The extent of this pattern should not be exaggerated, and should certainly not be taken as necessary evidence for continuity of settlement at the sites in question. But it does suggest that over long periods of time the same general locations appealed to local people, for practical and perhaps other reasons, as sites for settlements. The settlements which appear to have been the foci for Domesday vills were perhaps often located in places which had been favoured for centuries.

Early territories

A Domesday vill was not only a place, a settlement. It was a territory, and one which by the eleventh century had a taxation assessment based on its notional area, implying at least some fixed and recognisable bounds. But, as we have seen, there were other settlements in the area at the time of Domesday which were not accounted 'vills' but paid their taxes through, and were administered from, some neighbouring place: and although tenurially dependent, these too presumably had their own agricultural territories. It may be possible, at least in part, to use post-medieval sources to reconstruct late Saxon patterns of territorial organisation – to draw the boundaries of the various diminutive vills described in Domesday, and perhaps of the agricultural territories of those places not individually described.

The parish of Sutton, as we have seen, was constructed out of at least four Domesday vills: Stockerland, Hoo, Udeham, and Sutton itself. Assuming that the main focus of the latter place was somewhere in the vicinity of the parish church, we know the probable location of all of these places: Stockerland at Ferry Farm; Hoo at Little Haugh, near Sutton Hoo; and Udeham at Wood Hall. Using the distribution of properties shown on Haiward's map, surveyed in 1629 (IRO HA 24: 50/19/1.11), it is possible to suggest the configuration of the territories attached to some at least of these places. But before we do so, some further discussion of this important source is required.

Haiward's map shows *ownership*, and ownership in the modern sense. It does not concern itself with who occupied and farmed the land; nor does it describe which land belonged to the various manors in the parish, which comprised, by this date, Sutton Hall, Wood Hall, Stockerland, Fen Hall, Osmonds, and Pettistree, together with detached parts of Hollesley manor and of Talvas manor in Shottisham. Indeed, the only references to older, manorial forms of organisation made by the survey concern a number of parcels of land in the centre of the parish which are described as 'nativi' – that is, customary or bond land, held by copyhold (and originally by villein) tenure. There may have been other land in the parish which was of this archaic character but if so, the map does not show it, and it is probable that most was by this stage owned as freehold land, akin to private property in the modern sense.

Some land in the parish may always, even in the Middle Ages, have been held freely. Many of the occupiers of land in the various vills – particularly Sutton – were described by Domesday as free men and, while many will have declined in status in the wake of the Conquest, some free tenures probably survived right through the Middle Ages.

Most of the freehold land in the parish in 1629, however, probably began as villein, later copyhold, land, and was only converted to freehold property in the course of the fifteenth and sixteenth centuries. In the period after the Black Death – as the population fell, and as new ideas and concepts of ownership developed – manorial lords everywhere were keen to take vacant land back in hand and to absorb it, in effect, into their demesnes. In the course of the fifteenth and sixteenth centuries this drive to absorb old-fashioned copyholds continued, but was now carried out through systematic engrossment. As copyhold tenancies came up for renewal, usually at the death of the tenant, the inheritance would be prevented by one of several courses of action, depending on the customs of the manor in question, which varied considerably from district to district and from place to place. Some copyholds were relatively secure forms of tenure, little different in practice from freeholds, others were less so. Local practice (recorded in the late sixteenth century at Alderton and Rendlesham, for example) seems normally to have been that the 'fines' charged when heirs took over their father's property were 'arbitrable', that is, negotiable rather than fixed (MacCulloch 1976). The lord could thus prevail on his manorial court to increase the 'fine' payable by the heir to the point where he simply could not afford to take over the holding, relinquishing it back into his lord's hands.

One way or another, wherever copyholds were relatively insecure in character they were steadily taken into the control of manorial lords in the course of the fifteenth, sixteenth and seventeenth centuries. The land could then either be farmed 'in hand' by the lord, or be granted out to tenants, not now as customary land, but by a lease, the terms of which were individually negotiated rather then being fixed by custom. Of course, this was not the only way in which the large, consolidated blocks of property shown on Haiward's map developed. Freehold farmers, where they existed, might simply have been bought out. Many small owner-occupiers found it difficult to make a living, especially on poor land like this, and at times of low grain prices, such as the later fourteenth and fifteenth centuries. Even when agricultural fortunes revived, in the sixteenth century, they found it hard to compete with larger producers. At varying rates over the centuries, small properties everywhere passed to larger owners.

Nevertheless, in the case of Sutton, there are signs that engrossment by the absorption of copyholds was the main way in which the principal blocks of freehold property shown on Haiward's map had been created, for the largest of all were in the hands of two men, Miles Fernley and Francis Burwell, who were between them lords of all the main manors in the parish. The legend on Haiward's map reads: 'A description and plotte of the town of Sutton in the Countye of Suffolk Wherein Miles Ferneley Esq hath the manors of Suttonhall, Woodhall and Stokerland all sited w[i]thin this parish and … Francis Burwell hath …': the rest is illegible, but a court book from Fen Hall (IRO HB10:427/12(2)), dated 1632–61, gives Francis Burwell as lord of that manor, which his family seem to have acquired in the 1550s, buying the neighbouring manor of Osmonds in 1589.

In addition to the formation of these large blocks of property, owned by men like Burwell and Fernley, parcels of freehold land, large and small, were presumably bought and sold over the years between other, small and medium-sized landowners. All this worked to blur and obscure the older, medieval arrangement of properties. Nevertheless, careful examination of Haiward's map reveals what are probably its residual traces. As already noted, in spite of steady engrossment some small areas of 'bond' land – some relating to the manor of Fen Hall, some to the manor of Sutton, some to the manor of Hollesley (which held scattered parcels in the parish), and some attached to unspecified manors – still remained in 1629. All lay, intermixed with other properties, in one restricted area of the parish, to the south and south-west of the church. The sites of three of the principal manors marked by Haiward – Sutton, Fen Hall, Osmonds – were also in this general area, together with land of Shottisham Rectory (Sutton Hall, it should be noted, lay at this time close to the parish church: the present site of the hall, nearly a kilometre to the south, is only marked as a farm on Haiward's map). Although some areas of unenclosed open arable survived in this area, much of the land lay in consolidated blocks (Fig. 35).

Immediately to the east of this area, on the far side of the stream running roughly north–south through the central–southern portion of Sutton parish, patterns of landholding were significantly different. There was no bond land here, and there were no manorial sites (Fig. 35). Moreover, far more of the property lay intermixed, in small strips. This was especially true on the higher ground, where the Newport 2 soils gave way to the sandier, more acidic soils of the Newport 4 Association. Some of the large landowners – Miles Fernley, Francis Burwell – held parcels here, but most of the land was in the hands of small or medium-sized owners. While some of these individuals also owned property in the area to the south-west of the church – intermixed with the bond land of Sutton, Fen Hall and the rest – they did not, for the most part, have land elsewhere in the parish. Together, these two areas of land – the concentration of bond land and manorial sites, and the area of very fragmented property lying to its east – made up a single sub-rectangular unit of land, ranged roughly south-west to north-east, which extended from the low-lying ground

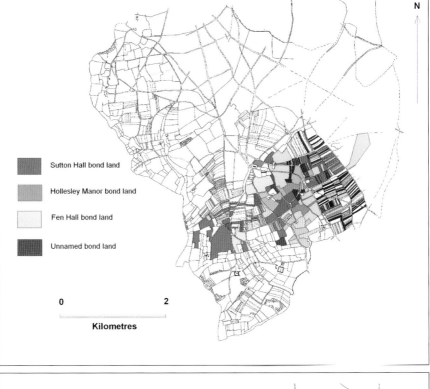

FIGURE 35. Haiward's map of Sutton, showing how the distribution of bond (copyhold) land and the properties of selected small owners serve to define a block of land which probably represents the Domesday vill of Sutton (the owners are Henry Halfen, Robert Cooper, Mrs Coitmer, Widow Camplin, Jeffrey Hedges, Mrs Girling, Robert Campbell, Joseph Hawes, Joseph Martin and Jeffrey Cooper).

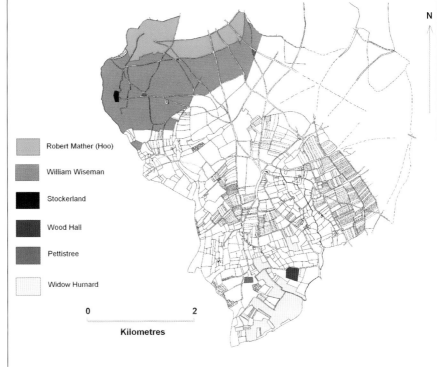

FIGURE 36. Other Domesday vills in Sutton, apparently defined by properties shown on Haiward's map of 1629. In the far north, Robert Mather's land corresponds approximately with Hoo, and William Wiseman's with Stockerland (the site of Stockerland manor is shown). In the far south, the manor sites of Pettistree and Wood Hall, and the holding of Widow Hurnard, indicate the location of Udeham.

by the estuary of the Deben up onto the higher, heathier soils inland. The line marking the southern edge of this block was remarkably sharp, even in 1629, although it did not correspond with any natural topographic feature, such as a stream, nor even with a human one, such as a road. Given that the lands of Sutton manor were concentrated in this block of land, and that Sutton church lay on its northern edge, this area evidently represents the original Domesday vill of Sutton.

To the south of this area there was evidently, in the early Middle Ages, a quite distinct territory. Haiward shows that none of the bond land of Sutton manor, nor any belonging to Fen Hall, lay here. But the sites of two other manors – Pettistree and Wood Hall – were found here. The latter, as we have seen, can be identified with the Domesday vill of Udeham, and this was probably the name originally applied to this whole area of land. By 1629 engrossment had ensured that only three large landowners held property here. One was Mr Burwell, whose family had acquired Pettistree manor in 1589; another was Mr Fernley, whose family had obtained the manor of Wood Hall in 1553 (Copinger 1911, 269–71). Their land in the south of the parish was clearly concentrated in blocks around the respective manor sites. But these men also, as previously noted, possessed much property elsewhere in the parish, so that their land spilled over, without interruption, northwards into the old vill of Sutton. The third landowner in the south of the parish, however – one widow Hurnard – was different. Her property was not associated with any manor and had presumably developed from the systematic acquisition of small free holdings. It was more clearly concentrated in this southern portion of the parish, with only a few small pieces of land north of the boundary, in Sutton proper (Fig. 36). The lands of Udeham were, like those of Sutton, laid out at right angles to the river but did not extend in the same way up onto the higher, sandier land to the interior, instead terminating at the watercourse forming the parish boundary with Shottisham.

Two other vills which came to form the parish of Sutton are immediately recognisable on Haiward's map although, once again, their boundaries had by this stage become somewhat blurred through the amalgamation, buying and selling of properties. In the far north the lands of Robert Mather formed a single, undivided block which included the site of Little Haugh Farm. This must, in broad outline at least, represent the lands of the diminutive vill of Hoo recorded in Domesday. Mather held no land anywhere else in the parish, although he did have property to the north, across the parish boundary in Bromeswell. The parish boundary may have been changed here at some stage in the past, for it takes an awkward, slightly zig-zag course: perhaps Bromeswell had somehow managed to annex a portion of the ancient vill of Hoo. Either way, to the south of this distinct block there was another large, unitary area of land, owned in 1629 by William Wiseman. Haiward's map shows that this included the site of the manor of Stockerland, now Ferry Farm, and so this property must approximate to the Domesday vill of that name. Both Hoo farm, and Stockerland, lay within a few hundred metres of the river. Once again, their land appears to have extended, strip-like, to the east, much of it lying on the poor upland soils of the Newport 4 Association (Fig. 36).

Udeham and Sutton in the south; Hoo and Stockerland in the north. The areas occupied by these former vills can be identified with relative ease. Between Sutton and Stockerland, however, in the centre of the parish, the situation is more confused. The configuration of landholding in 1629 clearly suggests that a different and distinct territory lay between these two vills and – on analogy with the situation in Hoo and Stockerland to the north – this was presumably focused on Methersgate Hall and Trotts Farm, close to the river (Haiward shows a number of other dwellings loosely concentrated in this area, which have now disappeared). A large area around Methersgate is occupied by buildings and paddocks, but a high density of medieval sherds was recovered by John Newman in the adjacent arable fields. There was a clear concentration of property in this area in 1629. Mr Blosse owned a substantial tract of land here, as did Mr Redgrave; Robert Gayton had a smaller farm, Thomas Mather a mere two fields. None of these men held any property elsewhere in the parish. The diminutive holding of Thomas Marsh was also largely restricted to this area, although it included a single outlying field to the south, in Sutton. Yet the boundary with the early vills to the north and the south is by no means distinct, partly because (yet again) of the acquisitions of the Burwells and the Fernleys, and of their predecessors as manorial lords. In particular, by 1629 these men owned substantial blocks of what ought to have been the eastern portion of this missing territory, on the higher ground to the east. Moreover, no manorial site is shown here by Haiward (although in later times, certainly, Methersgate was dignified with the epithet 'hall') and we have no missing manor which might be identified with it, so we have no idea what this putative territory might have been called. It was possibly part of Sutton at the time of Domesday, an agriculturally distinct but tenurially dependent territory. But it is tempting to suggest that it is one of the several 'lost' Domesday vills in the area. Possible candidates include *Hundesthoft, -tuf,* – a tiny place with a recorded population of three free men, its lordship divided in 1086 between Robert Malet and the Abbey of Ely; *Laneburc, -burgh,* with five free men under the lordship of Malet; or, more probably, Littlecross, a more substantial holding of forty acres. This contained seven villein farms and no free men, yet it was not described by Domesday as a manor. It was entirely under the control of Robert Malet and it is easy to see how, at an early date, it could have been united for administrative purposes with Malet's main manor in Sutton.

We are fortunate that, more or less at the same time as Haiward made his map of Sutton, he also surveyed the adjacent parish of Shottisham (IRO JA1/54 (1)). We are less fortunate in that in a number of ways this survey is less informative. The legend on the map itself informs us that tenants of the manors here held their land 'as well free as customary', but the different sorts of tenure were only set down in a lost field book, for figures on the map are described as being 'for reference to the book, where at the like figure you shall find those grounds set downe more at large & by what tenure they are holdeth'. Moreover, although the demesne land of the two main manors is shown, this was so extensive that it must have included considerable amounts of land which, in medieval times, would have been held by customary tenants, and which had been taken into the hands of the manorial lords during the previous centuries in the manner already described. Lastly, while the map legend informs us that the manors of Hollesley, and of Fen Hall in Sutton, extended into the parish, Haiward provides us with no clues as to which land was theirs. Instead, what he provides, once again, is simply a map of freehold ownership. Nevertheless, here too the distribution of properties must bear some relationship to the medieval pattern from which it evolved.

Shottisham is a very different parish to Sutton. Apart from the fact that it is much smaller, it also lies inland – set well back from the Deben – and a higher proportion of its area is occupied by soils of the Newport 4 Association. The eastern side of the parish is occupied by the valley of a minor watercourse which forms the boundary with the neighbouring parish of Sutton: on the sides of this are limited areas of Newport 2 soils. The church stands on a hill immediately above and to the east of this, today associated with a rather larger nucleated settlement than existed when Haiward's map was made. A small stream, a tributary to this watercourse, flows south-west to north-east across the southern section of the parish, and here too areas of Newport 2 soils are found. The present site of Shottisham Manor lies here (in an interesting parallel with Sutton, the site of the principal manor appears to have moved some time in the post-medieval period, away from the church – where Haiward shows it – to the site of what was then a farm, a kilometre to the south, where it now stands). A third stream, the Black Ditch, has its headwaters in the far north-east of the parish, thence flowing eastwards into the adjacent parish of Hollesley. Here too there is an isolated settlement, called – since at least the seventeenth century – 'Brew House'.

The largest property in the parish in 1631, the 'demesne' of Shottisham manor, was (like much of the land in Sutton) owned by the Fernley family, who had acquired the manor in c.1541. It lay entirely in the south of the parish, as did the demesne of Talvas manor, which they also owned. Together the two estates accounted for the overwhelming majority of land in the south of the parish, but a number of smaller ownerships also survived here: the diminutive farms of John Ward, John Cotwin, John Cooper, and Elizabeth Whitman, together with the lands of Shottisham Rectory (Fig. 38). All, without exception, lay entirely in the southern half of the parish. In the north of Shottisham, in contrast – more or less the area lying to the north of the parish church – a quite different collection of people held land. Most of this area was owned by Robert Bourne, whose properties extended into the adjacent parts of Sutton, while William Fox and Charles Allen held more modest farms, and a small area in the north was simply described as pertaining to 'Brew House'. One or two

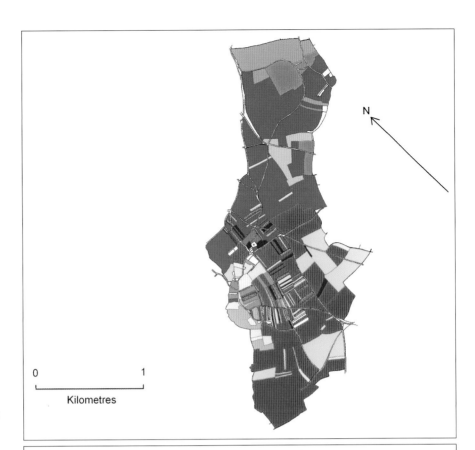

FIGURE 37. The various properties in Shottisham in 1631, as recorded by William Haiward.

FIGURE 38. The pattern of landholding in Shottisham, 1631. Holdings in the south-west of the parish: the demesne of Shottisham manor (red), the demesne of Talvas manor (green), lands of Shottisham Rectory (purple); and the properties of Robert Osbourne, John Ward, John Cotwin, Joseph Bourne, and Elizabeth Whitman.

other people held single strips, or small groups of strips, here: but once again, none held land in the south of the parish (Fig. 39). It is hard to see how this marked division of the parish could have developed in post-medieval times. It must represent a simplified version of a tenurial split going back into the early Middle Ages. In terms of landholding Shottisham was evidently, even in the seventeenth century, two different places.

At the time of Domesday most of Shottisham, like Sutton, formed part of the extensive holdings of Robert Malet. It consisted of a manor held from Robert by Walter the Crossbowman, comprising forty-four acres, which before the Conquest had been in the hands of one Osmond. It had a single under-tenant, a bordar; together with a number of groups of attached free men, totalling in all twenty individuals: the largest of these groups comprised fifteen men holding eighty acres. In addition, Ely Abbey held a single acre, and the patronage of one and a half free men. By late medieval times – certainly by the fifteenth century – the second manor in the parish, Talvas, had come into existence. This may have been formed in the immediate post-Conquest period out of the largest group of free men, with their eighty acres; more probably, it was a simple division, or sub-infeudation, of the main manor dating to the twelfth or early thirteenth century. Certainly, the demesnes of the two manors, to judge from the 1631 map, were fairly extensively intermingled, especially in the far south of the parish. The Domesday entries for Shottisham probably account for only the southern portion of the parish: it was here that the main manorial lands, and the various free tenancies, were concentrated. The northern section must therefore have comprised a separate vill, presumably based on the settlement represented on Haiward's map by the farm and small group of cottages at Brew House in the far north-east. Brew House is, almost certainly, a corruption of 'Bruery House', 'the heath house', a name of no great antiquity. It may be one of the 'lost' Domesday vills in the area, such as *Halgestou*, *Hundesthoft*, or *Laneburc* – probably the first, which Darby (although for no very clear reason) places in Shottisham although it only had a population of two. Shottisham, a smaller parish than Sutton, is thus simpler in its territorial composition, yet similar in that it contains – or was constructed out of – more than one ancient land unit, each with its own quite separate layout of farms and properties. The same was probably true of most of the other parishes in the area, given that Shottisham was amongst the smallest.

Historical geographers and landscape historians often make a distinction between the 'regular' field systems of the Midlands, and the more 'irregular' open fields found in many parts of the south and east of the country, in which holdings were usually clustered in particular parts of the fields of a parish. We can now see one of the ways in which these latter arrangements might evolve: where settlement failed to develop into large nucleations, parishes might contain a number of small hamlets, each with its own diminutive area of open arable, so that the lands of each tenants were perforce restricted to particular areas. But some readers may be wondering what relevance any of this can have to the main issue we are supposed to be addressing – the landscape context of the Sutton Hoo cemetery. The open fields of Sutton, Shottisham and other parishes were probably in existence by the time of Domesday, but not in the early seventh century. Nor do we have any good evidence that the territories whose layout was 'ghosted' by the distribution of properties within them can be traced back any further than the later Saxon period (although the notable continuity of occupation evident at a number of places, from the fifth through to the eleventh century, suggests that some may have had very ancient origins). The relevance of all this lies in the arrangement of these territories in relation to local soils and topography, and what this might suggest about earlier patterns of resource exploitation.

The territories of Sutton, Stockerland and Hoo were all arranged in such a way that they incorporated a range of resources: they ran from the shoreline, with areas of former salt marsh and mudflats; across the moderately fertile Newport 2 soils; and up onto the poor, sandy uplands. In Shottisham – an inland vill, with no coastal frontage – the situation was only slightly different, the two ancient land units here running from low-lying fen and meadow grounds beside the stream which now forms the parish boundary with Sutton, across the moderately fertile soils, onto the heathy uplands. The parishes in the area tend to do the same, their boundaries converging and narrowing, sometimes to a point, towards the centre of the main upland masses. Given that parishes were created by grouping together a number of these early land units, this similarity of layout is hardly surprising: parish boundaries represent the combination of the outer edges of several of these ancient territories. Of course, not *all* parishes are laid out like this, for topographic circumstances sometimes made it impossible for all the main environmental zones to be included within their bounds. Bawdsey, as its name suggests (Old English -*eg*, 'island') was virtually an island, and composed entirely of Newport 2 soils, surrounded by marsh. It had no access to the upland heaths. In a similar way, Udeham in the south of Sutton occupied a triangle of low-lying land between the Deben and the stream forming the parish boundary with Shottisham, and thus again had no direct access to Newport 4 soils. But for the most part, the pattern is clear enough.

The Newport 2 soils were evidently, in all periods, the core areas of arable land, although presumably when population levels were low not all the area which they occupied was under cultivation. The manner in which the less fertile Newport 4 soils, on the higher ground, were exploited is more complex. On their margins, as we have seen, settlements of all periods can be found, but further onto the main blocks of high ground they are rare. In all periods, the core areas of these poor soils were presumably left uncultivated – soil profiles from within Staverton Park, for example, indicate that the area has never been ploughed (Peterken 1968). But on their margins the frontier of cultivation seems to have fluctuated. Carver's excavations at Sutton Hoo – more or less at the junction of the two soil types – revealed that a co-axial field system had been

0   1

Kilometres

FIGURE 39. The pattern
of landholding in
Shottisham, 1631.
Holdings in the north-
east of the parish: the
Brew House (green);
and the lands of Robert
Bourne, Thomas
Silvester, Charles Allen,
and William Fox.

laid out in the later Iron Age in the area later occupied by the cemetery. This
had continued in cultivation into the Roman period, but had subsequently
been abandoned. The land here then remained as heath, only sporadically
cultivated, throughout the post-Roman period. But elsewhere on the margins
of the Newport 4 soils there are signs that the frontiers of cultivation land
re-expanded in later Saxon times. In particular, it is possible that the survival
of small owners, holding intermixed properties, on these poor soils in Sutton
(above, p.72) indicates that it was here that the majority of free tenancies had
been concentrated since the early Middle Ages, for land of this kind was more
resistant than that held by copyhold to absorption into the larger holdings
created by manorial lords like Fernley or Burwell. This may in turn suggest that
as land on the edges of the sandy uplands was being opened up for cultivation
once again, as population expanded in the course of the Saxon period, it was
granted out to enterprising colonists in the form of free tenancies, a procedure
known from many areas of England.

Heath and woodland

Not only will the extent of cultivation on the upland soils have fluctuated over time, largely in response to variations in demographic pressure. So too will the intensity with which these areas were grazed or otherwise exploited: and this in turn will have affected their ecology and appearance. It is easy to assume that the upland heaths were created in prehistoric times and subsequently remained largely unchanged until recent centuries. This, certainly, was the case with many areas of heathland in England. But there are grounds for suggesting that, far from comprising areas of open heathland, extensive tracts of woodland and wood pasture may have existed here in the early and middle Saxon periods, either because the land in question had never been cleared, or because trees had reclaimed it as population fell, and the intensity of land use declined, in the immediate post-Roman period.

Trees certainly return to the heaths quite quickly once the intensity of grazing and other forms of exploitation are reduced. Much of the surviving portion of Sutton Heath, for example, open and treeless in the late nineteenth century, has regenerated to scrub and secondary woodland in the course of the twentieth. Hawthorn, birch or oak find it relatively easy to establish themselves once grazing is reduced, moving into the patches of open soil left between over-mature stands of heather. Once the trees become established they shade out the heather: eventually *Quercus-Betula-Deschampsia* woodland, the natural climax vegetation on these poor soils, develops (Rodwell 1991, 377). In the post-Roman period open land could quite easily and rapidly have reverted to wood in this way. But some areas of woodland on the uplands may never have been cleared.

It has long been appreciated that at least one great East Anglian heath, Mousehold near Norwich, continued to be occupied by woodland well into the Middle Ages (Rackham 1986, 299–302). Domesday implies that there was a substantial wood here in the eleventh century and the element 'hold' derives from *holt*, an Old English term for 'wood'. In the thirteenth century the agent of the bishop of Norwich complained that it was proving difficult to restrain the tenants' use of the wood – which was common land – and that as a result the trees were disappearing. By the end of the thirteenth century, documents simply refer to Mousehold *Heath*. Recent research suggests that other areas of heathland in East Anglia, especially those situated on areas of Newport 4 soils – like those on the tract of fluvioglacial sands and gravels immediately to the north of Norwich, and along the moraine ridge between Holt and Cromer in the far north of Norfolk – carried areas of managed wood pasture well into the post-medieval period. Some of this comprised wooded commons, some was enclosed as private deer parks. Moreover, fieldwork has revealed a number of places where remnants of these heathland wood pastures still survive. On the Bayfield estate in north Norfolk, for example, over thirty ancient pollarded oaks – some *Quercus robur*, some *Q. petraea* – are buried within estate plantations on dry, leached soils of the Newport 4 Association. The youngest of these trees may be less than 300 years in age but the largest, the so-called 'Bayfield Oak', is probably around 700 years old. Similar concentrations of pollarded oaks are found on the Letheringsett estate, some 1.5 kilometres to the east, again buried within an eighteenth-century plantation ('Pereer's Hills'). Other examples come from the Green Sand ridge to the north of King's Lynn, again preserved within the eighteenth- and nineteenth-century woodland around Ken Hill House (centred on TF679349), and at Refley Wood, immediately to the west of King's Lynn. Several other areas of wood pasture are known from patches of acid, sandy soils in various places within East Anglia (Dallas *et al.* 2007).

It is within this wider, regional context that we need to consider the strange, evocative landscape of Staverton Park, an area of over eighty hectares of woodland which lies on the sandy uplands, on the boundary between the parishes of Wantisden and Eyke, a mere six kilometres to the east of Sutton Hoo (Fig. 40). This is an ancient wood pasture, characterised by pollarded oaks which were managed in the traditional manner – cropped at intervals of ten to twenty years – into the eighteenth century. There is, today, also a shrub layer consisting of hawthorn, birch, rowan and – in particular – holly. This may have become denser since the decline of regular and intensive grazing in the eighteenth century, although as early as 1764 Kirby was able to describe the 'vast' quantities of holly growing here (Kirby 1764, 25). As already noted, to judge from soil profiles the area has never been cultivated (Peterken 1968). The park, its later history at least, is reasonably well documented. It is first mentioned in 1268 but almost certainly has much earlier origins. It was the property of the Bigod family until 1306 when, on the death of Roger Bigod, it reverted to the Crown and was subsequently granted to the Earl of Norfolk. It remained in the hands of successive earls until 1529, when it was sold to Butley Priory. Accounts show that in the fourteenth century the park was used for grazing and for pannage, and as a source of bracken, as well as being exploited for wood and timber. There was also a rabbit warren here. But by the early fourteenth century, if not before, deer had ceased to be kept within it – an Inquisition Post Mortem for 1322 describing the park as 'without deer, now greatly broken down'. It does not ever seem to have been restocked. Following the Dissolution of Butley Priory, as it passed through a number of different hands, the park continued to be grazed, and to serve as a major source of wood and timber. Accounts show that the perimeter pale continued to be maintained, that oaks, poplars and alders were regularly felled, and that poles, 'cropewood' and faggots were cut from the pollards (Hoppitt 1992, 174–6). Henry VIII's sister Mary visited with her entourage in 1528: the company ate their dinner *sub Quercubus* – under the oaks – with 'fun and games'. In the late sixteenth century the park was acquired by the Stanhope family, which is why it is depicted on Norden's survey of 1601 (IRO V5/22/1). At that time it was densely filled with trees, but by 1779, to judge from a map surveyed by Isaac Johnson, it had become more open in character, while the eastern side had now been fenced off and incorporated within the adjacent sheep walk, and the southern and western edges had been ploughed

(IRO HD 11/475/W; Hoppitt 1992). Even then, however, the contrast with the surrounding areas of heathland, just beyond the pale, was marked, for these were entirely bleak and treeless. Yet the park boundary does not correspond with any change in soil type or drainage characteristics. And this, of course, raises the possibility that, in early medieval times, parts at least of the surrounding heathland likewise carried a significant amount of tree cover.

Staverton was not the only medieval deer park in the district. Another appears to have existed at Hollesley. Its site is uncertain but it was probably located somewhere on the poor upland soils, rather than on the more amenable soils of the lower ground (Rosemary Hoppitt, *pers. comm.*). It too was the property of the Earl Bigod, and is mentioned in the Patent Rolls for 1283 as one of ten or more Bigod parks which had recently been broken into. It may not have lasted long – no other references to it have been traced, and its location is not obviously indicated by field or minor place-names. Hollesley features in the itinerary of Roger IV Bigod in 1267, 1271 1271, and 1293, and his visits may have been for hunting. Certainly, it seems a strange place for a great magnate to come to on progresses which included visits to such places as Westminster, Woodstock and Chepstow (Rosemary Hoppitt, *pers comm.*).

By the thirteenth century, when these two parks are first documented, there can have been little woodland remaining in the district. Indeed, even at the time of Domesday there was very little in the locality. But the evidence of place-names strongly suggests that, in earlier periods, woodland had been quite extensive. The name of Hollesley itself means 'The clearing in the hollow'; nearby Butley means 'Butta's woodland clearing' or 'the woodland clearing by a mound' (Watts 2004, 106, 310). Ramsholt is the 'wild garlic wood' (OE *hramsa*, wild garlic), an interesting name in that wild garlic tends to be a plant of woodland edges. The settlement, to judge from the location of its medieval church, stood on the edge of the Newport 4 soils and thus perhaps on the margins of the upland woods. At least two of the lost Domesday vills in the district likewise have names with woodland associations. *Culeslea*, probably on the higher ground in Alderton, is 'Cula's clearing'; while Stockerland in Sutton is probably a compound of Old English *stocc*, 'tree stump', and either *land* or *lundr*, 'wood'. All these places lie on the edge of the upland soils and contain within their boundaries large tracts of such soils (Fig. 41). This somewhat surprising concentration of names indicating woodland, in an area characterised by light, sandy soils, has been largely ignored by modern historians and archaeologists, but it did not escape the attention of Arnott who, as long ago as 1946, drew attention to the large number of such names in the Sandlings as a whole: 'It would seem … that East Suffolk may once have been a district of forest land rather than open heath' (Arnott 1946, 1).

Further examples of such names are recorded on early maps. Norden's 1601 survey of the Stanhope estate shows, at c.TM31804930, a tract of heathland called 'Hatheles', a name almost certainly derived from *hæd leah*, 'the heathy clearing' (Smith 1956, 219). A short distance away, at c.TM31804940, 'Hasellande

Dale' comes from *hæsel land*, 'land grown with hazels', or perhaps *hæsel lundr* , 'hazel wood' (Smith 1956, 218). At TM347500 another area of open heath, not far from Staverton Park, is simply labelled 'Woodlande'; while at TM33005045 'Cookesley Pitt' probably derives its name from *cocc leah*, 'the clearing where the wood-cocks are' (Smith 1956, 104). Norden's map is a particularly useful source because the location of the various places to which these names refer is clear, and because it was surveyed at such an early date. Later maps are less helpful: many traditional names for areas of heathland were replaced in the course of the eighteenth and nineteenth centuries, although some survived. Hatchley Barn in Bromeswell, shown on the First Edition Ordnance Survey 6″ but which has since disappeared (TM318490), is recorded as *Hachlea* (*Haec's clearing*) in 1454 (Arnott 1946, 58).

The early extents – for Kingston, Rendlesham and Butley – are more difficult to interpret in this respect. The areas covered by the first two include clay soils as well as acid sands, and the precise location of many of the named places remains unclear: Figure 41, in other words, considerably underestimates the number of names referring to woodland in the area. The Kingston extent thus refers to a piece of land called 'Freth', and to 'Freth Pightel Hill' (OE *frid*, 'wood'), in Bromeswell, probably on Newport 4 soils at c. TM29004990; while

FIGURE 40. The ancient wood pasture of Staverton Park, some six kilometres to the east of Sutton Hoo. Large areas of the higher, poorer land in the district seem to have been wooded at the time the cemetery was in use.

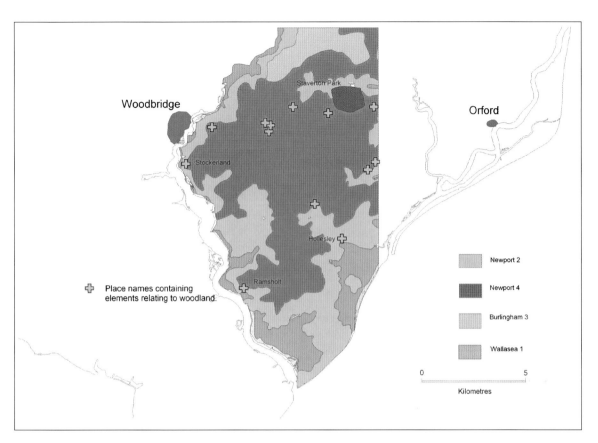

FIGURE 41. Place-names relating to woodland in the area around Sutton Hoo.

the Rendlesham survey refers to Tunley ('the farm clearing'), Wrangtunley and Overtunley, Northwood Croft and Close, and Netherwood Croft, all in contexts which probably suggest light rather than heavy soil. The survey of the manors of Butley, Boyton and Tangham mentions a number of extant woods – Ashholte, Homewood, Bellgoddwins, Waterie Wood, Little Heie Wood, Ha11eclose Wood, and Tangham Wood 'whereof various parts are pasture' – together with such suggestive field names as Home Park, Wood House, Le Frith, Great and Little Frith, and Stuckings (from *Stocc*, a tree stump, a term usually associated with medieval woodland clearance). Only a few of these can be identified on the ground. The clear implication of all these names is that in early and middle Saxon times the heaths around Sutton Hoo, far from being open and treeless environments, were to a significant extent tree-covered. Extensive tracts may well have looked more like Staverton Park than the surviving areas of open heathland on Sutton Common. Although the plantations established across much of the high ground in the area by the Forestry Commission in the course of the twentieth century are very different in their composition to the natural woodland which the heaths replaced, in some ways they may represent a return to the conditions of the early Saxon period.

Movement and exploitation

This woodland would have been exploited in a variety of ways in the early and middle Saxon periods. At this early date it is unlikely that much if any would have taken the form of coppice with standards, or would even have been managed as stands of pollarded trees, like Staverton Park. Such arduous forms of management probably only became common as the extent of woodland dwindled in the locality in the course of the Saxon period. These areas would, nevertheless, have supplied local communities with wood and timber, extracted on a more casual basis. Their most important role in the local economy, however, was probably as a source of grazing. Domesday records the remaining woods in the Sandlings, as elsewhere in Suffolk, in terms of the numbers of swine which they could support, and while this was probably by this stage often no more than a notional form of measurement, in earlier periods herds of pigs were doubtless driven into the woods in the autumn, to fatten on the harvest of acorns. But woods provided sustenance for other kinds of livestock. We usually think of sheep as animals that live on pastures, but they will eat a wide range of shrubs and trees, as also – although to a lesser extent – will cattle. Low-growing shrubs and the lower branches of trees could be consumed directly, while higher trees might be lopped to provide browse. 'Leafy hay' might also be cut from the trees and stored as winter feed, an ancient practice, but one which continued in some districts well into post-medieval times (Rackham 1980, 173–5). Even without cutting and storing, cattle and sheep will find much to consume in a wood in the depths of winter, happily eating bare twigs, and evergreens such as ivy and holly (the latter may have been particularly prominent in the local woods, to judge from the present-day vegetation of Staverton). As late as the sixteenth century Thomas Tusser, an Essex man, could recommend the use of oak as winter feed:

> If frost doo continue, this leson doth well,
> For comfort of cattell the fewell to fell;
> From eurie tree the superfluous bows
> Now prune for thy neat therupon to go browse

(Grison 1984, 74)

Woods and wood pastures would thus have provided ample sustenance for flocks and herds at times of the year when conventional grassland offered little. They may also have provided another resource: quarry for the hunter. Hunting was an activity which was, throughout Europe, increasingly reserved to the social elite in the course of the early medieval period, as the area under trees everywhere contracted, and as society itself became more hierarchical in character (Wickham 1994, 159–61). It is not impossible that Staverton Park was already being preserved as a hunting reserve in middle Saxon times. It is certainly a curious coincidence that the only surviving area of wood pasture on the whole of the Sandlings coast should be found here, a mere three kilometres from the residence of the East Anglian kings at Rendlesham.

Although it is likely that substantial areas of woodland thus existed on the poor upland soils in early Saxon times, this would probably not have formed a continuous and uninterrupted blanket of trees as dense as that at Staverton. Towards the margins, to judge from the evidence from the Sutton Hoo excavations, as well as from the distribution of known settlements, the landscape was probably park-like in character, while even in the interior there were probably some tracts of open ground – 'leahs' or clearings – which were constantly being expanded by the grazing of stock.

The various economic roles of the uplands, especially as grazing grounds, explains the importance evidently placed on securing a reasonable share of them when territorial boundaries were being laid out. But, as we have seen, care was also taken – where possible – to ensure access to the shore line, beside either the Deben estuary or the sea, and especially to the areas of salt marsh formed in the lea of the sand spits. These areas would have provided a wide range of resources, even before medieval embanking and reclamation. They afforded a rich store of wildlife which could be trapped: the seventeenth-century Suffolk writer Richard Reyce refers to 'those we call seapies, coots, pewits, curlews, teal, wiggeon, brents, duck, mallard, wild goose, heron, crane, and barnacle' caught on the Suffolk coast (Hervey 1902, 35). The unimproved marshes, together with the adjacent areas of mudflats and open water, were also a source of fish and shellfish: the remains of a fish trap of probable middle Saxon date has recently been discovered in Holbrook Bay. It is composed of two rows of paired posts (once probably supporting a wattle fence) which meet at a point, forming a 'V' (Hegarty and Newsome 2005, 61–3). On the foreshore immediately below Sutton Hoo what were possibly more fragmentary remains of earlier traps, radiocarbon dated to the late Roman or early Saxon periods, were discovered during a survey of the intertidal zone in 2003 (Loader and Everett 2004). Oysters occurred naturally on the floors of the local creeks and estuaries and were presumably caught by dredging from small boats from an early date. Norden's 1601 survey of the Stanhope estates shows two 'oyster boates' at work on the Butley river (IRO EE5/11/). But in addition, the coastal salt marshes, characterised by salt-tolerant vegetation such as sea fern-grass (*Catapodium marinum*) and red fescue, afforded some grazing for livestock, especially sheep, although in contrast to the grazing in the upland wood pastures this would mainly have been in the summer months, when the weather was less harsh, and water levels generally lower. Some of the Anglo-Saxon wooden structures found during the foreshore survey at Sutton Hoo in 2003 may conceivably have been employed in some way in the management of stock.

The natural resources exploited by early communities in the area thus lay in irregular bands arranged roughly parallel to the shore of the Deben estuary and the North Sea. This will have had a strong influence on patterns of movement through the landscape, just as it had on the disposition of early agricultural territories. Sheep and other stock needed to be walked, on a seasonal basis, from the low-lying salt marshes to the wooded uplands, and back again. Sheep would

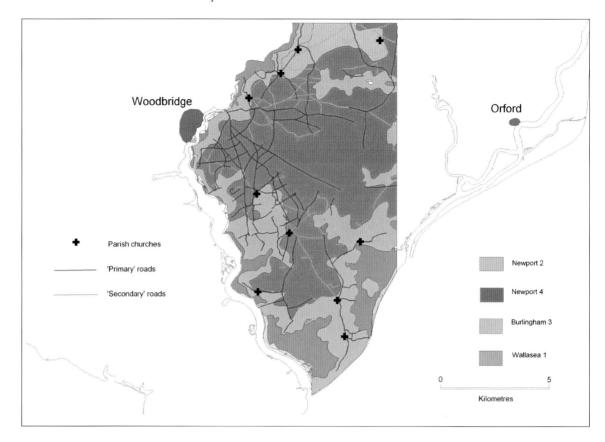

Woodbridge

Orford

✠ Parish churches

—————— 'Primary' roads

—————— 'Secondary' roads

Newport 2

Newport 4

Burlingham 3

Wallasea 1

0   5

Kilometres

also, in all probability, be moved on a daily basis, from the grazing grounds to the folds on the arable fields. Swine would be driven in the autumn up to the woodlands, and timber and wood brought down to the settlements on lower ground. Regular trips would be made from settlements down to the shoreline, in order to catch fish and gather shellfish, as well as to the river and sea themselves, via which more distant places would be reached by boat. The patterns of daily and seasonal life thus, in a wide range of ways, ebbed and flowed at right angles to the shoreline of the estuary and the sea.

Local roads are difficult or impossible to date in absolute terms. But is sometimes possible to suggest a *relative* chronology for them – that is, to identify which roads are likely to be earlier features of the landscape than others. Those which the earliest maps show lying 'unconformably' with other features – 'secondary' roads, which cut across the pattern of the open-field furlongs at an angle, or which are diverted around the margins of individual enclosures – are in general likely to be later in date than those which are 'conformable' – 'primary' roads, which share the same orientation as the boundaries of the surrounding fields and furlongs, which they are thus either contemporary with, or earlier than (Fig. 42). Some of the 'primary' roads clearly lead to important settlements of late Saxon date, settlements which often form part of multi-

FIGURE 42. 'Primary' and 'secondary' roads in the area around Sutton Hoo.

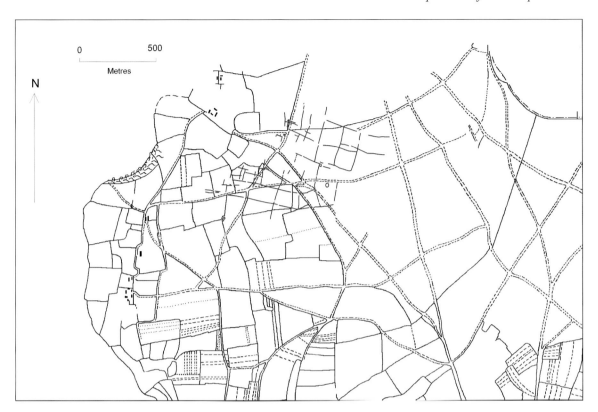

FIGURE 43. The relationship between 'co-axial' fields and roads shown on Haiward's 1629 survey of Sutton, and the prehistoric co-axial field system in the area around and beneath the Sutton Hoo cemetery.

period 'clusters'. Many roads of this kind, however, do not lead in any obvious way to early settlements, or indeed to settlements of any date. Instead they simply run from the shore line up onto the acid soils on higher ground: they are 'resource linkage routes' (Harrison 2005), created by the regular patterns of movement – and especially movements of livestock – just outlined.

Where the topography is relatively uncomplicated – that is, where there are no areas of low-lying marsh running for any distance back from the coast, and where the banding of resources (coast, arable soils, uplands) is thus strong and simple – these tracks lie parallel to each other, as across much of Sutton parish. The field and furlong boundaries lying conformably with them – running parallel or at right angles – thus form a rough brickwork-like pattern of the kind sometimes described as 'co-axial' by archaeologists. The regular patterns of ancient movement are here most clearly and indelibly etched into the fabric of the landscape.

The inherited landscape

In some parts of the country it has been suggested that field patterns like these, because they closely resemble a form of land division often found in prehistoric contexts, actually developed directly from prehistoric field systems (Williamson 1998) (Fig. 43). One such prehistoric co-axial system – of late Iron Age date

– was excavated by Martin Carver and his team beneath the Sutton Hoo barrows, and what may have been its continuation was observed during the excavation of the Tranmer House cemetery, some 600 metres to the north. In this case, there does not appear to be any direct continuity between an ancient field system and the co-axial layout of the medieval and later landscape. The boundaries shown on the earliest map of the area, Haiward's survey of 1629, lie on a similar but nevertheless slightly different alignment to that of the excavated features. We should, however, be a little cautious here, for the excavated fields lie entirely on poor Newport 4 Association soils and much of this area was apparently abandoned for cultivation, and occupied by undivided grazing, at the end of the Roman period. There may have been more continuity of boundary patterns on the lower, more fertile ground. Indeed, in the area to the west of the two excavations, towards the river, some of the roads and boundaries shown by Haiward do appear to have an alignment rather closer to that of the excavated boundaries. Moreover, aerial photographs reveal other areas of co-axial fields and tracks in the parish – as in the area around TM2955046770 – which do seem to share the same alignment as roads and furlongs shown in the same area on Haiward's map: these, too lie on lower ground. It is thus *possible* that where land remained in cultivation in the immediate post-Roman period, early co-axial landscapes formed the basis for later ones, whereas where land was abandoned, new patterns of roads, and boundaries, were laid out on slightly different alignments as land was brought back into cultivation in the later Saxon period. Either way, the similarity of orientation displayed by the road and boundary patterns shown on Haiward's map, and the Iron Age fields excavated at Tranmer House and beneath the Sutton Hoo mounds, clearly suggests that in the Iron Age as in early medieval times the dominant axis of movement in the landscape was the same – at right angles to the banding of resources.

There is some other evidence that parts of the medieval pattern of roads and tracks in the area around Sutton Hoo may have been inherited from the prehistoric and Roman period, and that some of these routeways therefore formed elements in the early and middle Saxon landscape. When the location of Romano-British sites is compared with the layout of the roads shown on the earliest available maps, it is noticeable that rather more lie close to those of 'primary' than of 'secondary' character (Figs 44 and 45). Given that the latter are fewer in number, and that sites of all periods tend, as noted, to cluster in the same fairly restricted areas, we should not make too much of this. But it remains possible that – on the lower and more fertile ground at least – the early and middle Saxon inhabitants of the district may have inherited, and maintained, more from their predecessors than the grass-grown banks of abandoned fields of the kind excavated at Sutton Hoo.

The people burying their dead at Sutton Hoo, and in the nearby cemetery at Tranmer House, certainly inherited another kind of feature from the distant past, which they will almost certainly have invested with some degree of symbolic significance. Throughout England Bronze Age round barrows were utilised as sites for burial by the Anglo-Saxons, or formed a focus for their cemeteries (Lucy 2000, 124–30; Williams 1998). A number of round barrows of probable Bronze Age date are known from the local area, either surviving as upstanding features, or visible from the air as the distinctive cropmarks known as 'ring-ditches'. It is possible that there were once much larger numbers of round barrows in the area, many of which survived into the early modern period before being levelled by the expansion of cultivation. As already noted, Norden's survey of 1601 marks the Sutton Hoo cemetery with the word 'Mathershoe', and with four rather irregular green mounds. Similar symbols occur elsewhere on his maps. A string of them thus extends to the north of Sutton Hoo, on the high ground above the Deben, all the way to Wilford Bridge (Fig. 46). It is not unreasonable to assume that these were likewise barrows: and at least two (although *only* two) of his symbols – at TM375528, and TM379569 – do seem to correspond roughly with known barrows or ring-ditch sites. Martin Carver has, however, proposed an alternative explanation for the symbols, based on the fact that a number are shown within the area marked by Norden as a warren on Dunningworth Heath: that they represent 'pillow mounds' used to provide accommodation for rabbits (above, pp.56–7). In fact, neither explanation appears very likely, for one simple reason. Norden was an excellent map-maker and most of the features he depicts, with the exception of ships out at sea, are clearly drawn to scale. Trees and houses are shown in elevation, but generally in sensible proportion to each other, and to the surrounding features depicted in plan. They are dwarfed by the mounds, which are generally huge: indicating, as Bruce-Mitford in fact suggested long ago, that they were a rough and ready way of depicting topography, marking places with noticeable hills and slopes. It is noteworthy how the symbols generally occur towards the edges of the upland plateau, where the ground falls away towards the Deben (the line running to the north of Sutton Hoo, already described); where the plateau is cut by the valley of the Butley River, to the north of Staverton Park; or, as in the area around Orford and Sudbourne, where it is more generally dissected. The fact that the mounds are not only very large, but also rather irregular in shape, supports such an interpretation. The mounds at 'Mathershoe' are rather smaller than most of those depicted by Norden. Nevertheless, even here it is just possible that the symbols are supposed to be, not the barrows themselves, but the steep slope immediately to their west. The name may have been a general one for the area, derived from the barrows but more widely applied. Nevertheless, while we may discount Norden's mounds as evidence for lost round barrows, there is no doubt that these monuments survived in some numbers in the area into the Anglo-Saxon period. Although relatively few certain examples are known, this may in part be a consequence of the fact that much of the higher ground in the area is now afforested. Not only will large-scale tree planting in the middle decades of the twentieth century have served to level the traces of barrows up till then unnoticed by the Ordnance Survey and local archaeologists. In addition, the current extent of tree cover precludes the discovery of such sites surviving only as crop or soil marks.

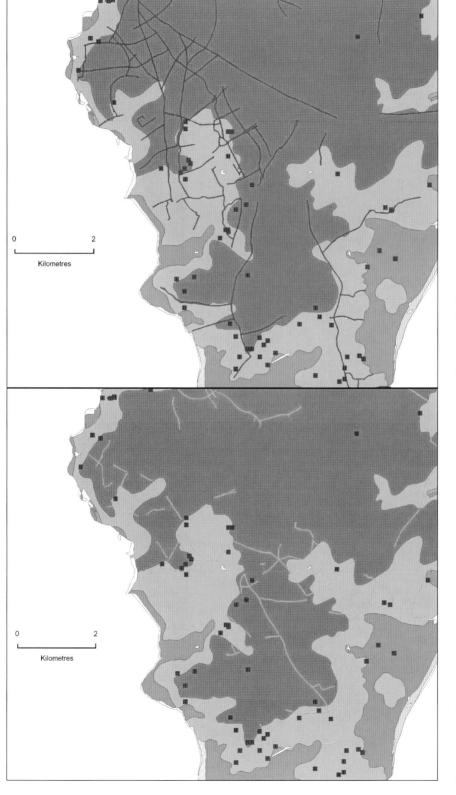

FIGURE 44. The relationship between Roman sites and 'primary' roads in the area around Sutton and Shottisham (soil key as for Figure 42).

FIGURE 45. The relationship between Roman sites and 'secondary' roads in the area around Sutton and Shottisham (soil key as for Figure 42).

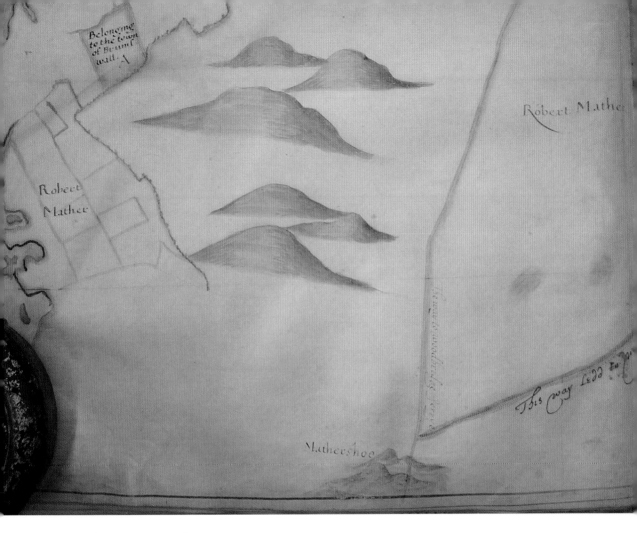

Within the image, handwritten map labels:
- Belonging to the town of Bromswall. A
- Robert Mather
- Robert Mather
- This way £33 fo[...]
- Mathershoo

FIGURE 46. 'Mathers Hoe' – the Sutton Hoo cemetery – and other mounds to the north, as depicted on Norden's survey of the Stanhope estates, 1601.

Conclusion

It might be useful, before turning to a more detailed consideration of the site of the Sutton Hoo cemetery, to summarise briefly the foregoing argument. From late prehistoric to early medieval times certain locales were especially favoured for settlement in the Sutton Hoo area. In some places settlement *may* have been continuous over several centuries, and some fragments of early road and boundary patterns may have survived right through the post-Roman period. Some of the places which formed the foci for the territorial units described in Domesday Book had probably been in existence for a considerable period of time. Using the evidence of post-medieval surveys it is possible to reconstruct the probable outlines of some of these early land units, two or more of which were usually combined to form ecclesiastical parishes and townships in the course of the Middle Ages. The evident stability of such units for five centuries or more after the time of Domesday does not, of course, mean that they had remained in existence, unchanged, for four centuries or so *before* it. But the systems of resource allocation which their layout implies (a pattern replicated, in simplified form, by the parishes which were constructed out of them) probably does provide an indication of rather earlier economic and agrarian arrangements.

The landscape comprised three main kinds of resource, arranged in irregular bands from low ground to high, *viz*: coast and salt marsh; moderately fertile soils suitable for arable cultivation; and the uplands, onto the margins of which cultivation expanded during periods of demographic growth but which, for the most part, were always occupied by grazing grounds and woodland – the latter apparently much more extensive in early Saxon times than has usually been assumed. The recurrent patterns of movement – of people, livestock and commodities – between these various ecological zones ensured, in some places, that a pattern of parallel tracks and boundaries, running at right angles to the coast, was etched into the medieval and early modern landscape, and to some extent survives today.

I noted earlier (above, p.27) that how people in the past experienced and thought about their local landscapes was shaped not simply by any intrinsic natural qualities which these might possess (such as the shapes of landforms) but also by the ways in which they were exploited, and by the patterns of regular movement that arose from this. In the area around Sutton Hoo, not only were these patterns arranged predominantly at right angles to the estuary of the Deben. There was, in addition, a marked contrast between the river itself and the farmed and settled territory around it; and the more sparsely inhabited, spatially marginal uplands, with their lonely woods and pastures.

The distinction was not merely, however, between the busy and settled core and the remote and lonely periphery. It also involved important sensory differences. Today it is perhaps only possible to recapture something of the ways that contemporaries may have experienced the uplands by standing in the depths of the ancient wood pasture at Staverton. Here, the sky is only partially visible through the canopy of trees. Views are limited in all directions by the vegetation; it is difficult to obtain a clear idea of the natural landforms. Sounds do not travel far. Although the feeling is not exactly one of claustrophobia, it is certainly one of seclusion and isolation. Admittedly, the uplands at the time of Sutton Hoo would not all have been as densely treed as this, but given the relatively muted topography even a moderate scatter of fully-grown trees and scrub would have served to limit the extent of the prospect. The way in which the nearby estuary of the Deben might have been experienced in the remote past is easier to recapture. Spaciousness, distant views, movement, airiness and – on all but the darkest day – light. It is easier to appreciate the natural landforms, and these are anyway more dramatic than on the rolling interfluves for the ground generally falls away steeply to the river's edge. This was the essential configuration of spaces and experiences which must have shaped the mental geography of the Anglo-Saxon inhabitants of the area.

CHAPTER FOUR

The Wuffingas' River

River and wold

The kind of pattern explored in the last chapter, in which the lives of local communities were shaped by the exploitation of banded resources arranged parallel to a major river, is one which has been discussed by a number of historians in the past, most notably Alan Everitt and Charles Phythian Adams. The former coined the term 'river and wold' for such arrangements, which formed the basis for a more general model he proposed of early settlement development, one which applies well to many areas in southern Britain. In very general terms, from the later Iron Age through to Saxon times the main settlements, and the principal arable areas, tended to be located within the larger valleys, where good supplies of running water were available, together with well-watered pastures for livestock. In most districts, moreover – as around Sutton Hoo – the most fertile and/or the most easily cultivated soils also tended to be found on the valley sides. The high interfluves lying between the principal valleys, in contrast, were generally occupied by intractable clays or poor, acidic sands, and often – again, as in the Sutton Hoo area – lacked dependable water supplies. When population densities were low these uplands tended to be occupied by woods and pastures, sometimes exploited by seasonally occupied settlements. In most cases, as population rose, the uplands were brought into cultivation and they came to be permanently occupied, but even then they generally remained dependent – tenurially, economically and socially – on settlements in the neighbouring valleys. High ground between major valleys – interfluves and watersheds – thus represented cut-off zones between communities, and social territories tended, over time, to correspond with drainage basins (Everitt 1977; Phythian Adams 1987, 1993).

Where, in their lower reaches, rivers widened into tidal estuaries this geography of social contact often changed: here they might become barriers to regular social intercourse and thus develop as boundaries between social groups. The Thames estuary thus represented a major boundary in Saxon times between the kingdom of Kent and the East Saxons. It is unlikely that the Deben estuary functioned in this kind of way at the time of Sutton Hoo, however. It is neither a particularly wide, nor a particularly hazardous, body of water. Rendlesham, which was probably a major 'central place' by the early seventh century, lies only a short distance (around four kilometres) above the point where the river widens into an estuary, suggesting that the land the Wuffingas controlled extended down both sides of the latter. Although impossible to cross on foot or horseback, the estuary must at this time have represented, in some ways, a highway, easily traversed by small boat, and uniting rather than dividing the people dwelling on its opposed shores.

The contrast apparent in the vicinity of Sutton Hoo between the poor soils of the drift-covered uplands, characterised in the Saxon period by woodland and heath, and the more fertile lower ground, where most settlements and the majority of arable land were located, was replicated in the valleys of the two other major rivers draining through the sands and gravels of the Sandlings, and into the North Sea, the Blyth and the Alde. These, too, served as highways, and monasteries like Botolph's Iken were located where they were not primarily because their founders sought isolation and solitude, but because they wanted to reside beside, and only slightly distanced from, the social arteries of their world. Moreover, where these rivers ran, in their middle and upper reaches, back into the claylands to the west, a broadly similar pattern of early settlement and land use is evident. The valley floors were of course narrower here, and often occupied by areas of peat rather than alluvium; but the slopes of the valley sides were characterised by varieties of clay soil – those of the Burlingham Associations especially – which were more easily ploughed, drained and cultivated than the seasonally waterlogged and tenacious Beccles and Ragdale Association soils which characterised the level plateau above. Not surprisingly, settlements in these river valleys, and in some of their principal tributaries, often bear the kinds of name indicative of early estate centres, with suffixes in -ham or -ingham, or contain other kinds of archaic element. The plateau between, in contrast, is scattered with places bearing names with elements suggesting subsidiary, dependent status (*tun*, 'farm') or the presence of woodland and clearings (*feld, leah*).

Rendlesham

The importance of the lighter clay soils for early Anglo-Saxon settlement is most clearly demonstrated by the location of Rendlesham, the site of the Wuffingas' major residence. This lies a mere six kilometres from Sutton Hoo, but on the western fringes of the band of light soils making up the Sandlings proper. The bulk of the modern parish, including the probable area of the 'palace' site close to the church, in fact comprises light clay loams of the Burlingham Association. I have not yet discussed Rendlesham but – as many archaeologists have noted – it must form an important part of the Sutton Hoo story. It is first mentioned as a royal site in Bede's *Ecclesiastical History*: its name probably means 'little shore', emphasising once again the centrality in contemporary experience of the river Deben. Bruce-Mitford in 1974 speculated on the kinds of features which *might* have characterised a royal palace here in the early seventh century, largely on the basis of the evidence produced by the excavations at Yeavering, in Northumberland, carried out by Brian Hope Taylor (Bruce-Mitford 1974; Hope-Taylor1977). There, the residence of Edwin

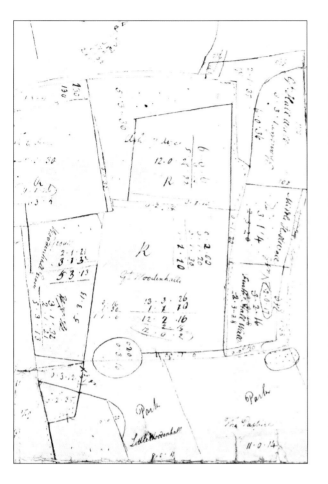

FIGURE 47. Survey of Rendlesham Park, made in 1828 by Isaac Johnson, showing the 'oval' corresponding to the earthwork supposedly associated with the Rendlesham 'palace'.

and his predecessor Northumbrian kings comprised an extensive collection of timber buildings, including a probable temple, a royal feasting hall and a complex amphitheatre-like structure. All this developed, in the later sixth and seventh century, close to a prehistoric site featuring a stone circle and at least one barrow. Whether a similar range of features ever existed at Rendlesham is unknown, because the site remains unexcavated. Bruce-Mitford's speculations were also made in the absence of any fieldwalking evidence, a deficiency remedied by John Newman, whose meticulous survey located a number of sites in the parish, including two distinct concentrations of early and middle Saxon material to the north and north-west of the church, both with evidence of Roman occupation (at TM32355300 and 32615292). These are among the most extensive Anglo-Saxon pottery scatters known from Suffolk. A third site (TM32505337) comprised a more diffuse scatter of Roman, early and middle Saxon material, perhaps the edge of a settlement largely obscured beneath the outbuildings around Naunton Hall, which by medieval times had become the location of the main manor in the parish.

The only features of the Rendlesham landscape which Bruce-Mitford actually discussed are the parish church; some round barrows; recorded finds of Anglo-Saxon burials suggesting a cemetery site; and an enigmatic earthwork enclosure buried in woodland to the north of Rendlesham Hall. The barrows (at TM335545) are undated, and perhaps located too far away from the scatters of debris recovered by Newman to have the kind of significance apparent at Yeavering. The probable cemetery occupies a low bluff of land called Hoo Hill (TM329535), overlooking the river, and has produced only limited finds (Bruce-Mitford 1974, 102–5). The earthwork enclosure merits a short digression. Bruce-Mitford described it as lying in a 'curious, roughly circular projection of trees into the arable and pasture' which extended out from Bush Covert, one of several woods in Rendlesham Park (a post-medieval designed landscape associated with Rendlesham Hall) (Bruce-Mitford 1974, 106–7). The edge of the projection formed the eastern half of an approximately oval earthwork which extended back, westwards, into the wood proper. 'The ring is defined by a shallow ditch and another shallow ditch divides it centrally along its east–west axis into two parts'. Bruce-Mitford acknowledged that 'it may prove to be

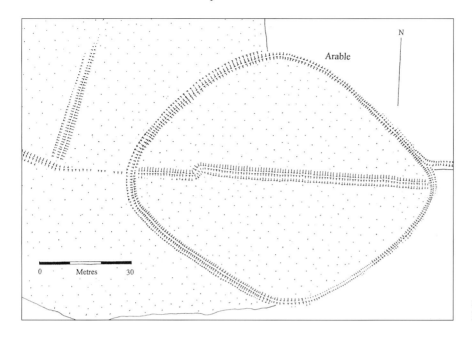

FIGURE 48. Plan of the
Rendlesham earthwork.

nothing more than an ornamental ring of trees such as exist elsewhere in the parkland', but noted the fact that a sketch map of 1828, made by the surveyor Isaac Johnson, gives the name 'Woodenhall Grove' to Bush Covert, and 'Great' and 'Little Woodenhalls' to neighbouring fields, names which he thought might preserve a dim memory of the halls of the Saxon palace (Bruce-Mitford 1974, 107). The map (Fig. 47) shows the oval as a free-standing feature, quite detached from the wood to the west, but subsequent expansion of the latter in the course of the nineteenth century has united the two. Bruce-Mitford was not the first to speculate on the earthwork. Thirteen years earlier Nicholas Pevsner, in the Suffolk volume of his *Buildings of England* series, had also noted the 'ring of trees defined by a shallow DITCH, with another shallow ditch dividing it from E to W' in 'Thirstley Belt' (Pevsner 1961, 374), and suggested an association with Saxon Rendlesham.

The enclosure now projects slightly less far out from the wood that it did in Bruce-Mitford's day, the latter having been extended over the years. Within the body of the wood the bank is around 0.2–0.3m high and 3m wide, and is flanked on the outside by a slight ditch, around 0.2–0.3m deep (Fig. 48). Where it projects out of the wood, and is thus surrounded by arable land, the ditch has largely disappeared. The transverse bank, running east–west through the centre of the oval, is 3–4 m wide and is flanked on the south, for most of its length, by a ditch which is generally between 0.1 and 0.2m deep. About four fifths of the way along, from the east, the bank kinks and changes direction slightly, but is otherwise roughly straight. What Bruce-Mitford failed to notice is that it also continues, in much degraded form, *beyond* the oval to the west, running through the woodland in a straight line to the corner of two other earthworks – banks and ditches which mark the old edge of Bush Covert/Woodenhall Grove, as shown on Isaac Johnson's map, before the wood was expanded eastwards in the course of the nineteenth century. More importantly, he failed to note the character of the vegetation associated with the earthworks. The transverse bank carries examples of coppiced sycamore, elm and maple which are clearly the remains of a hedge, the other constituent species of which have been shaded out by the dense tree canopy. The latter is largely supplied by regenerating stumps of long-felled lime trees which are completely restricted to the 'oval': not one occurs outside it, in the woodland to the west. The transverse bank is thus unquestionably the remains of a field boundary, presumably of post-medieval date; and the oval is evidently (as Bruce-Mitford clearly at times suspected) a typical parkland clump, surrounded by a bank to protect it from grazing, which was imposed upon the field boundary. The earthworks thus have nothing to do with the Anglo-Saxon 'palace', which presumably – to judge from the fieldwalking evidence – lay further south, nearer to the parish church.

The church is the other main feature of the Rendlesham landscape to which Bruce-Mitford drew attention (Fig. 49). It has no visible fabric earlier than the thirteenth century, but it carries a dedication which is almost certainly of some significance – to St Gregory, the Pope who initiated the Christian mission to England in the 590s. This is not a common dedication – there are only five other examples in East Anglia (two in Norfolk and three in Suffolk) – and it is difficult not to believe that it has a special significance at this particular location, possibly signifying the conversion, at an early date, of a major temple site. Bruce-Mitford found a possible parallel in the Swedish royal complex at Old Uppsala, where the church – lying immediately adjacent to the presumed site of the king's halls – was probably built immediately above a pagan temple (Bruce-Mitford 1974, 92). It is thus easy to assume that this was the site of the temple in which, to Bede's horror, Rædwald erected altars to both the Christian God, and to his traditional tribal deities. But it is worth sounding a note of caution. Although Rendlesham is often described as the site of 'Rædwald's palace', Bede never explicitly connects the two, instead referring to Rendlesham only in a rather later chronological context, as the place where the East Saxon King Swiðhelm was baptised by Bishop Cedd, with Æthelwald, brother of King Anna, acting as his sponsor. This was in 655, more than a quarter of a century after Rædwald's death. Rædwald may also have had his residence here, but we do not know this for sure. As the example of Yeavering shows, royal sites were not necessarily long-lived and, given the strong ritual character of palace complexes like this, or Uppsala, it is possible that the acceptance of Christianity may have encouraged the adoption of an entirely new site for the main royal residence. Moreover, Bede tells us that Aldwulf, Æthelwald's successor, later testified that Rædwald's temple 'had stood until his time, and that he had seen it when he was a boy', presumably some time in the 640s or 50s. While he may have meant by this that the building had by this time been converted into the church in which Swiðhelm was to be baptised a few years later, he does not actually say

so, and the passage could be taken to imply something very different – that the temple was a ruin, long abandoned, and located elsewhere. Nevertheless, even if the church at Rendlesham does not occupy the site of Rædwald's temple, its dedication makes it likely that it stands on the site of an early church associated with the palace, and was indeed the place where Swiðhelm accepted the faith in 655.

Although Bede described Rædwald's shrine as a building – and it clearly was one, given the character of Aldwulf's reminiscences – the majority of Anglo-Saxon sacred places were open-air sites. The two main kinds of shrine, distinguished by the Old English terms *hearg* ('harrow' in later names) and *wih* or *wēoh*, generally appear to have been places or enclosures, rather than buildings. Constructed temples, it has been suggested, only began to be built in the final stages of Old English paganism, as kings and kingdoms began to develop. In part this was because, like barrows, such built structures served to affirm the status of these new kinds of ruler, and in part perhaps because of the growing cultural influence of Christianity, a faith which had always employed buildings for worship (Blair 1995; 2005, 52). Prior to this, religious meeting places had been in the open, often beside natural features such as springs, or distinctive trees: Old English paganism, like many early religions, found spiritual significance in the natural landscape. To judge from the sites which the Anglo-Saxons chose for their burials, ancient burial mounds – round barrows from the Bronze Age – were also places of numinous awe, haunted perhaps by the ghosts of the ancestors. Indeed, it is probable that the Anglo-Saxon landscape was covered with a veneer of religious meaning, and that local people saw significance in a wide range of sites and features, just as their medieval Catholic Christian descendants were to do, with their multitude of wayside crosses, sacred wells and other shrines (Whyte 2006).

The possible locations of three Anglo-Saxon religious sites in the Sutton Hoo area have been preserved in medieval field names. Peter Warner noted one example, mentioned in the Melton/Bromeswell survey: folio 58b describes how

FIGURE 49. The parish church of St Gregory, Rendlesham, from the west.

Richard Wells held one pightle of copyhold land 'called Harrough Pightel lying in Bromeswell … near Wilford Bridge' (CUL MSS C 328, 311). The detailed description of the land's location provided by the survey makes it clear that it lay somewhere in the 'V' formed by what are now the main roads from Wilford Bridge to Bawdsey (B1083), and Rendlesham (B1084), at c.TM296499. Warner also drew attention to the field name 'Thurstow Went' on Norden's map, a short distance to the south-east of Bromeswell at c.TM314504, a name which may incorporate the name of the god Thor and the term 'stow', in the sense of 'meeting place' (Warner 1985, 18).

Another 'harrow' name occurs in the Rendlesham 'dragge', where folio 13 describes:

> A peece of land called the harrowe lieng between Tunley way on the north p[ar]t and the land of the said Rob[er]t and John Stav[er]ton on the south p[ar]t wherof the [ea]st head abutteth upon the land of the said Rob[er]t and the west head upon Tunley Way. (IRO HB 416/B4/1/30)

Its location is unfortunately unclear, but it seems to have been located some way from the possible temple site represented by the parish church.

Sutton Hoo, power and legitimation

Rendlesham may, or may not, have been a major royal residence at the time of Sutton Hoo, and the home of the family burying in the cemetery. Even if it was, we still need to explain why the two sites are separated by a distance of some five kilometres. The contrast with the situation at Scandinavian royal complexes like Uppsala, where palace and burial ground lie adjacent and form parts of a single ceremonial complex, is striking: but in England the spatial dissociation of the living and the dead was perhaps more usual than in Scandinavia. Most early Anglo-Saxon cemeteries appear to have been located at a distance from contemporary settlements – especially the large cremation cemeteries, found mainly in eastern England, which seem to have served as central repositories for widely dispersed communities (Arnold 1988, 41). But if tradition or belief necessitated the separation of the living and the dead, the central question remains: why was this point in space chosen for the site of the cemetery?

The answers advanced by archaeologists have to date mainly concerned concepts of status, display, and legitimation. As already noted, Howard Williams among others has emphasised that Anglo-Saxon burial sites often re-used monuments from earlier periods, especially barrows of Bronze Age date –'monument re-use was a widespread and frequent practice in early Anglo-Saxon England' (Williams 1998, 95) – and ancient earthworks like barrows continued to be used for isolated, wealthy burials into the seventh century. The reasons for this were complex:

> Ancient monuments were probably envisaged as powerful, liminal places, that may have been regarded as the dwellings of supernatural beings, ancient or ancestral

peoples … Consequently, the burial of the dead may have been an important statement by the living. This link with the past could have been significant in a variety of ways, supporting claims and rights over land, wealth, and other material and human resources … (Williams 1998, 103)

As hereditary local elites emerged in the later sixth and seventh centuries not only were ancient monuments still used as places for interment, but in addition entirely new barrows were now erected, something which may have been a form of emulation, an attempt by emergent rulers to identify themselves more closely with past elites, and thus to claim the legitimacy of power that continuity with antiquity conferred. In Williams' words, 'Perhaps the people who were buried with so many valuables in these graves were not venerating the ancient past; they were going one step further and trying to become the ancestors and deities that other groups had celebrated' (Williams 1998, 103), in an attempt to bolster their own claims to local supremacy.

It is thus possible that the site of Sutton Hoo was chosen because some ancient monument already stood there: and Martin Carver has indeed suggested that the actual placing of the mounds was influenced by the layout of the remains of the boundaries of the Iron Age and Roman field system, which survived at this stage as low turf banks. But, as Carver has noted, this prehistoric landscape 'although very old, was not funerary, monumental or even of a dramatic aspect' (Carver 2005, 457). Surviving remains may have influenced the disposition of the cemetery: they were less likely to have determined its site. Moreover, the excavations at Tranmer House in 2000 recovered further traces of a prehistoric field system, probably an extension of that discovered beneath the Sutton Hoo mounds, suggesting that in the sixth and seventh centuries the remains of early field boundaries might have been widespread in the area, which raises once again the question of why these *particular* sites were chosen as burial grounds. The excavations at the Tranmer House site also revealed a diminutive ring-ditch with central burial of Bronze Age date, whose presence may have influenced the location of the cemetery: but it was a tiny affair, a mere six metres in diameter, and as it lay within the area of the Iron Age field system it had almost certainly been ploughed flat long before the first Anglo-Saxon burials were made here. No traces of true prehistoric barrows have been made in the immediate vicinity of either cemetery and, as I argued earlier, the line of mound symbols to the north of Sutton Hoo shown on Norden's survey of 1601 does not seem to indicate a concentration of lost burial mounds.

To Williams, 'regardless of the presence or otherwise of an ancient monument on the Sutton Hoo site, building a new barrow may have served to manipulate conceptions of social meaning through the "antiquation" of funeral rites' (Williams 2001, 57–8); and if the site was newly chosen, then it was primarily because of its visibility. It occupied a topographically 'prominent' or 'commanding' position, visible from many places but in particular from the river Deben, from where it would be seen by people in ships passing upstream *en route*, perhaps for Rendlesham. Like other barrows in this period, those at Sutton Hoo 'were meant to be seen from a distance in specific ways' (Williams 2001, 57). Similar arguments, emphasising the desire of the family to display its presence in the wider landscape, have been advanced by other scholars. Evans, for example, has noted how the mounds 'would have been clearly visible from the river, and from the other side of the river where the land is lower than the plateau on whose edge the gravefield lies' (Evans 1986, 107). Webster has noted how the barrows, a 'statement of power', occupy 'a remote but dominant position in a ridge overlooking the Deben valley'; 'The Sutton Hoo barrows dominate the ridge' (Webster 1992, 77–8). Carver has emphasised that the mounds would originally have been considerably taller, and thus more visible from a distance, before they were truncated by later ploughing (Carver 2005, 198, 492, 465). Newton has gone so far as to state that the largest mounds could, perhaps, have been seen from the Saxon Shore fort at Walton Castle, at the mouth of the Deben some thirteen kilometres to the south (Newton 1993, 44). Other barrow sites of late sixth- and seventh-century date in England are similarly positioned in prominent locations, dynasties apparently affirming their power and control over the landscape. That at Taplow in Buckinghamshire occupies a terrace above the Thames, overlooking the river and the valley below; those at Cuddesdon and Astall in Oxfordshire are both similarly placed in a commanding position above the Thames; while the Broomfield barrow near Chelmsford in Essex stood on a terrace overlooking the river Chelmer (Webster 1992, 77–9).

All these explanations for the location of the Sutton Hoo cemetery thus emphasise the importance of prominence, visibility and display in the choice of its site, interpreting this as part of the cemetery's role in the legitimation and expression of the power, and the claims to power, of an emergent dynasty. This emphasis is reinforced by the links which many scholars have made between Sutton Hoo and various passages in the great Anglo-Saxon epic *Beowulf*. In particular, in his dying speech the hero asked to be buried 'in a splendid mound on the headland after my pyre; it shall be a reminder to my people, rising high on *Hronesnæsse*, so that seafarers will call it Beowulf's barrow' (ll.2802–2807). His wish was fulfilled, the poet describing how '… the Weder people built a mound on the hill, high and broad, widely visible to sea-farers; and in ten days the battle-leader's beacon was constructed' (ll.3156–3160). Not all scholars would necessarily share Sam Newton's views about the close connections between the Wuffingas and this poem, but few would argue with his assertion that 'Something of the ideal which this passage realises has clearly motivated the siting of … the East Anglian royal barrows at Sutton Hoo' (Newton 1993, 44).

But recent discoveries have made it harder to explain the siting of the cemetery in these kinds of terms. In particular, while the cemetery excavated at Tranmer House in 2000, only 600 metres to the north of Sutton Hoo (Fig. 50), included a number of high-status burials (inhumations with swords and a cremation in a bronze bowl) the site seems to represent a 'folk' cemetery, presumably the burial ground of the community from which the Wuffingas chose to separate themselves in the later sixth century – a proclamation of social distance and exclusivity evident in a number of areas in Europe at this time (Halsall 1995, 266). The Tranmer House site thus pre-dated Sutton Hoo; served a community, not just an elite; and lacked any substantial, monumental barrows. Yet it occupied a site virtually indistinguishable from it, in topographic terms, lying on the edge of the level shelf above the thirty-metre contour, immediately above the steep slope leading down to the Deben. Motivations of elite display, domination and the rest are scarcely applicable here, not least because – lacking as they did anything other than low mounds – the burials could never have been visible from any great distance. In short, if we only consider Sutton Hoo in isolation it is possible to argue that the barrows were placed where they are in order to dominate the landscape and, in particular, to signal the presence of the Wuffingas – or whoever was buried there – to ships passing up the Deben. If Sutton Hoo is examined within this wider context of local cemetery choice, however, a relationship with the river remains, but it requires some alternative explanation.

We might, moreover, legitimately question the extent to which ideas of power politics, domination, and the appropriation of territory and resources really were the sole or principal motivations behind choice of cemetery site – were, of necessity, the main concern of the bereaved in early Anglo-Saxon England. Death and burial did not simply provide opportunities for advancing the political fortunes of a dynasty. They were also occasions for experiencing loss and grief, and for dealing with the great questions of human existence. Religious and spiritual considerations may not loom large in the lives of modern archaeologists, but we should not assume that the same was necessarily true of the people whom they study.

Those who have emphasised the 'prominence' of the Sutton Hoo mounds, moreover, have not perhaps always paid enough attention to the particular characteristics of their site or, more importantly, to those of alternative places in the immediate vicinity in which they might just as easily have been placed. For the cemetery is not, like Beowulf's barrow, positioned on a commanding promontory, but rather at the head of a shallow embayment. While it is hard to imagine or reconstruct what the landscape would have been like in the late sixth and early seventh century – and in particular, how much tree cover there was at the time – we can use computer modelling to provide *some* indication of

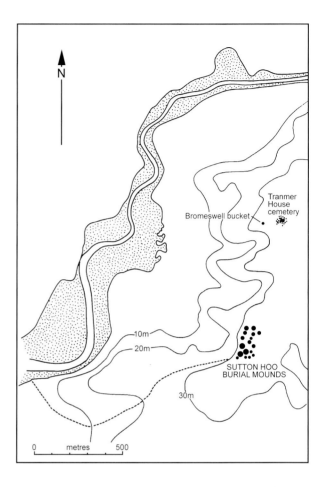

FIGURE 50. Map showing the location of the Sutton Hoo and Tranmer House cemeteries in relation to the river Deben (after Carver 2005).

the places and areas which might have been seen from the cemetery, and even from the locations of individual mounds within it – and *vice versa*. As Figure 51 illustrates, the earliest of the excavated mounds in the cemetery (3, 4, 5, 6, 7) could only ever have been visible along a very short stretch of the estuary; indeed, a location some fifty metres to the south-west, or the same distance to the north, would have ensured that they could have been seen across a wider area, and along a greater length of the approach to Rendlesham. Moving the cemetery still further from its actual site would have brought even greater benefits in this respect. If a location on the opposite shore of the Deben had been chosen, for example, around Drybridge Hill, then the mounds would probably have been visible for much of the approach up the estuary (Fig. 52).

The precise character of the visual relationship between the Sutton Hoo and Tranmer House cemeteries, and the river, is now rather difficult to appreciate because of the growth of the plantations established in the area since the later nineteenth century: in both cases the Deben can only now be distantly glimpsed, through the trees. In the case of Tranmer, however, it is clear that the view of the river was constricted or framed by the slopes of a shallow embayment or dry valley, at the head of which the cemetery is placed. From here, the eye would have been drawn to the river, as if to a performance. The view from Sutton Hoo would in some ways have been similar, and although the dip in the ground level represented by the embayment would have been less pronounced, the 'framing' effect would perhaps have been similar (Fig. 53). Nevertheless, if the view from both sites was to some extent framed or constricted, it was nevertheless clearly important. All this suggests that rather than concentrating on the ways in which the barrows might have been seen from the surrounding area, we need to consider the possible meaning of the views which could have been enjoyed from their site. Howard Williams, as well as emphasising the 'prominent' locations chosen for late sixth- and seventh-century burial mounds, has also acknowledged that:

> There may also have been a desire to locate barrows with particular kinds of views. In this sense, barrows were distinctive ways of seeing the landscape. (Williams 2001, 57)

It is also important in this context to emphasise the distinction between the height of the Sutton Hoo cemetery above sea level, and the prominence and visibility of the site: for in this district of rather gentle topography the two are not the same. If the cemetery had been placed on slightly lower ground, on the falling spur to the south-west for example, the burial mounds would have been much more visible, both from the river and from the opposite shore. Height in itself thus appears to have been of some importance to the users of the cemetery, as well as proximity to the river: and the same was evidently true of the community who established the earlier burial ground at Tranmer House. It is thus noteworthy that there is only a very limited area on the eastern bank of the Deben where the ground rises above the thirty-metre contour, as two slight but broad eminences above the wider, twenty-metre, plateau. These together cover less than four square kilometres, and at their broadest, north–south, are no more than two kilometres across. Between here and the sea, a distance of some twelve kilometres, no higher land occurs. It is surely not coincidence that the two cemeteries lie on the western margins of this diminutive upland.

River people

The view of the Sutton Hoo cemetery from the river was thus less important than the view of the river from the cemetery: and the same appears to have been true of the other, earlier burial ground, at Tranmer House. This in turn suggests that the river had some meaning for those who buried in these cemeteries. In this context, it is perhaps worth noting that the *hearg* field name discovered by Peter Warner in the Bromeswell survey – 'Harrow Pightel' – seems to have occupied a similar position, on the edge of the level uplands and looking down onto the river, as did the cemetery on Hoo Hill at Rendlesham and, perhaps, the site of 'Thurstow Went' in Bromeswell. Rendlesham church may, or may not, have been the site of Rædwald's temple, but it is noteworthy that although it is set well back from the Deben on a wide, level shelf of land, a slight embayment in the valley side again allows the river to be glimpsed in the middle distance.

The placing of cemeteries so that they had views towards, or across, a significant watercourse, while hardly standard practice, was by no means unknown in the early Anglo-Saxon period, particularly for the larger communal cemeteries, dominated by the rite of cremation, commonly found in East Anglia. Spong Hill in Norfolk commands an extensive prospect over the Black Water and its confluence with the river Wensum; the cemeteries at Castle Acre and West Acre seem to be similarly positioned above the river Nar; that at Walsingham enjoys views towards the Stiffkey; Brettenham looks out across the Thet; and, in the south of the county, the cemetery at Pewter Hill near Kirby Cane commands a distant prospect over the Waveney. In north-west Suffolk, some, at least, of the cemeteries along the Lark valley appear to have been placed in such a way that the view of the river, while sometimes distant, was nevertheless clear and uninterrupted. Such relationships may be accidental: cemeteries were located on the margins of the cleared and cultivated ground, which was concentrated in the valleys. But in many cases the placing appears to be intentional.

Of course, only a relatively small proportion of Anglo-Saxon cemeteries are so positioned. There were other preferred places for burial. Sometimes, for example, burial grounds were placed around, or on, some striking topographic feature, such as the esker at Old Hunstanton in north-west Norfolk. A wide range of factors, relating to the natural environment, the proximity of more ancient remains, and doubtless much else, could influence the choice of cemetery site: the early Anglo-Saxons seem to have drawn in a flexible manner on a shared collection of 'significant' associations when they chose places for their burial ground, just as they chose from a range of burial practices, making of them something that

FIGURE 51. 'Viewshed analysis' of the earliest of the excavated barrows (marked in black) at Sutton Hoo (Mounds 3, 4, 5, 6 and 7). The dark green shading shows the areas from which the mounds, originally between 2 and 2.5 metres in height, would have been visible.

FIGURE 52. If the main concern of the people who used the Sutton Hoo cemetery had been with visibility along the approach up the Deben to Rendlesham, then the best place to put the cemetery would probably have been near Drybridge Hill to the south-west of Woodbridge (dark green shading shows areas from which the mounds would have been visible).

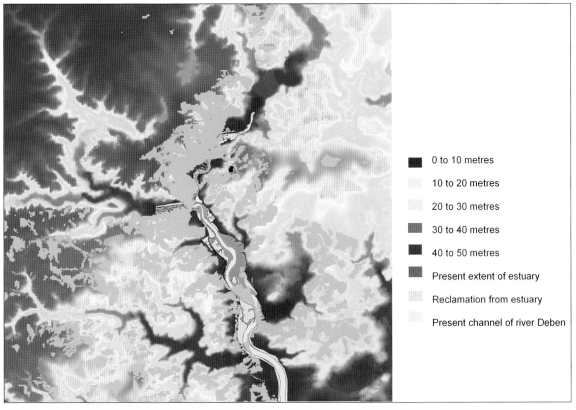

0 to 10 metres

10 to 20 metres

20 to 30 metres

30 to 40 metres

40 to 50 metres

Present extent of estuary

Reclamation from estuary

Present channel of river Deben

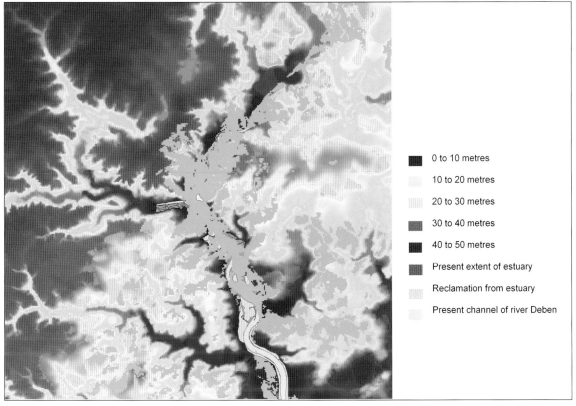

0 to 10 metres

10 to 20 metres

20 to 30 metres

30 to 40 metres

40 to 50 metres

Present extent of estuary

Reclamation from estuary

Present channel of river Deben

made sense in their own lives (Lucy 2000, 178–9; Filmer-Sankey and Pestell 2001, 262–4). In many cases cemetery location may have been decided by the significance of some feature which has now disappeared, and whose presence has left no archaeological trace: place-names, as well as the proclamations of the early church, thus attest the religious significance of trees in Anglo-Saxon paganism, and it is not inconceivable that burial grounds might have been placed close to prominent or particularly ancient examples. Such ephemeral influences perhaps explain such things as the curious placing of the cemetery at Snape, to the north-east of Sutton Hoo, which in spite of suggestions to the contrary is located in a position of very low visibility, in a slight concavity in a level heathland plateau (the discovery of a Bronze Age urn here might, alternatively, suggest that the cemetery was clustered near a lost round barrow). Nevertheless, all this said, elevated places with views across or towards rivers were clearly among the favoured locations for burying the dead in the fifth and sixth centuries.

This does not mean that rivers necessarily had any kind of religious identity, or even significance, to people living in the fifth or sixth centuries, in the way that – to judge from votive deposits – they possessed through much of prehistory (Bradley 2000b). But, given the patterns of movement, topography, and territorial organisation discussed earlier in this study it would not be surprising to learn that the Deben played a significant part in the emotional, imaginative and symbolic life of the people who buried their dead at Sutton Hoo. It was, with its great estuary, a presence impossible to ignore in a world in which patterns of movement ensured that much time was spent walking towards or away from it. Even today, when travel by land is channelled along a diversity of alternative routes, and the landscape is cut up by a myriad of other visually strong lines, the Deben still makes a profound emotional impact on the observer. How much greater would that impact have been at a time when high, uninhabited, and probably largely wooded interfluves separated those who dwelt beside it from those living beside the next river draining into the sea, to north or south. The Deben ran – like the other great rivers in the locality – through a ribbon of open, settled land, where wide views could be enjoyed: on the higher ground away from it, in contrast, occupied by the lonely woods and pastures, prospects in any direction were more constricted by the extent of tree cover. And the river may well have had another significance, one expressed clearly enough by the ship burials within Mounds 1 and 2. It was a highway which linked those living near its banks together, but which at the same time provided a gateway to places more distant. Moreover, whether the ancestors of the Wuffingas came from Denmark, or from some other part of northern Europe, they must have first arrived in this district along this inviting estuary. The location of the Sutton Hoo and Tranmer House cemeteries, together with the presence within some of the Sutton Hoo mounds of ships, may thus have referenced a lost origin-myth, describing how the people living in this area had first arrived here. In short, in innumerable ways the river would have been the centre of the imaginative and experienced world of those who dwelt beside it.

In some other contexts, rivers in Anglo-Saxon England seem to have acquired an almost totemic significance: or at least, groups of people identified so closely with a particular watercourse that they actually took their name from it. One striking example relates to another river which drains off the claylands of central Suffolk, through the Sandlings and into the sea via a visually striking estuary, a short distance (around forty kilometres) to the north of the Deben. Peter Warner has cogently argued that the hundred of Blything, which approximates more or less to the drainage basin of the river Blyth, was in origin the tribal territory of the *Blythingas*, the 'people of the river Blyth' (Blythburgh, the site of the early monastery at which King Anna was reputedly buried, was the 'monastic enclosure by the Blyth': Blyth itself means 'the merry river', or something along those lines)(Warner 1996, 120–1). In a similar way, the *Beningas*, an early tribe in eastern Hertfordshire who gave their name to the parishes of Benington and Bengeo, took their name from the river Beane; Avening in Gloucestershire was named after the 'people of the river Avon'; Dorking in Surrey takes its name from the *Dorcingas*, the 'people of the river Dorc', an old name for the river Mole. Of course, not all the place-names incorporating the term *-ingas* ('the people of') relate to tribal groups and territories dating back to the sixth or seventh centuries – the term was used for smaller and much later social units, such as extended kin-groups living in a particular locality (Everitt 1986, 162–3, 322). But names of this kind, which relate to topographic features, do for the most part appear to be ancient and tribal in character, and such an identification with natural landforms is apparent in early tribal names of other types: the *Chilternsætan*, for example, were 'the people who dwell by the Chilterns; the *Wrocsætan*, 'the people of the Wrekin'.

Identification with rivers, watercourses and estuaries is a particular feature of the early social nomenclature of East Anglia, presumably because of the paucity of other clearly defined topographic incidents in the landscape. Ten kilometres north of the river Blyth – and occupying all that north-eastern corner of Suffolk beyond Lowestoft – lies the hundred of Lothingland, often referred to as the 'Island' of Lothingland, bounded as it is by the North Sea to the east, the river Waveney to the west, and the inlet known as Lake Lothing to the south. There are grounds for believing that Lothing originally formed a single territory with the hundred of Mutford to the south (the two were reunited administratively in 1773) so that Lake Lothing, a visually prominent inlet from the sea, originally lay at its centre. The *Lothingas* almost certainly took their name from it: *Hlud* means something like 'the loud one', referring presumably to the noise made in the inlet by the incoming tide. A short distance to the west, across the county boundary and into Norfolk, Loddon Hundred is named, not after the town of Loddon which lies within it, but from another early tribal group, the *Lodningas*, 'the people of the *Ludne*' – the latter an early name for the river Chet, a small river which flows in a well-defined valley into what is now the Waveney, but which was then a vast estuary extending across what is now the Halvergate marshes (Watts 2004, 378–9). On the other side of Norfolk the *Wissa*, a tribal

group living on the edge of the Fens who are mentioned in the eighth-century *Life* of Saint Guthlac, similarly took their name from the river Wissey, a name which probably simply means 'river' in Old English (Ekwall 1962, 465–7). In north Norfolk, the villages of Great and Little Snoring preserve the name of the *Snoringas*, who may have derived their name from an ancient name for the river Stiffkey, the *Sneare*, 'the swift one' (Ekwall 1962, 61). Tribal names of this kind are, it should be noted, indistinguishable in character from those more common *-ingas* compounds, such as Happing in Norfolk – 'the people of *Hæpp*' – which seem to indicate the notional descent of a clan or tribe from a common ancestor, real or legendary (Watts 2004, 277). Perhaps in these cases rivers really did have a kind of totemic significance, embodying, in some sense, the spirit of a people.

I would not want to give the impression that tribal river-names of this kind are ubiquitous. Early social groups were more likely to take their name from individuals, or from other kinds of topographic feature: Chevening in Kent, for example, takes its name from the *Cheveningas*, 'the people of the ridge' (Watts 2004, 132). River names often seem to have been used where well-defined, significant river basins, containing extensive areas of tractable soils, are separated from other areas suitable for early settlement by particular wide and uninviting interfluves; and/or where rivers flow via striking but visually coherent estuaries into the sea. But such names may once have been more common than we think, and other examples may lurk unidentified in the pages of the English Place-Name Society volumes. This is because river names were often changed in the course

FIGURE 53. The view of the Deben from the Sutton Hoo barrows is now obscured by the trees of Top Hat Wood. This photograph, taken from the edge of the thirty-metre 'shelf' a little to the north, captures something of the prospect which would otherwise be enjoyed from the site.

FIGURE 54. Mound 2, reconstructed to its original height following excavation.

of the Middle Ages, and sometimes later still: and if the original name is lost then place-name specialists might well interpret some now obscure first element of an *ingas* name in the locality, in their customary way, as a lost personal name (even if such a name is not evidenced in any other context). Many river names in East Anglia, and elsewhere, were changed by the process of 'back-formation': that is, when a watercourse takes a new name from a settlement located along it, often near its source or its mouth. In many East Anglian examples of this phenomenon the new name replaced, not one with Old English origins, but a survival from the Roman or Celtic past – a name which perhaps had become awkward to pronounce or meaningless to later generations. The river Nar in Norfolk thus takes its name from the village of Narford, but was originally called the Pante (Welsh *pant*, 'valley') (Ekwall 1962, 299). The Yare is a back-formation from Yarmouth: its early medieval name was the Gerne, derived from the British *Gariennos* or *Gariannos*, 'the loud one' (Ekwall 1962, 477–8). The Wissey, as already noted, takes its name from the Old English term *wissa*, 'river': but its British name *Wigora*, 'the winding one', survived long enough to be preserved in the name of the village of Wereham (*Wigorham* in a charter of 1060). The name of the Chet is a back-formation from Chedgrave (Ekwall 1962, 77). Its earlier name, as already noted, was the Ludne, from British *Ludna*, 'muddy river' (Ekwall 1962, 258). It is noteworthy how, in this last case, an early Anglo-Saxon tribe, the *Lodningas*, took their name from a *British* river name.

The name of the river Deben, it might be worth noting at this point, is itself a back-formation: the river takes its name from the town of Debenham, which is located close to its source. The name, sometimes in the shortened form *Deane* (as in Reyce's 1618 *Breviary of Suffolk*: Hervey 1902, 12), is first recorded in the sixteenth century. In the words of W.G. Arnott, writing in his *Place-Names of the Deben Valley Parishes* of 1946: 'What the Deben was called originally, will probably never be known although the name of some river-side meadow or ford may be found to occur in other riparian villages and thus provide the clue' (Arnott 1946, 2–3).

'Beyond the evidence': the mounds and the river

The discussion so far, while not perhaps backed up with hard, irrefutable proof, has a certain logic which readers may, or may not, find persuasive. In essence, the cemeteries at Sutton Hoo and Tranmer were placed where they were because the people who used them had an affinity with, felt some kind of association with, the Deben, and – for purposes of burial – placed a particular value on high places from which that river could be viewed. In identifying in some way with their local river they were not entirely unique: some other tribal groups in East Anglia and beyond seem to have had similar attitudes to prominent watercourses flowing through the centre of their own territories, sometimes expressing this in the names they gave themselves, imperfectly preserved in modern place names. In the pages that follow I will develop these ideas, quite consciously going still further 'beyond the evidence' in ways that are even less susceptible to rigorous testing. Readers should be warned that what follows *is* a short exercise in speculation, of the kind in which prehistorians seem increasingly happy to indulge but which medievalists rightly, for the most part, avoid. But such speculations can, I believe, at least suggest ways in which we might think about the relationships between landscape, burial, and social change at the time of Sutton Hoo.

Of the nineteen mounds in the Sutton Hoo cemetery, less than half have been fully excavated in modern times. Leaving aside Mound 14, which covered a female inhumation made in the mid-seventh century, after the main period of use of the cemetery, the barrows fall into two main groups. The first comprises Mounds 3, 5, 6 and 7, all of which were raised in the decades either side of AD 600. All originally contained wealthy grave goods and single cremations, in bronze bowls or, in the case of Mound 3, on a wooden trough or boat. All these mounds appear to have originally been between 14 and 20 metres in diameter and between 1.7 and 2.5 metres high. Mounds 4 and 18 also belong to this phase but were probably smaller than the others (the latter was no more than a slight rise in the ground surface at the time it was excavated), and perhaps represent family members of lesser status: both mounds had been robbed in the remote past and badly damaged by ploughing, but had contained cremated remains in bronze bowls (in the former those of a man, woman and horse, in the latter a single individual) (Carver 2005).

The second group comprises mounds 1, 2 and 17. Mound 17 was raised some time between c.600 and 620 and contained the inhumation of a warrior accompanied by grave goods showing the influence not only of Scandinavian but also of Frankish custom and tradition. It was followed by Mounds 1 and 2, roughly contemporary with each other and dating to around 630 (Carver 2005, 489–92). The former was larger than any of the previous mounds at Sutton Hoo. It was some thirty metres in diameter and may have stood as much as four metres high (Carver 2005, 197). It contained the great ship burial, a rite displaying clear Scandinavian affinities, but also the wealthy grave goods from Francia, Byzantium and Rome noted in Chapter One. It likewise covered an inhumation rather than a cremation. The badly robbed Mound 2 was also a substantial feature – around 22 metres in diameter and between 2.7 and 3.8 metres high (Fig. 54). It covered an inhumation and a boat burial, and again probably contained grave goods with wider European rather than specifically Scandinavian associations.

The two main groups of barrows thus display marked differences in burial rite, and in the character of the grave goods they contained. The earlier group, in Carver's words, 'signalled high status and affiliation to the cultural practices of Scandinavia and north Germany' (Carver 2005, 490). The grave goods in the later mounds, in contrast, while still affirming an allegiance with Scandinavian traditions, display a greater range of contacts with the European mainland: with Francia and the world of late antiquity. The adoption of inhumation rather than cremation might also signal the growing influence of this latter world (see above, pp.16–17).

What is striking is that the two groups of barrows appear to have a different relationships with the surrounding landscape. The cemetery as a whole is arranged around a rough south-south-west/north-north-east axis, which broadly mirrors the orientation of the river, some 500 metres to the west. What are probably the main mounds of the first phase, however – 3, 5, 6 and 7 – form an accurate line running through the middle of the cemetery, more closely parallel to the river's course (Figs 55 and 56). We must be cautious here – the 'subsidiary' status of Mounds 4 and 18 is difficult to demonstrate with any certainty, given the extent to which they had been damaged by ploughing and robbing, and the character of unexcavated mounds remains unclear, so it is possible that the 'line' is more fortuitous than real. Nevertheless, it remains a noticeable feature of the site, and it may be significant that Carver's careful analysis of the dating evidence suggests that it developed from north-east to south-west (Carver 2005, 490–1) – the chronological order of the mounds thus mimicking the direction of flow of the Deben, out towards the sea. The river, indeed, was visible from each of the mounds in the line but, had they been placed only a few metres further to the east, away from the edge of the shelf, it would not have been (Fig. 57). The location of the later barrows was different. These were all placed to the west of the prominent 'line' of existing barrows, nearer to the river: Mound 2 only slightly so, but Mounds 1 and 17 on the very edge of the shelf. They did not continue – were not added to – the developing 'line' – assuming once again

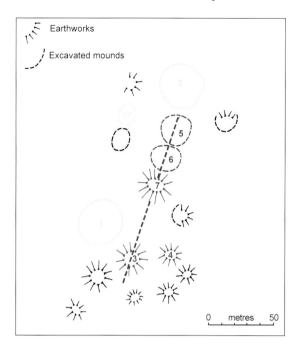

FIGURE 55. What appear to have been the most important barrows constructed in the period before c.610 were arranged in an accurate line lying parallel with the Deben. The line developed from north-east to south-west, with the flow of the river.

that this is indeed a significant feature, and not an illusion.

We might perhaps speculate that the line of barrows in some sense represented an attempt by an emerging elite, burying in a new and spatially distinct cemetery, to identify with (to appropriate?) the river which had long served as a focus for group identity; and that by breaking this line the later mounds, as to some extent their contents, expressed a further distancing from the world of the *folk*. What is certainly clear is that the seventh-century barrows were placed in positions that made them more prominent and visible in the landscape than the mounds in the earlier group – not greatly so, especially in terms of their visibility from the Deben, for this could only have been achieved by burying elsewhere, but enough to make a significant difference (Fig. 58). In this context we should note again that Mounds 1 and 2 were considerably larger than the earlier barrows in the cemetery. Status display, rather than (perhaps) association with the main topographic feature in the locality, was now of greatest importance to those who buried at the cemetery.

We do not, of course, know precisely who *was* interred in any of these mounds, and Martin Carver has rightly cautioned against trying to guess (Carver 2005, 503). But few have managed to resist the temptation, and I will not try: for by speculating about the relationship between the cemetery and its surrounding landscape, we may perhaps view this question in a slightly different light. The character of the grave goods – the Christian references in spoons and perhaps bowls, the dating of the coins and other artefacts – perhaps make it likely, as most people have long accepted, that Rædwald himself (who died around 625) was buried in Mound 1; his son Rægenhere, killed at the battle of the river Idle in 616, would be a possible candidate for Mound 17 (although it is admittedly a long way to bring a body); while Mound 2 might conceivably have contained Rædwald's other son Eorpwald, who died around 627. Although (according to Bede) the latter embraced the Christian faith more wholeheartedly than his father this would not – at this initial stage of the Conversion – necessarily have meant that he was buried without traditional grave goods, or even away from the burial ground of his ancestors (Hoggett 2007). In Christian Francia, grave goods continued to be employed into the eighth century (Halsall 1995, 266): even burial mounds might still be erected, in northern parts of the Frankish world at least, until as late as c.800, only then being specifically identified as a pagan practice (Effros 2003, 199–200). Eorpwald's successors, however – men more actively involved in the Christian mission – would surely have been less likely to have been interred here. While some family members continued to use the Sutton Hoo burial ground into the middle of the seventh century, both Sigeberht and Anna would almost certainly have been laid to rest in the monasteries which would henceforth be the spiritual focus, and the place of interment, of the royal elites emerging across England.

Looked at in this way, in terms of its relationship with the landscape, the development of the cemetery can thus be read as part of a process by which the Wuffingas distanced themselves from the wider community of a *folk* dwelling

FIGURE 56. The 'line' is now less apparent due to the levelling of Mound 5, in the foreground (beyond the edge of Mound 2, just visible). Mounds 6, 7, and 3 align in the distance.

on the banks of the Deben. But the family had once formed a part of that community, and it is possible that the name they bore originally applied to the tribe as a whole, rather than to one section of it. As we have seen, Bede tells us that the Wuffingas derived their name from Uffa or Wuffa, Rædwald's 'grandfather': a genealogy supported by the pedigree of the eighth-century King Ælfwald. Sam Newton, as we have also seen, has persuasively argued that Uffa was a mythical figure (Newton 1993, 105). Yet this leaves one minor problem – the name of Ufford, which lies just over three kilometres to the north of Sutton Hoo, directly across the Deben from Rendlesham. It is possible, as Parker Pearson *et al.* have suggested (1993, 29), that the village takes its name from some other person called Uffa: but this would be a remarkable coincidence. The name may, of course, have been given to the place as part of a story told about the mythical founder-figure of the dynasty – the place where he fought a great battle, for example. But there is another possibility.

Ufford appears in Domesday Book in two versions: *Uffeworða*, and *Uffeforda*, 'Uffa's enclosure' and 'Uffa's ford' respectively. Such early confusion of, and drift between, names ending in *-ford* and *-worth* is common in place-names. There are a number of examples of names which originally ended in *-worth* which were gradually changed to ones ending in *-ford*, such as Pampisford in Cambridgeshire (*Pampisworth* in Domesday Book). Conversely, there are names which early charters or Domesday have ending in *-ford* which, by the later Middle Ages, had changed to ones in *-worth*, such as Panxworth in Norfolk. In the case of Ufford, there can be little doubt about the original form, for the village stands close to a prominent crossing place, where the Deben's floodplain narrows appreciably. It may well have been the lowest fording place in early Saxon times, the ford at Wilford, some two kilometres downstream, only developing as relative sea levels dropped after the ninth century and (perhaps) as the amount of silting in the upper estuary increased.

Many place-names which incorporate the term 'ford' have as their first element the name of an individual. In rather more cases, the initial element serves to describe some characteristic of the ford in question, or refers to a neighbouring topographic feature. Wilford is thus 'the ford where the willows grow'; Chillesford, some nine kilometres east of Sutton Hoo, is the 'gravelley ford' (Gelling and Cole 2000, 75, 73). A small minority, however, have as their first element the name of the river across which they provided a passage. The nearest example is Blyford, the 'ford on the river Blyth', which lies some forty kilometres to the north of Sutton Hoo (Gelling and Cole 2000, 76). In some of these cases the old name for the river has been replaced by the process of back-formation (as described earlier: above, p.111), yet lives on in a place-name derived from a ford which crossed it. The river Glaven in north Norfolk, for example, is a back-formation from the village of Glandford, but it is probable that the latter incorporates the earlier name for the river, *Glan*, from the Old Welsh term meaning 'pure' – very suitable for this chalk stream (Ekwall 1962, 174).

'Ford' names of this kind, incorporating the name of a river, are often associated

FIGURE 57. This 'viewshed' shows how the river would have been virtually invisible from the line of early mounds if they had been located ten metres further away from the edge of the 'shelf'. Their visibility from the far shore of the Deben, however, would have been unchanged (dark green shading shows areas from which the mounds would have been visible; compare with Figure 51).

FIGURE 58. Mounds 1, 2 and 17 were placed closer to the edge of the 'shelf' than the earlier 'line', perhaps to ensure that they were visible across a wider area and along a marginally longer stretch of the approach up the Deben (dark green shading shows areas from which the mounds would have been visible).

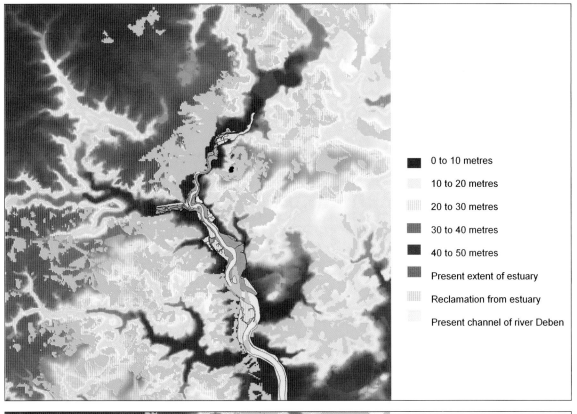

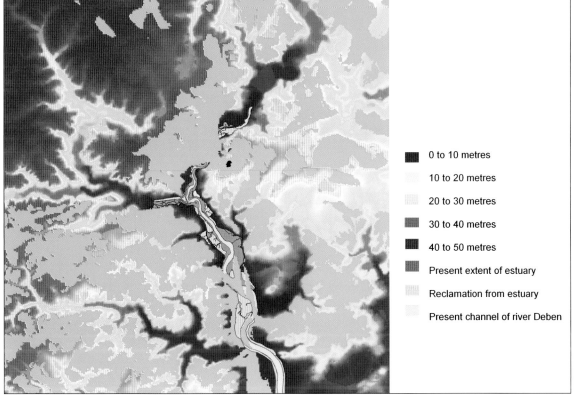

with its lowest fording point. Blyford was always the lowest ford on the Blyth; Glandford the lowest on the Glaven; and Sleaford in Lincolnshire was, in Saxon times, probably the lowest place where the Slea could be crossed without a boat. Crayford and Dartford in Kent both lie a few kilometres above where the rivers Cray and Dart flow into the Thames, while Ilford in Essex is similarly located on the northern side of the Thames, at the head of Barking Creek, the mouth of the river Rothing, formerly the *Hyle* (Gelling and Cole 2000, 76). There are, it should be noted, other topographic circumstances which encouraged this kind of name: for example, where a major road, especially a Roman road, crossed a river (such as Lydford in Somerset, where the river Lyd is crossed by Fosse Way (Gelling and Cole 2000, 76)). But names of this type do seem to have been thought particularly appropriate to fording places close to the point where a river widened out into an estuary, or fed into a more substantial watercourse.

It is just possible, then, that Ufford likewise originally incorporated a river name: it was the fording place on a river called something like the Uff or Wuff. This first element might have the kind of derivation suggested by Newton for the family name of the Wuffingas, and have meant 'wolf' or 'little wolf', but this seems a curious name for a river. It is more probable that, like many other lost river names in East Anglia, it was of Celtic origin. The river Worf in Wiltshire offers a possible parallel: early recorded versions of this name are *Worfe* in a late copy of a mid-eighth-century charter; and *Wurf* in a tenth-century charter. Ekwall suggested that it derives from a British term *verb, meaning 'the winding one', 'the bending one' (Ekwall 1961, 469–70). The same term occurs in the name of the river Wharfe in the West Riding of Yorkshire (earliest forms *Weorf* and *Werf*) (Ekwall 1962, 454–5). Such a name *might* – just might – have arisen from the marked bends made by the river immediately below Woodbridge.

If the name of Ufford does indeed derive from the lost name of the river Deben, then so too did the name of the Wuffingas. What Ufford was to the Deben, Blyford was to the Blyth; and what the Blythingas were to the Blyth, the Wuffingas were to the Deben. Like them and like the *Lodningas* or the *Wissa*, the Wuffingas were a river people. *Wuffingas* was not, in origin, a dynastic name, but a tribal one. It was gradually transformed from the latter into the former – became the name of one particular family group within what may in origin have been a clan of more widely related individuals; and as this happened a false etymology for the name and, perhaps, a false family history was invented, and apparently at a very early date. Both Bede's *History*, and the pedigree of King Ælfwald, were originally written down in the first half of the eighth century.

This chapter has, as I promised, concluded with a number of essentially untestable hypotheses – with speculations based on the most tenuous of evidence. I hope that this will not damage the credibility of the wider arguments advanced earlier in this section concerning Sutton Hoo and its landscape, and above all the suggestions about the importance, and the character, of the relationship between the cemetery and the river Deben.

CHAPTER FIVE

Territory and Topography

The Essex connection

In the opening chapter of this study I suggested that the Sutton Hoo burial mounds need to be considered in two distinct landscape contexts. Firstly, we need to understand why they were placed precisely where they were within this particular locality. But secondly, we need to explain why they are in this general area, a somewhat remote corner of south-eastern Suffolk, rather than anywhere else in East Anglia, perhaps more centrally placed. The first question has been addressed, at least after a fashion, in the previous chapters. I now want to turn to the second, and this involves – as it were – panning back, and looking at the cemetery within a more extensive geographical context. It also involves – again, as already intimated – adopting perhaps more conventional archaeological and historical approaches, examining broad patterns of settlement, land use, exchange networks and political power, rather than essentially *local* patterns of landscape experience.

To explain why the Sutton Hoo cemetery is located here in the far south-east of Suffolk is really to explain why a group of people originating in this district came to dominate the whole of the East Anglian kingdom. As I have already emphasised, the cemetery does not stand alone, but instead forms part of a tight cluster of sixth- and seventh-century sites with royal connections: Rendlesham, Iken, Walton, Burgh (if this was indeed the site of *Cnobheresburgh*), perhaps Ufford, together with the *wic* at Ipswich. No other area of East Anglia can boast such a collection. Yet the southern Sandlings is unquestionably a district which, by the time we get a clear picture of administrative geography in the late Saxon period, lay on the very edge of the kingdom of East Anglia, of the land of the East Angles. Indeed, so marginal are the Sutton Hoo barrows to the generally accepted area of the kingdom that some archaeologists have doubted whether they really have anything to do with it, or with the Wuffingas, at all. In an important article published in 1993 Michael Parker Pearson, Robert Van de Noort and Alex Woolf challenged 'the underlying assumption that the burials at Sutton Hoo belong to an East Anglian political, social and economic milieu' (Parker Pearson *et al.* 1993, 27). They threw doubt on the significance of the places lying near to the cemetery which apparently had connections with the Wuffingas. They thus argued that while Bede, in his account of the baptism in 655 of the East Saxon King Swidelm, clearly states that Rendlesham lay within 'the province of the East Angles', the wording makes it unclear whether he meant that he was talking about the situation then, or at the time he himself was writing – i.e., in the early eighth century. The proximity of the mounds to the village of Ufford they dismissed as mere coincidence – the name 'was one of six Uffa derivatives, the others being nowhere near East Anglia' (*ibid.*, 29). Political boundaries were fluid at this time, they suggested, so that 'we should be wary of interpreting it [the site of Sutton Hoo] as clearly within a political territory of the time'. Indeed, the place might have stood 'in a boundary zone' between the kingdom of the East Angles, and that of the East Saxons.

Parker Pearson and his colleagues argued that the burial in Mound 1 was perhaps slightly earlier in date than numismatic scholars such as Kent (1975) or Brown (1981) had suggested on the basis of the coin evidence; that the grave goods showed closer affinities with Essex and south-eastern England than with East Anglia; and that the burials formed part of a wider European distribution of 'princely burials' peripheral to the core zone of Merovingian power in northern France, which indicated that the areas in question – including Kent and much of south-eastern England – lay 'within the realm of Frankish influence, if not under direct Frankish political and economic control' (Parker Pearson *et al.* 1993, 32). The Sutton Hoo cemetery, considered in this wider European context, would be better interpreted as the resting place of the East Saxon rather than the East Anglian royal family, and Parker Pearson and his colleagues identified the burial in Mound 1 as that of King Sæberht, who was baptised in 604, died in 616, and whose sons had then repudiated both the Christian faith and the political hegemony of Kent over the East Saxons with which this had been associated. The magnificence of the funeral, the scale of the mound and the vast wealth of the grave goods were intended as a 'political gesture' on the part of Sæberht's successors 'to restate the nature of the boundary with the East Angles (including East Saxon control of the Deben) and to dispose of all those items redolent of his [Sæberht's] ties with Christianity and Kentish overlordship' (Parker Pearson *et al.* 1993, 47–8).

Parker Pearson and his collaborators agreed, in the conclusion to their article, that they had been 'unable to disprove that Rædwald and the East Anglian royal dynasty were buried at Sutton Hoo', *or* to prove that Sæberht and the East Saxons had been buried there. There intention was to robustly challenge accepted views, and this they achieved with some success. Nevertheless, their arguments have for the most part been disputed or – more usually – virtually ignored in subsequent studies (e.g. Carver 2005), and they can indeed be challenged on a number of grounds. In particular, the local context of the cemetery is not fully taken into account, in the sense that the strong association of the Wuffingas with places close to Sutton Hoo, like Iken and Walton, is either ignored, or unconvincingly disputed. The contention that the proximity of a place called 'Uffa's ford' to the burial ground of a group called 'Uffa's people' is simply a coincidence seems unreasonable; while it is hard indeed to read the passage in Bede dealing with Swiðelm's baptism by Cedd in 655 to mean

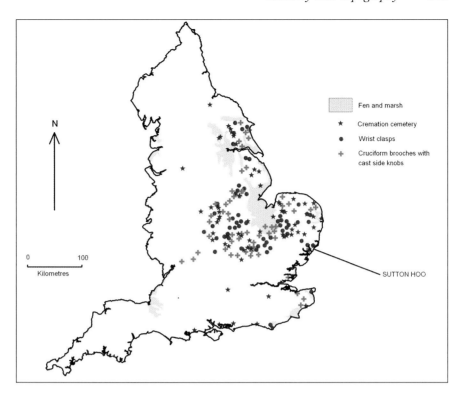

FIGURE 59. The distribution of typical 'Anglian' artefacts (after Parker Pearson *et al.* 1993) and cremation cemeteries.

anything other than that Rendlesham was, *at that time*, 'in the province of the East Angles' – not least because we are told that 'Æthelberht, king of the East Angles, brother to Anna, king of the same people', was Swiđelm's godfather at the ceremony. Nevertheless, the article does raise a number of important questions about the wider cultural and political context of the Sutton Hoo cemetery which we do need to briefly explore.

Firstly, it is true that the grave goods found not only in Mound 1, but also those associated with the burials more recently excavated by Martin Carver, show associations with Essex and the south as much as, if not more than, with East Anglia. Variations in the kinds of pottery and metalwork used by the early Anglo-Saxons, and mainly recovered from furnished burials, used to be interpreted by archaeologists in fairly straightforward 'ethnic' terms (Lucy 2000, 11–14; examples include Hawkes 1956). Certain kinds of artefact were considered 'Anglian', or 'Saxon', or 'Jutish', because they were found in those parts of the country which, according to Bede's account of the fifth and sixth centuries, were settled by members of these ethnic groups. The invaders, he tells us in a famous passage:

> Came from three very powerful Germanic tribes, the Saxons, the Angles, and the Jutes. The people of Kent and the inhabitants of the Isle of Wight are of Jutish origin, and also those opposite the Isle of Wight, that part of the Kingdom of Wessex which is still today called the nation of the Jutes. From the Saxon country, that is,

the district now known as Old Saxony, came the East Saxons, the South Saxons, and the West Saxons. Besides this, from the country of the Angles, that is the land between the kingdoms of the Jutes and the Saxons, which is called *Angulus*, came the East Angles, the Middle Angles, the Mercians, and all the Northumbrian race … as well as the other Anglian tribes … (McClure and Collins 1994, 27)

Types of fifth- and sixth-century artefact found within the areas later occupied by the kingdoms of Mercia, Northumbria, and the East Angles – essentially the Midlands, north-east England and East Anglia – were therefore thought to be specifically 'Anglian' in character. Others kinds of artefact, in contrast, were considered 'Saxon' because they were found primarily in southern England, including Essex, and in the Thames basin. Modern archaeologists, for the most part, do not accept such neat ethnic labels, nor the elegant simplicity of Bede's account which was, after all, written more than two centuries after the *Adventus Saxonum*. The modern orthodoxy is that the Germanic settlers were, in fact, culturally diverse and ethnically mixed. In the words of Sam Lucy:

> The immediate post-Roman period in Britain, and indeed in the whole of Europe, was a time when identities were in an extreme state of flux … when charismatic leaders could gather strong bands of followers around them and gain control of often extensive tracts of territory … (Lucy 2000, 4)

In the very process of migration, people from a wide area of northern Germany and southern Scandinavia might have become incorporated within the same war band. Nevertheless, the material culture of the period does display, at least to a degree, the kind of geographical character outlined above, and this requires some form of explanation. So-called 'Anglian' material, largely restricted to East Anglia, the Midlands and the north, is typified by the artefacts known as 'wrist clasps', and by particular styles of brooch – those classified by archaeologists as 'equal armed', 'cruciform' and 'annular', together with most of the 'square-headed' variety. As we shall see, the rite of cremation was also particularly favoured in these areas (Fig. 59). In 'Saxon' areas, in contrast, wrist clasps are largely absent and different forms of brooch predominate – a particular kind of square-headed ('Group VIII'), quoit and radiate-headed (Hills 1998, 184; Parker Pearson *et al.* 1993, 34–6; Hines 1984). In fact, it has long been recognised that 'Saxon' material occurs widely in 'Anglian' areas, although the inverse is rather less true. Whether or not these variations have any connection with the homelands of immigrant peoples settling in different parts of England, they certainly hint at regional variations in the style of dress in the fifth and sixth centuries. 'In East Anglia, the East Midlands and Yorkshire, women wore cruciform and annular brooches, and fastened their sleeves with metal clasps. In southern England, in Sussex, Wessex and Essex, they preferred round brooches and did not use clasps' (Hills 1998, 184). The relevant point here is that, as Parker Pearson *et al.* note with regard to the finds made in Mound 1: 'There are *no* artefacts in the burial of a specifically Anglian style (as opposed to Saxon, Kentish or broadly English styles)' (Parker Pearson *et al.* 1993, 41). Conversely, some of the artefacts found in Mound 1, such as the clay bottle turned on a slow wheel or some of the spear-heads of leaf-shaped type, are more typical of southern England than they are of East Anglia. This argument is not perhaps as strong as it seems, however, because – as Helen Geake has shown – the early seventh century was a time in which the kinds of regional variation described above were fast disappearing, and a more uniform material culture was coming to be adopted (Geake 1997). In Carver's words, in this period artefacts 'became unspecific to locality and signify a more national community' (Carver 2005, 497). Moreover, the grave goods found at Sutton Hoo came from a wide range of places, as far afield as Byzantium, especially those associated with the later burials, and the lack of clear regional/ethnic markers may have been another signal of the way that the people burying here were an elite, consciously distancing themselves from the wider culture of the *folk*. But this said, the character of the assemblages does perhaps reflect the way in which the users of Sutton Hoo were marginal to the main distributions of 'Anglian' material culture, just as they were unquestionably marginal to the area of the East Anglian kingdom itself.

The two Suffolks

We do not know the precise boundaries of the East Anglian kingdom, and in its early years at any rate these may have fluctuated depending on the strength and military success of its individual rulers. While it is easily assumed that the boundaries of those medieval counties of England which came to bear the names of Anglo-Saxon kingdoms provide some guide to the extent of those polities, this is by no means certain, and in East Anglia especially. The settlement of much of northern East Anglia by Danish invaders in the later ninth century, and the region's subsequent reconquest by the West Saxon kings and incorporation into the unified English kingdom, may well have led to significant reorganisation of territories and boundaries. Indeed, we have no clear idea of where the county boundaries of Norfolk or Suffolk ran in the period before the Domesday survey; and their character suggests that they were not then of any great antiquity. The present boundary between Essex and Suffolk – along the river Stour – thus features a number of curious anomalies. For example, the vill, and later parish, of Bures St Mary lies on the Suffolk side of the Stour, but Mount Bures lies on the Essex side, as does Bures Hamlet – although it is part of the parish of the Bures St Mary (Round 1903, 408). True, by medieval times the boundary between the Diocese of London – established to serve the kingdom of the East Saxons – and that for East Anglia, based in medieval times on Norwich, but in the Saxon period located variously at *Dommoc*, Elmham, and Thetford – ran along the line of the river Stour. But again, we do not know the antiquity of this arrangement and it, too, might only date back to the time of the West Saxon reconquest in the tenth century.

The issue is complicated by the fact that a major cultural boundary – or boundary zone – ran, in most historical periods, diagonally through the middle of Suffolk from Bury St Edmunds to Ipswich, roughly along the line of the Lark and Gipping valleys or, more usually, on the high ground just to the north of this. In many ways and in many periods the material culture of north and east Suffolk had more in common with that of Norfolk than with that of the areas to the south-west of the 'line', which in turn shared much in common with Essex. Such quintessential 'East Anglian' phenomena as early medieval round church towers, or the habit of placing two or more parish churches in the same or adjacent churchyards, are thus most common in the north and east of the region, relatively rare in the south and west, their distribution fading out along a line drawn roughly from Bury to Ipswich (Williamson 2006, 90–1). Aspects of medieval and post-medieval vernacular architecture display similar patterns. Late medieval houses with queen post (as opposed to crown post) roofs, or the tendency – when open halls were being floored over during the sixteenth century – to place the chimney stack between the hall and the parlour, rather than at the lower end of the hall, are thus a feature of both north-east Suffolk and Norfolk, but rare in south-west Suffolk, as in Essex (Coleman and Barnard 1999). Pantiles – the distinctive tiles with a section like a shallow 'S' which were introduced from the Low Countries in the seventeenth century – likewise have a distribution which fades away rapidly towards the south-west of Suffolk (Lucas 1993; Williamson 2006, 98–106). There are many other examples of this pattern (Fig. 60).

What is striking is that a number of pre-medieval archaeological distributions also cut off along this same general line (Williamson 2006, 36–45). In the later Iron Age, for example, the material culture of south-west Suffolk, like that of the adjacent areas of Essex and Hertfordshire, indicates close contacts with the Roman world. It features wealthy burials, furnished with grave goods including amphorae and other exotic imports; fairly sophisticated, wheel-turned pottery; the early use of coinage; and the development of large, sprawling agglomerations of settlement, defended by linear earthworks, such as Colchester in Essex or Braughing in Hertfordshire, which archaeologists usually term 'oppida'. North and east of the Lark–Gipping corridor, in contrast, wheel-thrown pottery did not really become current until after the Claudian conquest, wealthy burials and rich imports are virtually unknown, and few if any sites of 'oppida' type existed. This difference in culture and economics is associated, although just how closely is uncertain, with a political division. Northern East Anglia was the land of the Iceni, whose leading families remained hostile to the Roman world even after the Conquest – famously mounting, under the leadership of Boudicca, the great revolt of AD 61. Southern East Anglia – Essex, and south-western Suffolk, together with the eastern parts of Hertfordshire – was the land of the Trinovantes. The 'boundary' between these two tribal areas, to judge from the distribution of certain distinctive artefact types, and of the coinage produced by the two groups, lay once again roughly along a line running diagonally through the county from around Bury St Edmunds to the vicinity of Ipswich (Fig. 61) (Martin 1999, 83–90; Haselgrove 1982; Cunliffe 1995, 58–97).

FIGURE 60. In both the medieval and the post-medieval periods north-east Suffolk often had, in terms of its vernacular architecture and material culture, much in common with Norfolk. The south-west of the county, conversely, displayed strong similarities with Essex. This map shows three aspects of this divide: the distribution of round-towered churches, of shared and proximate churchyards, and of pantile roofs.

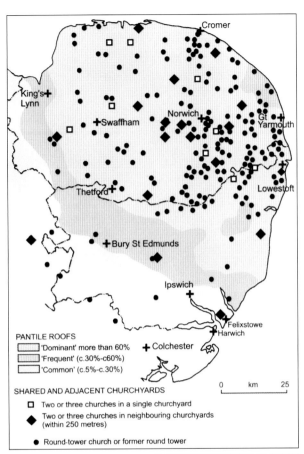

FIGURE 61. The same cultural boundary, running roughly along the line of the rivers Lark and Gipping, is apparent in many archaeological distributions. In the Iron Age, Icenian coins were found in the north and east of East Anglia, and cemeteries of the 'Aylesford-Swarling culture', containing wealthy imports for continental Europe, were characteristic of the south-west (after Rippon 2007).

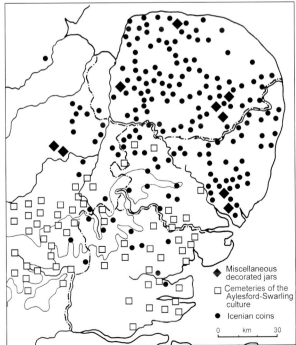

More significant in the present context is the fact that the same essential division reappears in the post-Roman period. 'Anglian' dress ornaments, of the kinds already noted, thus seem to be more a feature of Norfolk, and of northern and eastern Suffolk, than of the south-west of the latter county (Newman 1992b). Moreover, in the middle Saxon period the distribution of Ipswich Ware – made at Ipswich and probably distributed through some kind of elite gift exchange, rather than via a true market economy – also tends to fade off on the Lark–Gipping line (Fig. 62). This last example may, in fact, suggest that in middle Saxon times south-west Suffolk was not only culturally distinct from the rest of East Anglia, but also lay *politically* outside East Anglia, and within the kingdom of Essex.

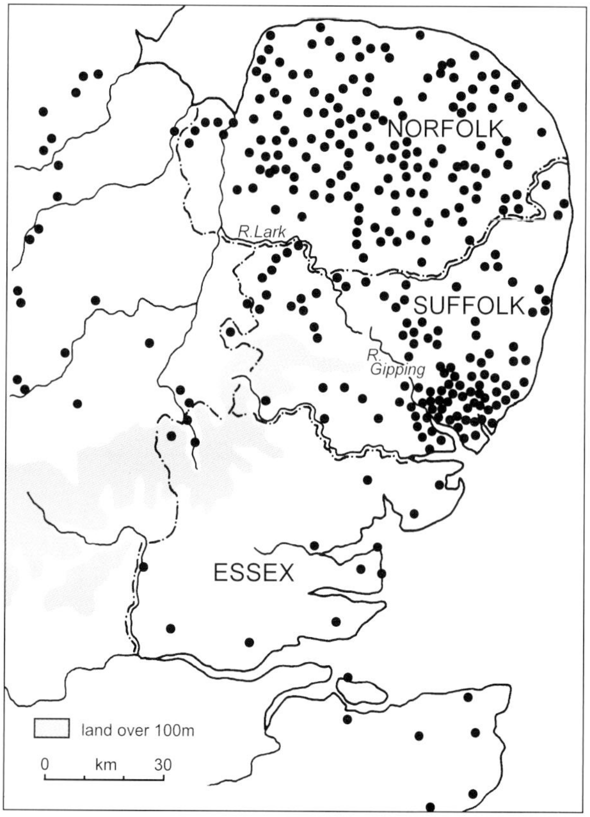

Yet it is also likely that, at least by the middle of the seventh century, the kingdom extended to the west of the present boundary of the two counties, embracing much of what is now the Cambridgeshire Fenland, for the Diocese of Norwich extended as far as the Isle of Ely (Warner 1996, 94). The chronicles of Ely Abbey record that the island of Ely was given to St Etheldreda, daughter of King Anna, when she married the prince of a subsidiary tribal group, Tondbert (Bede describes it as part of a *regio* within the province of East Anglia) (Mclure and Collins 1994, 202–3; Warner 1996, 155–6). All this means that the position of Rendlesham, Sutton Hoo and the rest would thus have been even *more* marginal to the kingdom the Wuffingas ruled than might appear from a simple perusal of the present county boundaries.

FIGURE 62. The distribution of middle Saxon Ipswich Ware (after Blinkhorn 1999).

Landscape and territory

The fact that the same north-west/south-east line running through the middle of Suffolk formed not only a significant cultural boundary, but also probably some kind of political frontier, in both the later Iron Age and the middle Saxon period might be interpreted as evidence for a significant degree of long-term territorial continuity: and some people have indeed suggested that the tribal territories of the Iron Age, transformed into administrative divisions within the Roman province of *Britannia*, in some case re-emerged in the post-Roman period as fully independent entities, albeit ones now controlled by new immigrant elites (Bassett 1989, 24; Blair 1947; Brooks 1989, 57–8). Such an argument would suggest that the East Anglians were simply the Iceni under a new name, while the East Saxons developed from the Trinovantes. Those scholars like Stephen Bassett (1989) or Chris Scull (1992, 22) who believe that the fifth and sixth centuries were periods of advanced political fragmentation would reject such arguments for direct political continuity at this kind of regional level, and the evidence already discussed for the close association of the Wuffingas with a very circumscribed area of south-eastern Suffolk strongly suggests that if there *was* any kind of broad continuity in regional cultural identities, this was not reflected in *political* structures. The early Wuffingas could only grant land to monasteries in this area, were only associated by name with places in this area, because this was the only district which – initially at least – they directly controlled. Whatever broader cultural affinities and identities they may have shared with their neighbours further north in East Anglia, those neighbours, in the period before the middle of the sixth century at least, were politically independent. We cannot, unfortunately, reconstruct these various early territories with any certainty, or in any detail. But we can get some idea of the character of early social and political geography by examining archaeological distributions, the location of places known to have been important centres of authority in middle Saxon times, and place-names, against patterns of topography and soils.

It is often stated, in rather simple terms, that as the population declined in the immediate post-Roman period settlement retreated from heavy clay soils – in East Anglia as elsewhere in England – and retrenched onto areas of light, easily worked land (Newman 1992a; Newman 2005, 483; Brown and Foard 1998, 73–5; Williamson 2003, 29–30). Fieldwalking surveys consistently show that Roman (and late Iron Age) sites can be found widely scattered across the heavy soils of the clay plateaux in both Norfolk and Suffolk. Early Anglo-Saxon sites, in contrast – settlements and, in particular, the far more archaeologically 'visible' cemeteries – are relatively rare on the claylands (Warner 1996, 65–6). The bulk of the evidence for early Anglo-Saxon settlement in East Anglia, especially in the form of cemeteries, comes from the principal areas of light, freely draining, and easily cultivated soil. In the case of Suffolk, this essentially means the district in the north-west of the county known as Breckland; and the Sandlings in the east. Only in the course of the middle and later Saxon periods did settlement expand once more onto the heavier soils which occupy most of the interior of the county (Wade 1989; West 1989).

While there is a great deal of truth in this 'light soil/clay soil' model, we have already seen that – in the area around Sutton Hoo at least – matters were in fact rather more complicated. Here, not *all* of the light, freely draining soils were equally attractive to early Saxon farmers. Certain types were particularly favoured – principally those of the Newport 2 Association, more calcareous and fertile than the poor sandy podzols of the Newport 4 Association which blanketed the uplands, and which were largely occupied by tracts of woodland or pasture in this period. Conversely, not all areas of clay soil were equally shunned by sixth- and seventh-century settlers, for the parish of Rendlesham largely comprises clay soils of the Burlingham 3 Association. In just the same way that important variations exist between different kinds of light soil, so likewise there are different types of clay soil, and in particular a contrast between the relatively light clay loams found in the principal valleys, and the intractable, poorly draining stagnogleys which characterise the plateaux between them.

Rather than viewing southern East Anglia simply in terms of the contrast between 'light' and 'heavy' soils, in other words, when studying the environmental context of early and middle Saxon settlement, it is more useful to make a rather more subtle distinction: between comparatively light, loamy clays, moderately calcareous sands, and other light loams on the one hand; and heavy impervious clays, and acid, leached and infertile sands on the other. In the first category we would place the clay soils defined by the Soil Survey as the various Burlingham Associations and Ashley Association; the chalky soils of the Newmarket 1 and 2 and Swaffham Prior Associations; the sandy loams of the Newport 2 and 3 Associations; and the Ludford, Melford and Moulton Associations – well-drained argillic brown earths and sands formed in a variety of deposits found in the valleys cutting through the boulder clay plateau – aeolian drift, chalk and various glacial deposits (Hodge *et al.* 1984, 96–7, 132–5, 237–9, 245–7, 261–3, 270–7, 316–19, 365–70). The sandy yet calcareous soils of the Methwold Association, generally occurring around the fringes of the main Breckland plateaux, should also be included in this first category (Hodge *et al.* 1984, 249–53). These various soils generally form ribbons or pockets, on the sides of the principal valleys and on other low ground. The higher ground in between, in contrast, is occupied by the poorly-draining stagnogleys of the Beccles, Ragdale and Hanslope Associations (in the centre of the county); by the leached, acid sands of the Newport 4 or Worlington Associations (in Breckland and the Sandlings); and the silty and sandy, yet seasonally waterlogged, soils of the Tendring Association (in the south) (Hodge *et al.* 1984, 117–19, 209–12, 277–9, 322–8).

The importance of this more subtle distinction in soils types, rather than that more usually advanced, immediately becomes apparent when we consider the distribution of pagan Saxon cemeteries, or of known political or administrative centres of middle Saxon date – such as Hoxne, Blythburgh, Bury St Edmunds, Ipswich and Dunwich (Wade 1989) (Figs 63 and 64). Fieldwork and chance finds suggest, in particular, marked concentrations of early Saxon activity all along the valleys of the river Fynn, from Martlesham through to Witnesham; and in that of the Lark and the Dove in the north of Suffolk. Interestingly, it is also on, or beside, these pockets of relatively amenable ground that we find the only examples in the region of place-names thought to incorporate some Romano-British elements. Wickham – a compound of the Old English word *-ham*, 'estate', and the Latin *vicus*, by late Roman times probably used simply to mean a small settlement – is found in the names Wickham Market, Wickham Skeith, and (less certainly) Wickhambrook. The Latin word *campus*, 'field', occurs in the name Campsey Ashe and probably in that of Bulcamp near Blythburgh, the traditional site of Anna's battle with Penda of Mercia. The precise significance

FIGURE 63. Selected soil types, and the distribution of early cemeteries and place-names incorporating Latin elements (Wickham Skeith, Wickham Market, Campsey Ashe, and Bulcamp) in southern East Anglia. Light clay loams, as well as the more fertile soils formed in sand and chalk, formed the main areas of fifth- and sixth-century settlement. Acid sands as much as heavy clays were shunned by early Saxon farmers.

FIGURE 64. The upland clays and sands, away from the ribbons of easily worked soils, were occupied by woods and pastures in the early Saxon period.

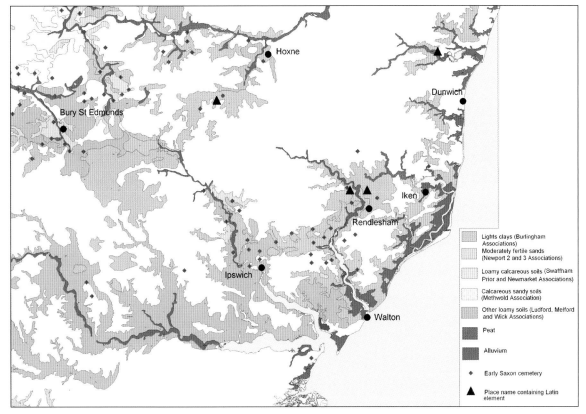

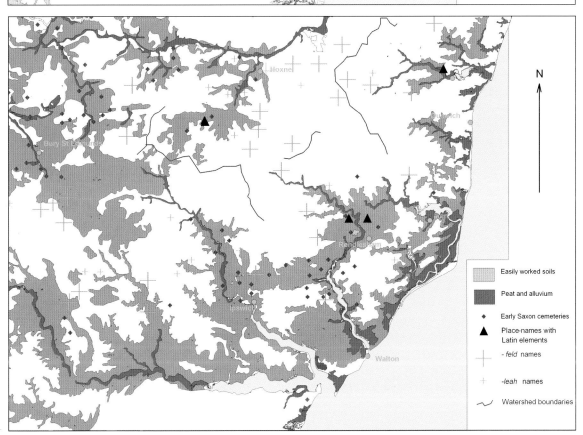

of such names is uncertain, but it has been suggested by Margaret Gelling and others that they indicate some degree of 'continuity' (that dangerous term!), perhaps the peaceful co-existence of native and intrusive populations. Whatever their precise meaning, it is surely significant that Rendlesham should lie close to two examples of such names – Campsey Ashe and Wickham Market – all three places being associated with the same substantial tract of relatively light clay soils of the Burlingham Association lying on either side of the river Deben, inland from the belt of sandy soils running down the coast. This area of relatively fertile and amenable soils, rather than the acid sands of the Sandlings themselves, may represent the real core of the Wuffingas' homeland, and – in effect – the agrarian aspect of their power base.

In a number of places continuous lines of parish boundary, and/or hundred boundary, run across the high, drift-covered interfluves and appear to form the outer boundaries of territories based on particular valleys and drainage systems, perhaps indicating that late Saxon administrative divisions made extensive use of existing lines in the landscape, which had originated as territorial boundaries in early Saxon times. The long boundary between Hartismere Hundred to the north, and Bosmere and Claydon Hundreds, and Stow Hundred, to the south, is a noteworthy example, closely following the line of the watershed between the Gipping and the Dove (Fig. 64). The boundary of the Blything Hundred, studied in some detail by Peter Warner, is particularly noteworthy in this respect (Warner 1996, 157–8). Where interfluves are wide, place-names incorporating the element *-feld* are common, like the marked concentrations of contiguous parishes on the flat claylands in the north-east of the county – one comprising Fressingfield, Metfield, Wingfield, Laxfield, Cratfield and Huntingfield, the other Bedingfield, Bedfield, Redlingfield and (slightly detached) Ashfield (Fig. 64) (Scarfe 1986, 13–26). Such names are generally considered to indicate extensive areas of relatively open land, pasture or wood pasture, within an otherwise more densely wooded environment – openings larger than the clearings indicated by place-names incorporating the element *-leah*, 'ley', which in contrast tend to be found towards the edge of the clayland plateau, or where (especially towards the south-west of the county) it is more extensively dissected by river valleys (Gelling 1984, 235–6; Martin 1999; Warner 1996, 205). The fact that six of the *-feld* names (Stanningfield, Fressingfield, Waldringfield, Bedingfield, Redlingfield and Huntingfield) have as their first element the term *-ingas* may indicate that these were seasonal grazing grounds used by the named groups, whose settlements were located on more fertile, lower ground.

The 'North Sea Province'

The contrast between drift-covered upland and more fertile lower ground – between 'river' and 'wold' – is thus deeply etched into the early medieval landscape of southern East Anglia. Zones of well-watered valley land, with tractable and at least moderately fertile soils, formed the cores of social territories which extended up onto the infertile uplands, where tracts of ground were exploited as grazing and woodland. Such an observation is neither new, nor surprising. What was true at a local and regional level, however, was also true at a national level. Patterns of major watersheds, and drainage basins, determined wider patterns of communication and contact, patterns which shaped the distributions of artefacts mapped by archaeologists and, perhaps, structured wider senses of identity in the early Saxon period.

I noted earlier the major cultural boundary, or boundary zone, which appears in many periods, running diagonally across Suffolk from the area around Bury St Edmunds to the district around Ipswich. In early Anglo-Saxon times this seems to mark the boundary between areas in which 'Anglian' and 'Saxon' metalwork and dress-fittings were popular. But it also has another significance in this period. As already noted, the Anglo-Saxons in the fifth, sixth and early seventh centuries disposed of their dead in two main ways: by inhumation, usually with grave goods; or by cremation, with the burnt bones and ashes (together with the remains of grave goods and food put on the pyre) placed in the ground in a pottery urn or other receptacle. Both rites, as we have also seen, are represented at Sutton Hoo. In very general terms, in the course of time cremation tended to decline in favour of inhumation. It is possible that this indicates – like the changes in the character of grave-goods in the later sixth and seventh centuries discussed by Helen Geake (1997) – the increasing influence of ideas from the Frankish and Mediterranean world, where cremation was rarely practised, and the decline in traditions deriving from north Germany and Scandinavia, where cremation had long been widespread. This was part of a shift in the character of European cultural influences upon southern and eastern England which arguably climaxed in the adoption of Christianity in the course of the seventh century. Of more interest in the present context, however, are the *spatial* variations in the relative importance of these two rites of disposal.

In northern East Anglia pagan cemeteries are widespread, especially on the lighter soils, and cemeteries dominated by cremations are common. But in south-west Suffolk and Essex pagan cemeteries are fewer in number and cremation cemeteries in particular are virtually unknown. This division is part of a much broader one. In this case (although not necessarily in others) the Lark–Gipping 'corridor' defines the edge of distributions which extend far beyond East Anglia, and which broadly correspond with those of 'Anglian' and 'Saxon' artefacts already discussed. Cremation, and in particular large cemeteries in which cremation is the sole or overwhelmingly dominant rite, is thus a feature of the 'Anglian' lands – of East Anglia, the Midlands, and north-east England – although inhumation was of course also practised here, and became more important with the passing of time. Cremation cemeteries are by no means unknown in the south and in the Thames valley, but they are rare and generally small in size (Hills 1998, 183–4). Here inhumation was, from the fifth century onwards, the dominant rite. In addition, while across most of northern East Anglia, the Midlands, and the north-east of England cemeteries – cremation, inhumation, or mixed – are widely scattered, and with gaps in their distribution which are usually explicable in terms of environmental factors (areas of high, drift-covered uplands, tracts of heavy, intractable clay or waterlogged fens), this is perhaps less true in the south and south-east. Here large areas of fertile and relatively easily worked land, as in east Hertfordshire, have failed to produce any kinds of 'Anglo-Saxon' burials, suggesting that some people in the fifth and sixth centuries may have employed forms of burial rite that have left no clear archaeological traces, like many of their predecessors in Roman Britain (Fig. 65).

As I noted earlier, an older generation of archaeologists had little trouble in explaining patterns like these. Cremation was essentially an 'Anglian' practice, in just the same way that particular kinds of metalwork were 'Anglian' in character. Cremation cemeteries were concentrated within, although not entirely restricted to, those areas which Bede believed had been settled by people coming from Angeln in Schleswig-Holstein – East Anglia, Mercia and Northumbria. Modern archaeologists reject these simple ethnic labels and explanations: but the spatial patterning in the data remains, and perhaps requires more consideration than it usually receives.

The significance of these patterns becomes rather clearer when we consider them against the broad sweeps of regional topography. For it was not only at a local level that patterns of cultural and social identity may have been influenced, moulded, by natural topography. At a much larger scale, situations in which contact and communication between individuals and groups of people was easy and regular tended to engender, if not a measure of social or political identity, then at least some sharing of beliefs, language and material culture. Where contact was restricted, in contrast – for topographic or other reasons – there was more divergence in social and cultural development. River systems, with their well-settled, fertile soils, evidently represented in many topographic situations the arteries along which ideas, styles and fashions moved, exchanged from group to group and person to person: while rivers themselves were, in their navigable lower reaches at least, physical paths of movement, for it was generally easier to transport men and materials by river than over land.

But there is another aspect to all this. In the fifth, sixth and seventh centuries England was, perhaps more than at any other time before or since, subject to the movement of people, artefacts and ideas coming from foreign lands – from Ireland, Scotland, and above all from the European mainland. Where the principal English rivers entered the sea – which direction their valley-systems and associated hierarchies of social territories faced – is thus also a matter of some importance. Looked at in a wider European context England can thus usefully be considered as comprising three great 'provinces', facing the North Sea, the Irish Sea, and the Channel and Thames estuary, respectively (Fig. 66).

These three 'provinces' were, and indeed are, separated from each other by interfluves and watersheds of varying magnitude and significance. The boundary between the 'North Sea Province' and the 'Channel Province', for example, is defined all along its course between the vicinity of Tring in Hertfordshire,

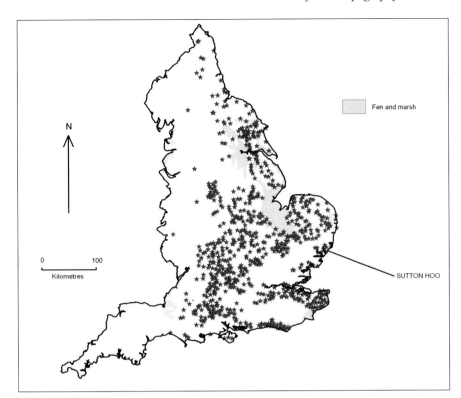

FIGURE 65. The distribution of early Saxon cemeteries in England (after Lucy 2000).

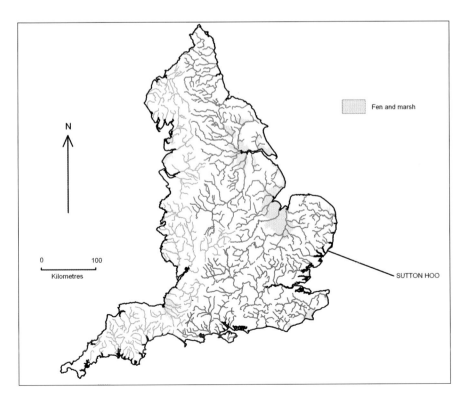

FIGURE 66. The 'three provinces' of England, defined by patterns of drainage basins and watersheds. Red, the 'North Sea Province'; Blue, the 'Channel Province'; green, the 'Irish Sea Province'.

and a point a little to the south of Newmarket in Suffolk, by the impressive escarpment of the Chiltern Hills and its more diminutive (but still physically striking) north-eastern continuation, the so-called 'East Anglian Heights'. Much of the high watershed here is still occupied by extensive tracts of woodland, and concentrations of 'woodland' place-names indicate where more extensive areas were cleared and settled in the course of the Anglo-Saxon period. But at either end of this well-defined section the line dividing the two 'Provinces' is less physically obvious. To the west, the line of division leaves the Chiltern escarpment and, tracking north through north Buckinghamshire, follows the watershed dividing rivers like the Thame draining westwards into the Thames, and those flowing eastwards into the Great Ouse, running along only moderately high ground, although ground peppered with a scatter of 'woodland' names – Wingrave, Stewkley, Mursley, Horwood – and on through Whaddon Chase. The line then swings south of Buckingham, and runs northwards through western Northamptonshire. To the east of the strongly defined Chiltern/East Anglian Heights section the boundary is more diffuse still and, to judge from archaeological distributions, perhaps more permeable in character. It picks its way, in a slightly convoluted manner, along the high ground of west Suffolk, passing to the south of Bury St Edmunds, but then turning northwards and following, to the south-east, the high ground lying just to the north of the river Gipping. On this section of its course it thus forms, quite unsurprisingly, the line of the strong cultural boundary discussed earlier, which in many periods divided the northern and eastern portions of East Anglia, from the southern and western. The line continues towards the North Sea but becomes less distinct in this more muted topography, and fades out on the high ground lying between the Deben and the Orwell. Looked at in this way the Deben has – if only just – an outfall into the North Sea, while the combined mouth of the Orwell and the Stour together form – again, only just – the northern edge of the Thames estuary.

The watersheds defining the boundaries of the other topographic provinces are similarly varied. Sometimes they correspond with dramatic ranges of hills, obvious barriers to contact and communication; sometimes to more muted topographic incidents. But while the latter may have been more permeable in character, in all cases these major watersheds constituted the edges of major cultural distributions in the early Saxon period. 'Anglian' England – with its cremation cemeteries and distinctive artefacts like wrist clasps – thus clearly corresponds with the North Sea Province. Its distinctive character must in part reflect the fact that it faces out across the North Sea to regions which had never been within the Roman *limes* (Fig. 67). 'Saxon' England, in contrast – essentially, what I have defined here as the Channel Province – faces France and the southern Low Countries, lands which *had* formed parts of the Roman Empire. The absence of large cremation cemeteries from this region may, perhaps, indicate that it was less subject to major cultural influences from 'barbarian' lands, and perhaps less affected by 'barbarian' immigration in the immediate post-Roman period. Indeed, the appearance in this region in the fifth century of cemeteries containing inhumations with grave goods may have been the consequence of indigenous developments within late Roman society, rather than representing, in any simple and straightforward way, the signature of 'invaders'. In Hills' words:

> Late Roman burials were mostly unfurnished inhumations, but the later fourth century saw the appearance in Britain and northern Gaul of inhumations accompanied by weapons and belt fittings. Although these have often been interpreted as the burials of Germanic mercenary soldiers, there is not really any reason to see them purely in ethnic terms, although it does seem to have been a fashion prevalent amongst a military elite, which included men of Germanic origins. These burials may have contributed to the development of the rite [i.e., inhumation burial with grave goods] seen throughout western Europe and southern Britain between the fifth and seventh centuries. (Hills 1998, 184)

Not that the appearance of cremation cemeteries, and other aspects of an intrusive culture, should be viewed even within 'Anglian' England simply as a sign that new people were arriving *en masse* from northern Europe. The fact that distributions of 'Anglian' material and cremation cemeteries tend to break at major watersheds suggests, not that invaders found these some kind of insurmountable topographic obstacle to conquest, but rather that these things represent only the archaeologically visible aspects of a wider package of shared ideas and fashions, that spread as much by emulation as by the actual displacement of one group of people by another. In other words, the apparent correlation of archaeological distributions with aspects of the natural topography lends some support to those archaeologists who believe that the major changes in material culture apparent in the fifth and sixth centuries represent, not so much outright conquest and a mass population movement from northern Europe, but rather the more general adoption of new fashions and beliefs, and new ways of life, derived from the barbarian north, as the social, economic and ideological influence of Rome and the south waned. New people unquestionably arrived from the Continent, but not necessarily in vast numbers. Nor was this new pattern of cultural influences something operating over a short period of time; or even solely in one direction. As Hills again has noted:

> People did not get into their boats and sail to England, never to return. The communities on both sides of the North Sea remained in contact. The connections between them could have owed as much to the exchange of ideas and goods through trade, religion and political relationships as to migration. (Hills 1998, 183)

And as John Hines has showed, such contacts between Scandinavia and 'Anglian' England continued through the sixth and into the seventh centuries, and perhaps beyond (Hines 1984, 286–301). The Scandinavian influences evident at the Sutton Hoo cemetery, both in terms of grave goods deposited and the rituals employed, need to be seen within this much more extended chronology of cultural contact.

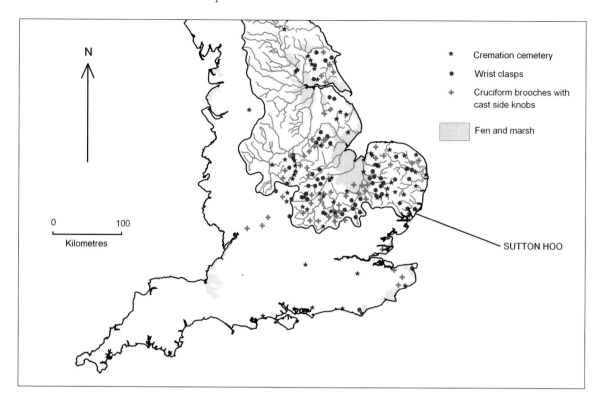

Indeed, it is arguable that the distinction between the 'North Sea' and 'Channel' Provinces reappeared even more strongly in the ninth century. In the 860s and 70s, following more than seven decades of summer raiding, Viking forces from Denmark began to remain for longer periods in England, occupying East Anglia in 865, Northumbria and Mercia in 866. In 870 the 'host', in the words of the *Anglo-Saxon Chronicle*:

> Rode across Mercia into East Anglia, and took winter-quarters at Thetford: and the same winter King Edmund fought against them, and the Danes won the victory, and they slew the king and overran the entire kingdom. (Swanton 1996)

From here they raided into the east Midlands, sacking the monastery at Peterborough, and into Wessex, fighting armies led by Æthelred and Alfred at a number of places, before making peace. The 'Great Army' then withdrew to London and made peace with the Mercians. But the following year it was on the move again, progressing first to Northumbria, and then into Lindsey, before dividing: one portion returning to Northumbria, the other (under Guthrum) going on to Cambridge. This phase of activity culminated in systematic land grabbing. Northumbria was 'shared out' in 876; Mercia was partitioned in 877, and the Danish portion similarly 'shared'; while East Anglia was 'shared out' in 879. We have no certain way of knowing precisely what the *Chronicle* means by this phase – whether estates and revenues were being partitioned amongst a warrior elite, or whether a peasant folk-movement was under way in the wake

FIGURE 67. The distribution of selected 'Anglian' artefacts, and cremation cemeteries, in relation to the 'North Sea Province' and its watershed boundary.

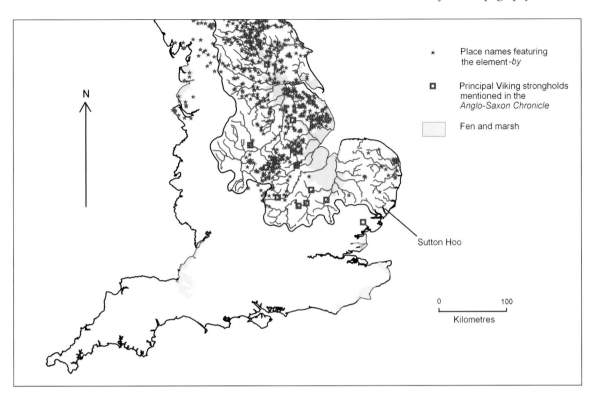

Sutton Hoo

Place names featuring
the element -*by*

Principal Viking strongholds
mentioned in the
Anglo-Saxon Chronicle

Fen and marsh

0   100
Kilometres

FIGURE 68. Distribution of selected Scandinavian place-names, and the location of major Viking strongholds, in relation to the 'North Sea Province'.

of the conquering armies – but the 'Great Army' wandering across the country, from winter quarters to winter quarters, is not heard of again.

It is often stated that the division between English England and the 'Danelaw' was fixed by a treaty made in 886 between Alfred and Guthrum, the terms of which survive: the frontier was to run along the river Thames, then up the river Lea, and then along the line of Watling Street. In fact, as David Dumville has cogently argued, this treaty probably represents, not the terms of a permanent settlement drawn up at Wedmore in 886, but only a temporary peace made following the battle of Edington in 878. More importantly, Dumville has drawn attention to the fact that the *Anglo-Saxon Chronicle*, while making it clear that eastern Mercia and East Anglia were over-run and settled by the Danes in the 870s and 80s, is much more circumspect in its treatment of Essex. Danish armies are mentioned in the north-east of the county, but 'When they wanted a safe base for their women or chattels, Essex was not [the Vikings'] first choice but East Anglia…. Essex was territory that was being debated' (Dumville 1992, 9). Most of the county seems to have remained in English hands, and one *Chronicle* entry, for 896, looking back to events earlier in the 880s and 890s, recalled the deaths of 'many of the king's best thegns' – including Brihtwulf, Ealdorman of Essex. Essex had been effectively incorporated into the West Saxon kingdom in the 820s, and that control was never in all probability subsequently relinquished, except in the north-east of the present county, in the area around Colchester. It is noteworthy that in 921, during the reconquest of East Anglia from the Danes,

Edward was able to gather a great force 'from Kent, Surrey, *and Essex*, and from all parts from the nearest fortresses', to attack Colchester (my italics).

The fact that Essex should have remained under English control, while Suffolk and Norfolk were lost to the Danes, is at first sight remarkable, given the fact that the area lay some way from the main centres of West Saxon power, had a long exposed sea coast, and was not divided from East Anglia proper by impassable hills or a major watercourse. Looked at in the topographic contexts already discussed, however, this situation becomes much more explicable. Essex, and probably south-western Suffolk, continued to form part of the 'Channel Province'; the core of Danish influence always remained within the 'North Sea Province'. This relationship between natural topography on the one hand, and patterns of ethnicity and political power on the other, is clear when the distribution of major Scandinavian place-names, and of the forts and towns described by the *Anglo-Saxon Chronicle* as major Viking strongholds, is mapped against the pattern of drainage basins and river catchments (Fig. 68). The same pattern of rivers and watersheds which structured, as I have argued, aspects of cultural variation in the fifth and sixth centuries now clearly affected patterns of Danish influence and settlement. This is not the place to discuss what this might imply about the true character of the 'Viking invasions': the point here is simply that, in the ninth century as in the fifth and sixth, the movement of people, artefacts and ideas coming from across the North Sea was strongly channelled within lowland England by the structures of natural topography.

The location of Sutton Hoo

The locations of the Sutton Hoo cemetery and of what appears to have been the Wuffingas' original territory were thus doubly marginal. They lay at the extreme southern edge of what was to become the kingdom of East Anglia; and also at the extreme southern margins of 'Anglian England', of the 'North Sea Province'. This simple observation has two important implications, the first concerning the rise of the Wuffingas to a position of regional dominance, the second relating to wider issue of ethnicity, identity and the character of territorial development in the fifth and sixth centuries.

Most scholars now accept Stephen Bassett's 'football knock-out competition' analogy for the development of territorial organisation in early and middle Saxon England (Bassett 1989), a model which applies well to the archaeological evidence from East Anglia (Scull 1992, 22). A myriad of small, largely autonomous tribal groups struggled with each other, some gradually dominating and absorbing their neighbours, so that more powerful leaders, of larger and more hierarchical polities, gradually emerged. These, too, vied with each other for supremacy, leading to further conquest and amalgamation, and so on until the eventual emergence of the kingdoms which we encounter in the pages of Bede's *History*. Tribal leaders and kings lived for war, and retained retinues of warriors by heaping rewards upon them. In time these came to take the form of gifts of land but initially prestige goods, exotic artefacts and precious metals were more important. These were in part obtained as plunder, and as tribute from conquered peoples; and in part through exchange with distant trading partners or political allies.

The later sixth century, the period when the Wuffingas were rising to dominance in East Anglia, was also a time when – to judge from the evidence of grave goods – there was an increasing interest on the part of elites throughout England in styles and fashions emanating from the land of the Franks and the Mediterranean world (Geake 1997 and 1999; Blair 2005, 40). In this context, the significance of the location of the Wuffingas' heartland, on the very edge of the Channel Province, immediately becomes apparent. It would have allowed them easier access to, and greater control over access to, the kinds of prestige goods which were now increasingly in demand than could be enjoyed by neighbouring groups in East Anglia: a geographical advantage which was subsequently developed further with the growth of the great emporium at Ipswich on the river Orwell. According to the 'knock-out competition' model, privileged access to desirable objects would have ensured that the Wuffingas were well supplied with warriors; and this in turn would have encouraged their domination of the surrounding territories and also, for a short while under Rædwald, their wider political supremacy in England.

Yet this raises a further interesting question. While the Wuffingas may have enjoyed some inherent economic and therefore military advantages over their neighbours, the 'knock-out competition' model suggests that the outlines of their kingdom ought to have been largely the result of chance. Random outcomes in the battlefield could have led to territorial expansion in one direction just as easily as in another. Or, to put it another way, the territory of the Wuffingas might have come to extend southwards into what is now Essex, rather than northwards into East Anglia: or could have embraced equally parts of both. Instead, as we have seen, it grew in a remarkably asymmetrical fashion, *only* to the north and north-west. Its boundaries to the south-west remained stubbornly co-terminus with that cultural and topographic frontier which I have discussed in some detail over the previous pages, between the 'North Sea Province' and the south.

This asymmetrical growth of power may tell us something important about the character of early English society. I noted earlier how modern scholars generally question the simple account of the ethnic origins of the various Anglo-Saxon kingdoms and peoples presented by Bede, arguing that the migration bands were already, in all probability, of very mixed origins before their arrival in Britain. According to this view, neat labels like 'the South Saxons' – and the origin-myths associated with these entities, so prominent in the early sections of the *Anglo-Saxon Chronicle* – only developed as larger territorial units emerged in the course of the later sixth and seventh centuries. A shared history, real or otherwise, served to increase the sense of solidarity and coherence of these new polities (Reynolds 1983; Lucy 2000, 157–8). The adoption of Christianity,

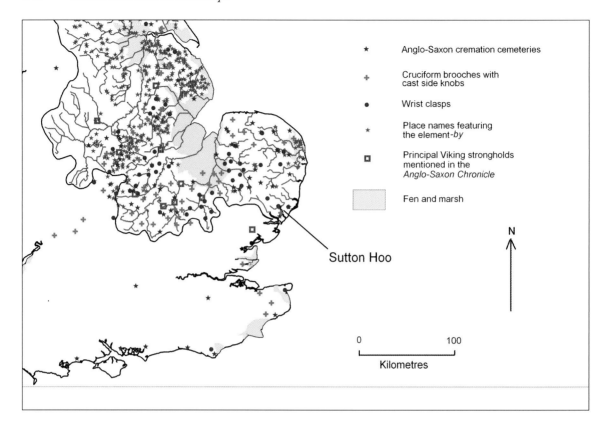

★ Anglo-Saxon cremation cemeteries

✦ Cruciform brooches with cast side knobs

● Wrist clasps

✶ Place names featuring the element-*by*

▫ Principal Viking strongholds mentioned in the *Anglo-Saxon Chronicle*

Fen and marsh

Sutton Hoo

N

0   100
Kilometres

FIGURE 69. The location of Sutton Hoo, on the south-eastern margins of the 'North Sea Province'.

as Susan Reynolds has urged, may have been a contributory factor: myths of common origins also served the 'desire of learned clerics both to find honourable origins for their own peoples and to make sense of the contemporary world in the light of classical and Christian learning' (Reynolds 1983, 375).

These are persuasive arguments, and it is indeed probable that ethnic identities and histories were to some extent forged, in the course of the sixth and seventh centuries, in the ways suggested. But labels like 'West Saxon' may not have been completely arbitrary in character. It is notable, for example, how the dynasties and peoples who identified themselves as 'Saxon' or 'Anglian' fall into neat geographical blocks, with one (East Saxons, Middle Saxons, South Saxons and West Saxons) in the south of England and the Thames basin, and the other (East Angles, Mercians, Northumbrians) in the Midlands, east and north-east. These areas, moreover, *do* correspond to a significant extent with variations in mortuary practice and material culture; *and* with the configuration of the topographic 'provinces' already discussed. 'Anglian' peoples really do seem to have shared, however weakly, an identity which separated them from their 'Saxon' neighbours, an identity perhaps born of topographic structures which ensured that they enjoyed – well after the invasions of the fifth century – closer contacts with the barbarian north.

Looked at in this way, the fact that the hegemony of the Wuffingas was gradually extended north, exclusively into the lands of Anglian neighbours, rather than south, suggests that the process of kingdom-building in the sixth and seventh centuries was perhaps more subtle and more complex, and less random in character, than Bassett's 'knock-out competition' model would seem to suggest. The Wuffingas, in effect, *only* rose to supremacy over people of their own kind: and this implies that their kingdom did not emerge simply or solely from the piecemeal, random conquest of smaller polities. Perhaps privileged access to prestige goods was also used to achieve political dominance in a range of other ways – though gifts, dowries, bribes – which worked most effectively on tribes and dynasties with whom Rædwald and his kin already shared familial links and certain aspects of a common culture, and which were correspondingly less effective in maintaining an ascendancy over 'Saxon' neighbours to the south. Whatever the precise explanation, the location of Sutton Hoo, Rendlesham and the rest on the very peripheries of the East Anglian kingdom is clearly of immense significance to our understanding of the character of ethnicity, and state-formation, in Anglo-Saxon England.

CHAPTER SIX

Conclusion

This short volume aspires to be no more than a footnote to the various more weighty academic tomes which have been produced on the subject of the Sutton Hoo burial ground (most notably Carver 2005). It is, in a sense, a meditation on the geography of a very special place. My intention has been a simple one: to throw some additional light on the meaning of the cemetery by considering its landscape context, and this I have attempted to do at a number of levels, and by adopting a number of theoretical perspectives, including – after a fashion – aspects of that approach usually described as 'phenomenology'.

These various ways of looking at the geographical location of the Sutton Hoo site are, however, united by a common theme. I have argued throughout that only by examining aspects of the natural environment can we understand not only the economic and agrarian aspects of early Saxon society, but also such matters as patterns of territorial organisation and the formation of social identities. Soils and topography not only influenced modes of settlement and land use. They also conditioned patterns of communication and contact, and thus the configuration of local societies, and of political units like kingdoms. But more importantly for our understanding of the Sutton Hoo burial ground, at a local level the environment helped to shape modes of movement, subsistence and exploitation, and thus the ways in which contemporaries thought about and experienced the land – determining which areas or features lay at the heart of community experience, for example, and which were peripheral.

Some readers may well have felt uneasy about the more speculative conclusions to Chapter Four, but I hope that such excesses will not have obscured its central argument: that the cemeteries at Sutton Hoo and Tranmer House were positioned where they were not to ensure that they could be viewed from the river, but so that the river could be seen from them. Their position, in other words, was chosen not for reasons of elite display, nor to legitimate the claims to power and territory of a particular ruling dynasty. The choice of site was made at an earlier time, and reflected the mentalities of a different kind of community – a folk, deeply rooted in its local landscape. That the river and its great outfall had some meaning for the people who used these cemeteries should cause us no surprise. Even today the great presence of the Deben – like that of the other major rivers cutting through the Sandlings to the sea – is striking. I have tried to show – albeit by employing in large part evidence relating to rather later periods – how its impact would have been far more profound in early Saxon times, when the surrounding uplands were partly wooded and largely devoid of cultivation and settlement, when local patterns of exploitation ensured that daily and seasonal movement was more often than not at right angles to its brooding presence, and when more infrequent, more specialised journeys would have been made by ship along its course – whether excursions of a local character, or the first stages in voyages to more distant lands. At one and the same time the river represented 'home', and a gateway to faraway places. Even in its higher reaches, running through the claylands above Ufford and Rendlesham, the Deben formed a ribbon of inhabited and cultivated land, separated from other lands by sparsely inhabited uplands characterised by tracts of woodland and pasture. The Deben formed the centre of the world for those who lived around it, and looked at in this way it is quite understandable that they should have chosen to bury their dead overlooking it.

'Phenomenological' approaches to landscape archaeology are often presented as quite distinct and separate from, if not in direct opposition to, more conventional perspectives: the former attempting to 'get inside the heads' of people in the past, to reconstruct the meanings which they gave to their environments; the latter driven by a mechanistic, 'top down', outsider's view, and seeing the structures of the past and the spaces between them as merely the by-products, the fossil traces, of social and economic activities. In reality, as I have argued here, the experience of landscape, in the present as much as in the past, is constructed to a significant extent by the ways in which land is used and exploited. It was this, as much as raw topographic form, which gave meaning to the environments of the past. The phenomenological mission may always be an over-reaching, over-optimistic enterprise, doomed to failure – based on an essential confusion, on the part of its practitioners, between our own experiences and those of people in the past. Indeed, parts of Chapter Four of this volume, in particular, might quite properly be criticised as yet another example of this tendency. But, insofar that we will ever be able to understand how past peoples thought about and gave meaning to their landscape, we will surely only do so when we have managed to reconstruct, if only in broad outline, its physical character and appearance, and the ways in which it was exploited.

Those landscape archaeologists who adopt phenomenological approaches, and perhaps others, whose main interests lie in the study of Anglo-Saxon society, may have another objection to the arguments presented here. It has become fashionable, as part of the post-processualist reaction, to downplay the influence of the environment on human affairs, and to view those who emphasise its importance as being guilty of 'environmental determinism'. To some archaeologists, a pronounced emphasis on the ways in which such things as soils and landforms shaped the lives of past peoples amounts to a negation of the role of individuals, placing them at the mercy – in Julian Thomas' memorable phrase – of the 'titanic forces', impersonal and unknowable, of economics and the environment. Yet to stress the ways in which both individual lives and communal experience were shaped by such things is to do no more than acknowledge the reality of the human condition, in all ages. For even today the world we know and experience is very different from the one in which we really live: and our lives are shaped by vastly complex forces – environmental, economic, demographic – which we can seldom fully understand, still less control.

Bibliography

Allen, J., Potter, V. and Poulter, M. (2002) *The Building of Orford Castle: a translation from the Pipe Rolls 1163–78*, Orford Museum, Orford.

Armstrong, P. (1973) 'Changes in the Suffolk Sandlings: a study of the disintegration of an eco-system', *Geography* 58, 1–8.

Arnold, C. (1988) *An Archaeology of the Anglo-Saxon Kingdoms*, Routledge, London.

Arnott, W.G. (1946) *The Place-Names of the Deben Valley Parishes*, Adlard, Ipswich.

Bailey, M. (1988) 'The rabbit and the medieval East Anglian economy', *Agricultural History Review* 36, 1, 1–20.

Bailey, M. (1990) 'Sand into gold: the evolution of the foldcourse system in west Suffolk, 1200–1600', *Agricultural History Review* 38, 40–57.

Barnes, G., Dallas, P., Thompson, H., Williamson, T. and Whyte, N. (2007) 'Heathland in Norfolk: ecology and landscape history', *British Wildlife* 18, 6, 395–403.

Barrett, J. (1994) *Fragments from Antiquity: an archaeology of social life in Britain, 2900–1200 BC*, Blackwell, Oxford.

Bassett, S. (1989) 'In search of the origins of Anglo-Saxon kingdoms', in S. Bassett (ed.) *The Origins of Anglo-Saxon Kingdoms*, Leicester University Press, Leicester.

Beardall, C. and Casey, D. (1995) *Suffolk's Changing Countryside*, Suffolk Wildlife Trust, Ipswich.

Bender, B. (1998) *Stonehenge: making space*, Berg, Oxford.

Blair, P.H. (1947) 'The Origins of Northumbria', *Archaeologia Aeliana* 25, 1–51.

Blair, J. (1995) 'Anglo-Saxon pagan shrines and their prototypes', *Anglo-Saxon Studies in Archaeology and History* 8, 1–28.

Blair, J. (2005) *The Church in Anglo-Saxon Society*, Oxford University Press, Oxford.

Blake, E.O. (ed.) (1962) *Liber Eliensis*, Camden Society, 3rd ser. 92.

Blinkhorn, P. (1999) 'Of Cabbages and Kings: production, trade and consumption in middle Saxon England', in M. Anderton (ed.) *Anglo-Saxon Tradint Centres: beyond the emporia*, Cruithne Press, Glasgow, 4–23.

Bradley, R. (1987) 'Time regained: the creation of continuity', *Journal of the British Archaeological Association* 140, 1–17.

Bradley, R. (1993) *Altering the Earth: the origins of monuments in Britain and Continental Europe*, Society of Antiquaries of Scotland Monograph Series 8, Edinburgh.

Bradley, R. (2000a) 'Mental and material landscapes in prehistoric Britain', in D. Hooke (ed.) *Landscape: the richest historical record*, Society for Landscape Studies, Supplementary Series 1, 1–11.

Bradley, R. (2000b) *The Archaeology of Natural Places*, Routledge, London.

Brooks, N. (1989) 'The creation and early structure of the kingdom of Kent', in S. Bassett (ed.) *The Origins of Anglo-Saxon Kingdoms*, Leicester University Press, Leicester, 55–74.

Brown, D. (1981) 'The dating of the Sutton Hoo coins', *Anglo-Saxon Studies in Archaeology and History* 2, 71–86.

Bruce-Mitford, R. (1975) (1978) and (1983) *The Sutton Hoo Ship Burial*, 3 vols, British Museum, London.

Bruce-Mitford, R. (1974) *Aspects of Anglo-Saxon Archaeology: Sutton Hoo and other discoveries*, Victor Gollancz, London.

Burrell, E. (1960) *An Historical Geography of the Sandlings before 1840*, unpublished MSc Thesis, University of London.

Butcher, R. (1941) *The Land of Britain: Suffolk (East and West)*, Land Utilisation Survey, London.

Campbell, J. (1979) 'Bede's words for places', in P. Sawyer (ed.) *Names, Words and Graves*, Leeds University Press, Leeds, 34–54.

Carver, M. (1992a) 'The Anglo-Saxon cemetery at Sutton Hoo: an interim report', in M. Carver (ed.) *The Age of Sutton Hoo: the seventh century in north-western Europe*, Boydell, Woodbridge, 343–72.

Carver, M. (1992b) 'Ideology and allegiance in East Anglia', in R. Farrell and C. Neuman de Vegvar (eds) *Sutton Hoo: fifty years after*, American Early Medieval Studies, Ohio.

Carver, M. (1998) *Sutton Hoo: burial ground of kings?* London.

Carver, M. (1985). *Sutton Hoo: a seventh-century princely burial ground and its context*, Reports of the Research Committee of the Society of Antiquaries of London No. 69, British Museum Press, London.

Chadwick, H.M. (1940) 'Who was he?' *Antiquity* 14, 76–87.

Chatwin, C.P. (1961) *British Regional Geology: East Anglia and Adjoining Areas*, HMSO, London.

Cole, A. and Gelling, M. (2000) *The Landscape of Place-Names*, Shaun Tyas, Stamford.

Coleman, S. (1999) 'Crown post roofs', in D. Dymond and E. Martin (eds) *An Historical Atlas of Suffolk*, 3rd edn, Suffolk County Council, Ipswich, 178–9.

Coleman, S. and Barnard, M. (1999) 'Raised aisled halls and queen post roofs', in D. Dymond and E. Martin (eds) *An Historical Atlas of Suffolk*, 3rd edn, Suffolk County Council, Ipswich, 180–1.

Copinger, W.A. (1911) *The Manors of Suffolk, Vol 7*, Unwin, London.

Cosgrove, D. (1984) *Social Formation and Symbolic Landscape*, Croom Helm, London.

Cosgrove, D. and Daniels, S. (1988) *The Iconography of Landscape: essays on the symbolic representation, design and use of past environments*, Cambridge University Press, Cambridge.

Cramp, R. (1984) 'The Iken cross-shaft', *Proceedings of the Suffolk Institute of Archaeology and History* 35, 4, 291–2.

Cunliffe, B. (1995) *Iron Age Britain*, Batsford, London.

Daniels, S. (1988) 'The political iconography of woodland in later eighteenth-century England', in C. Cosgrove and S. Daniels (eds) *The Iconography of Landscape*, 51–72.

Darby, H.C. (1957) *The Domesday Geography of Eastern England*, Cambridge University Press, Cambridge.

Darby, H.C. and Versey, G.R. (1975) *Domesday Gazetteer*, Cambridge University Press, Cambridge.

Dickens, A.G. (1951) *The Register or Chronicle of Butley Priory, Suffolk, 1510–1535*, Warren, Winchester.

Dimbleby, G.W. (1962) *The Development of British Heathlands and their Soils*, Oxford.

Dumville, D. (1992) *Wessex and England from Alfred to Edgar: six essays in political, cultural and ecclesiastical history*, Boydell and Brewer, Woodbridge.

Edmonds, M. (1999) *Ancestral Geographies of the Neolithic: landscape, monuments and memory*, Routledge, London.

Ekwall, E. (1962) *English River Names*, Clarendon Press, Oxford.

Evans, A.C. (1986) *The Sutton Hoo Ship Burial*, British Museum, London.

Everitt, A. (1977) 'River and wold: reflections on the historical origin of regions and *pays*', *Journal of Historical Geography* 3, 1–19.

Everitt, A. (1986) *Continuity and Colonisation: the evolution of Kentish settlement*, Leicester University Press, Leicester.

Eyre, S.R. (1955) 'The curving ploughland strip and its historical implications', *Agricultural History Review* 3, 80–94.

Fairclough, J. and Plunkett, S.J. (2000) 'Drawings of Walton Castle and other monuments in Walton and Felixstowe', *Proceedings of the Suffolk Institute of Archaeology and History* 39, 4, 419–59.

Fleming, A. (2006) 'Post-processual landscape archaeology: a critique', *Cambridge Archaeological Journal* 16,3, 267–80.

Fenwick, V. (1984) 'Insula de Burgh: excavations at Burrow Hill, Suffolk 1978–1981', *Anglo-Saxon Studies in Archaeology and History*, 3, 35–54.

Filmer-Sankey, W. and Pestell, T. (2001) *Snape Anglo-Saxon Cemetery: excavations and surveys 1824–1992*, East Anglian Archaeology 95.

Geake, H. (1992) 'Burial practices in seventh- and eighth-century England', in M. Carver (ed.) *The Age of Sutton Hoo: the seventh century in north-western Europe*, Boydell, Woodbridge, 83–94.

Geake, H. (1997) *The Use of Grave Goods in Conversion Period England, c.600–850*, British Archaeological Reports 261, Oxford.

Geake, H. (1999) 'Invisible kingdoms: the use of grave goods in seventh-century England', *Anglo-Saxon Studies in Archaeology and History* 10, 203–15.

Gelling, M. (1984) *Place-Names in the Landscape*, Dent, London.

Glyde, J. (1856) *Suffolk in the nineteenth century: physical, social, moral, religious and industrial*, Simpkins, London.

Grierson, P. (1952) 'The dating of the Sutton Hoo coins', *Antiquity* 26, 83–6.

Grigson, G. (ed.) (1984) *Thomas Tusser: the Fiver Hundred Good Points of Husbandry (1580 Edition)*, Oxford University Press, Oxford.

Halsall, G. (1995) *Settlement and Social Organisation: The Merovingian region of Metz*, Cambridge University Press, Cambridge.

Hanley, J.A. (1949) *Progressive Farming*, 4 vols, Caxton, London.

Harke, H. (1997) 'A context for the Saxon barrow [on Lowbury Hill]', *Archaeological Journal* 151, 158–211.

Harrison, S. (2005) *A History of Evolution and Interaction: man, roads and the landscape to c.1850*, unpublished PhD thesis, University of East Anglia.

Haslam, J. (1992) '*Dommoc* and Dunwich: a reappraisal', *Anglo-Saxon Studies in Archaeology and History* 5, 41–6.

Haselgrove, C. (1982) 'Wealth, prestige and power: the dynamics of late Iron Age political centralisation in England', in C. Renfrew and S. Shennan (eds) *Ranking, Resource and Exchange: aspects of the archaeology of early European society*, Cambridge University Press, Cambridge.

Hawkes, C.F.C. (1956) 'The Jutes of Kent', in D.B. Harden (ed.) *Dark Age Britain: studies presented to E.T. Leeds*, Methuen, London, 91–111.

Hegarty, C. and Newsome, S. (2005) *The Archaeology of the Suffolk Coast and Inter-Tidal Zone*, unpublished report for the national Mapping Programme, English Heritage and Suffolk County Council, Swindon.

Hervey, Lord F. (ed.) (1902) *Suffolk in the Seventeenth Century: the breviary of Suffolk by Robert Reyce*, London.

Hills, C. (1983) 'Economic and settlement background to Sutton Hoo in eastern England', in J.P. Lamm and H.A. Nordstrom (eds) *Vendel Period Studies: Transactions of the Boat-Grave Symposium in Stockholm, February 2–3, 1981*, Stockholm.

Hills, C. (1998) 'Early historic Britain', in J. Hunter and I. Ralston (eds) *The Archaeology of Britain: an introduction from the upper Palaeolithic to the Industrial Revolution*, Routledge, London, 176–93.

Hills, C. (2003) *Origins of the English*, Duckworth, London.

Hines, J. (1984) *The Scandinavian Character of Anglian England in the Pre-Viking Period*, British Archaeological Reports British Series 124, Oxford.

HMSO (1898) *Calendar of Inquisitions Post Mortem and Other Analogous Documents Preserved in the Public Record Office,* 2nd Series: Henry VII Vol. 1, London.

HMSO (1912) *Calendar of Inquisitions Post Mortem and Other Analogous Documents Preserved in the Public Record Office,* Vol. 3: 20–28. Edward I, London.

HMSO (1913) *Calendar of Inquisitions Post Mortem and Other Analogous Documents Preserved in the Public Record Office,* Vol. 4: 29–35, Edward I, London.

Hodge, C., Burton, R., Corbett, W., Evans, R. and Scale, R. (1984) *Soils and their Uses in Eastern England*, Soil Survey of England and Wales, Harpenden.

Hoggett, R.S. (2007) *Changing Beliefs: the archaeology of the East Anglian conversion*, unpublished PhD thesis, University of East Anglia.

Hope Taylor, B. (1977) *Yeavering: an Anglo-British centre of early Northumbria*, Department of the Environment, London.

Hoppitt, R. (1992) *The Development of Deer Parks in Suffolk from the Eleventh to the Seventeenth Century*, unpublished PhD thesis, University of East Anglia.

Hoppitt, R. (1999) 'Rabbit warrens', in D. Dymond and E. Martin (eds) *An Historical Atlas of Suffolk*, 3rd edn, Suffolk County Council, Ipswich, 68–9.

Kent, J.P.C. (1975) 'The coins and the date of the burial', in Bruce-Mitford, *Sutton Hoo Ship Burial* I, 578–647.

Kerridge, E. (1967) *The Agricultural Revolution*, Allen and Unwin, London.

Kirby, J. (1764) *The Suffolk Traveller*, London.

Kirby, J. (1829) *The Suffolk Traveller*, London.

Leeds, E.T. (1936) *Early Saxon Art and Archaeology*, Clarendon Press, Oxford.

Loader, T. and Everett, L. (2004) *Survey of the Intertidal Foreshore Below Sutton Hoo*, Unpublished Suffolk County Council Archaeological Service Report No. 2003/110.

Lucas, R. (1993) 'Studwork, early brick and clay-brick chimneys in Norfolk and Suffolk', *Vernacular Architecture* 24, 18–19.

Lucy, S. (1992) 'The significance of mortuary ritual in the political manipulation of landscape', *Archaeological Review from Cambridge* 11, 1, 93–105.

Lucy, S. (2000) *The Anglo-Saxon Way of Death: burial rites in early England*, Suttons, Stroud.

MacCulloch, D. (1976) *The Chorography of Suffolk*, Suffolk Records Society 19, Ipswich.

Martin, E. (1988) *Burgh: Iron Age and Roman enclosure*, East Anglian Archaeology 40.

Martin, E. (1999) 'Place-name patterns', in D. Dymond and E. Martin (eds) *An Historical Atlas of Suffolk*, 3rd edn, Suffolk County Council, Ipswich, 50–1.

Martin, E. (1999) 'Suffolk in the Iron Age', in J. Davies and T. Williamson (eds) *The Iron Age in Northern East Anglia*, Centre of East Anglian Studies, Norwich.

Martin, E. (1999) 'Hundreds and liberties', in D. Dymond and E. Martin (eds) *An Historical Atlas of Suffolk*, 3rd edn, Suffolk County Council, Ipswich, 26–7.

Martin, E. (2001) 'Rural settlement patterns in rural Suffolk', *Annual Report of the Medieval Settlement Research Group*, 15, 5–7.

McClure, J. and Collins, R. (eds) (1994) *Bede: the Ecclesiastical History of the English People*, Oxford University Press, Oxford.

Morley, C. and Cooper, E.R. (1922) 'The sea port of Frostenden', *Proceedings of the Suffolk Institute of Archaeology and History* 18, 167–79.

Nerman, B. (1948) 'Sutton Hoo: en Svensk Kunga eller Hovdinggrav?', *Fornvannen* 43, 65–93.

Newman, J. (1992a) 'The late Roman and Anglo-Saxon settlement pattern in the Sandlings of Suffolk', in M. Carver (ed.) *The Age of Sutton Hoo: the seventh century in north-western Europe*, Boydell, Woodbridge, 25–38.

Newman, J. (1992b) 'Sutton Hoo – East Anglian or East Saxon King?', *Saxon – the newsletter of the Sutton Hoo Society* 17, 4–5.

Newman, J. (2000) 'Sutton Hoo before Rædwald', *Current Archaeology* 180, 498–505.

Newman, J. (2005) 'Survey of the Deben valley', in M. Carver, *Sutton Hoo: a seventh-century princely burial ground*, 477–88.

Newton, S. (1993) *The Origins of Beowulf and the Pre-Viking Kingdom of East Anglia*, Boydell, Woodbridge.

Norden, J. (1618) *The Surveyor's Dialogue*, London.

Parker Pearson, M., van de Noort, R. and Woolf, A. (1993) 'Three men and a boat: Sutton Hoo and the East Anglian kingdom', *Anglo-Saxon England* 22, 27–50.

Pestell, T. (2004) *Landscapes of Monastic Foundation: the establishment of religious houses in East Anglia c.600–1200*, Boydell Press, Woodbridge.

Peterken, G.F. (1968) 'The development of vegetation in Staverton Park', *Field Studies* 2, 1–39.

Pevsner, N. (1961) *The Buildings of England: Suffolk*, Penguin, Harmondsworth.

Phillips, C.W. (1940) 'The Sutton Hoo ship burial', *Antiquity* 14, 6–27.

Phythian Adams, C. (1987) *Rethinking English Local History*, Leicester University Press, Leicester.

Phythian Adams, C. (1993) *Societies, Cultures and Kinship 1580–1850: Cultural Provinces and English Local History*, Leicester University Press, Leicester.

Rackham, O. (1980) *Ancient Woodland: its history, vegetation and uses in England*, Edward Arnold, London.

Rackham, O. (1986) *The History of the Countryside*, Dent, London.

Reynolds, S. (1983) 'Medieval *origenes gentium* and the community of the realm', *History* 68, 375–90.

Rigold, S.E. (1961) 'The supposed see of Dunwich', *Journal of the British Archaeological Association* 24, 55–9.

Rigold, S.E. (1974) 'Further evidence about the site of "Dommoc"', *Journal of the British Archaeological Association* 37, 97–102.

Rippon, S. (2007) 'Focus or frontier? The significance of estuaries in the landscape of southern Britain', *Landscapes* 8, 23–38.

Robinson, D.H. (1949) *Fream's Elements of Agriculture*, 13th edn., John Murray, London.

Rodwell, J.S. (1991) *British Plant Communities Volume 2: Mires and Heaths*, Cambridge University Press, Cambridge.

Rollison, D. (1992) *The Local Origins of Modern Society: Gloucestershire 1500–1800*, Routledge, London.

Round, J.H. (1903) 'Introduction to the Essex Domesday', in A.A. Doubleday (ed.) *Victoria County History of Essex*, Vol I, 333–426.

Scarfe, N. (1986) *Suffolk in the Middle Ages*, Boydell, Woodbridge.

Scarfe, N. (1988a) 'Domesday settlements and churches: the example of Colneis hundred', in D. Dymond and E. Martin (eds) *An Historical Atlas of Suffolk*, 1st edn, Suffolk County Council, Ipswich, 42–3.

Scarfe, N. (ed.) (1988b) *A Frenchman's Year in Suffolk: French impressions of Suffolk life in 1784*, Suffolk Records Society, Woodbridge.

Scull, C. (1992) 'Before Sutton Hoo: structures of power and society in early East Anglia', in M. Carver (ed.) *The Age of Sutton Hoo: the seventh century in north-western Europe*, Boydell, Woodbridge, 3–24.

Scull, C. (2002) 'Ipswich: development and contexts of an urban precursor in the seventh century', in B. Hardh and L. Larson (eds) *Central Places in the Migration and Merovingian Periods*, Acta Archaeologica Lundensia, Lund, 8, 39, 303–16.

Steers, J.A. (1925) 'Suffolk shore: Yarmouth to Aldeburgh', *Proceedings of the Suffolk Institute of Archaeology and History* 19, 1–14.

Steers, J.A. (1926) 'Orford Ness: a study in coastal physiography', *Proceedings of the Geologists Association* 37, 306–25.

Swanton, M. (ed.) (1996) *The Anglo-Saxon Chronicle*, Dent, London.

Taylor, C. (1983) *Village and Farmstead: a history of rural settlement in England*, George Philip, London.

Thomas, J. (1993) 'The politics of vision and the archaeologies of landscape', in B. Bender (ed.) *Landscape: politics and perspectives*, Berg, Providence.

Thomas, J. (1996) *Time, Culture and Identity: an interpretative archaeology*, Routledge, London.

Tilley, C. (1994) *A Phenomenology of Landscape: places, paths and monuments*, Berg, Oxford.

Tilley, C. (2004) *The Materiality of Stone: explorations in landscape phenomenology*, Berg, Oxford.

Trist, P.J.O. (1971) *A Survey of the Agriculture of Suffolk: Royal Agricultural Society of England County Agriculture Surveys No. 7*, Royal Agricultural Society, London.

Wade, K. (1988a) 'Ipswich', in R. Hodges and B. Hobley (eds) *The Rebirth of Towns in the West, AD 700–1050*, Council for British Archaeology Research Report 68, London, 93–100.

Wade, K. (1989) 'The later Anglo-Saxon period', in D.

Dymond and E. Martin (eds) *An Historical Atlas of Suffolk*, 2nd edn, Suffolk County Council, Ipswich, 46–7.

Wade, K. (1993) 'The urbanisation of East Anglia: the Ipswich perspective', in J. Gardiner (ed.) *Flatlands and Wetlands: current themes in East Anglian Archaeology*, East Anglian Archaeology 50, 144–51.

Warner, P. (1984) 'Sutton Hoo Research Project: documentary sources, Interim Report', unpublished report for the Sutton Hoo Research Project.

Warner, P. (1985) 'Documentary survey', *Sutton Hoo Research Committee Bulletin* 3, 17–18.

Warner, P. (1996) *The Origins of Suffolk*, Manchester University Press, Manchester.

Watts, V. (2004) *The Cambridge Dictionary of English Place Names*, Cambridge University Press, Cambridge.

Webster, L. (1992) 'Death's diplomacy: Sutton Hoo in the light of other male princely burials', in R. Farrell and C. Neuman de Vegvar (eds) *Sutton Hoo: fifty years after*, American Early Medieval Studies, Ohio, 75–82.

West, S. (1984) 'Iken, St Botolph, and the coming of East Anglian Christianity', *Proceedings of the Suffolk Institute of Archaeology and History* 35, 4, 279–301.

West, S. (1989) 'The early Anglo-Saxon period', in D. Dymond and E. Martin (eds) *An Historical Atlas of Suffolk*, 2nd edn, Suffolk County Council, Ipswich, 44–5.

White, W. (1885) *History, Gazetteer and Directory of Suffolk*, London.

Whitelock, D. (1972) 'The pre-Viking church in East Anglia', *Anglo-Saxon England* 1, 1–22.

Whyte, N. (2005) *Perceptions of the Norfolk Landscape c.1500–1750*, unpublished PhD Thesis, University of East Anglia.

Wickham, C. (1994) *Land and power: studies in Italian and European social history, 400–1200*, British School at Rome, London.

Williams, H. (1998) 'Monuments and the past in early Anglo-Saxon England', *World Archaeology* 30, 1, 90–108.

Williams, H. (2001) 'Death, memory and time: a consideration of the mortuary practices at Sutton Hoo, in C. Humphrey and W.M. Ormrod (eds) *Time in the Medieval World*, York Medieval Press, York, 35–71.

Williamson, T. (1998) 'The "Scole-Dickleburgh field system" revisited', *Landscape History* 20, 19–28.

Williamson, T. (2005) *Sandlands: the Suffolk coast and heaths*, Windgather Press, Macclesfield.

Williamson, T. (2006) *England's Landscape: East Anglia*, English Heritage and Harper Collins, London.

Wymer, J. (1999) 'Surface geology', in D. Dymond and E. Martin (eds) *An Historical Atlas of Suffolk*, 1st edn, Suffolk County Council, Ipswich, 18–19.

Yorke, B. (1990) *Kings and Kingdoms in Early Anglo-Saxon England*, Seaby, London.

Young, A. (1795) 'A fortnight's tour in East Suffolk', *Annals of Agriculture* 23, 38–40.

Young, A. (1797) *General View of the Agriculture of the County of Suffolk*, 1st edn, London.

Index